The Silver Road

How Spain and Latin America Helped to Win the American Revolutionary War

StorySellers Press & Media LLC

Contents

Chapter 1

Prequel to the American Revolution

On a warm June morning in 1762, a Spanish lieutenant peered through his spyglass from the high walls of Castillo del Morro in Havana. He was startled to see a huge fleet of ships near the Cuban coast, all flying British flags. He reported his sighting to his commanders, who impatiently dismissed his concerns, believing the massive fleet was on its way to Jamaica, a British colony about 90 miles south of Cuba.[1] Havana, the prized jewel of the Spanish New World, was highly secured. Morro fortress towered in the skyline on the Caribbean Sea as it still does today, guarding the precious city with massive walls six feet wide and fourteen feet high. Annoyed with the lieutenant, the commanders returned to Havana to enjoy their Sunday.

As the hours passed, the pilot appointed to watch the fleet became increasingly dismayed by what he saw. Over 200 ships – including 30 heavily armed warships – changed direction and were now heading directly for the city's harbor.[2] The sentries sounded the alarm that Havana was under attack. The sound of church bells clanging broke the calm afternoon. Unknown to the stunned commanders, the Spanish had joined the French in the Seven Years' War against the British in May 1762. The Spanish leadership in Cuba remained unaware of the outbreak of fighting as the British seized the Spanish mail ship that carried the news. In an age without satellite news or text messaging, the Spanish did not know that the British plans for invasion had begun or that the colossal British fleet was heading their way. One of the key battles of the Seven Years' War began on that summer day. This war was the prequel to the American Revolution that determined Spain's decision to finance and arm the struggling Americans to win against the British.

The invading British force comprised 28,400 men and included enslaved Africans, Native Americans from Canada, Europeans, and free Black militia from Britain and the Caribbean.[3] The British recruited thousands of troops from their North American colonies. Spanish officers estimated that 4,000 Americans arrived in late July.[4] The French, allies of the Spanish, had been fighting the British in the French and Indian War in the American colonies since 1754 and in the Seven Years' War since 1756. With the turbulence in Europe and in North America, the Spanish Crown reinforced Havana with artillery, munitions and warships between 1758 and 1761. Battle-tested veteran soldiers had arrived in Havana the previous year, but this seasoned garrison numbered only 2,330 men in June 1762. The British Regulars were about six times that number. The local militia companies, today's equivalent of the National Guard, were called to duty. These civilian soldiers were overwhelmed by the well-trained British.[5] The siege of Havana lasted over two months, with British troops suffering terrible casualties due to the tropical heat and unfamiliar diseases. The 18th century reporters wrote that both military veterans and fresh volunteers simply "dropped dead" of thirst and heat, and days passed during which thousands of the British were too ill to fight or even to stand.[6]

So many soldiers died in Castillo del Morro that the Spanish were forced to throw the bodies into the sea below. Afro-Cubans were a key factor in enabling the Spanish to hold out as long as they did,[7] and the carnage continued over the weeks. Juan de Prado y Portocarrero was the Spanish Governor and commander in charge of Havana's defense. The Spanish quickly organized resources and manpower throughout the island and across the sea in Mexico. The Spanish Navy scrambled to ship in artillery and to send its marines into battle and intentionally sunk ships to cut off British access to the port.

The British cut off the city's water supply, creating havoc and hardship for Habaneros, the citizens of Havana.[8] They shelled the city for weeks, sometimes shooting a hundred bombs in a single day.[9] The junta de guerra – council of war – appointed Juan Ignacio de Madariaga as sub-delegate of the governor. Madariaga organized supplies and materials throughout Cuba, and deployed all the available land and sea troops, as well as weapons, ammunition and gunpowder from nearby Matanzas, Santiago, and all the smaller outposts near Havana.[10] By early August, every male Habanero over 14 years of age was ordered to join the defense. Supplying the Spanish and Cuban defenders and remaining civilians was a logistical challenge. The military struggled to send 200 to 300 cavalry wagons from the countryside loaded with casaba, cornmeal, cattle, eggs and chickens.

Relief convoys of food and ammunition arrived from Campeche and Sisal in Mexico. The fighting continued, and the Spanish and Cubans remained stalwart.

The city was evacuated in early June, with between 10,000 and 30,000 people fleeing British troops[11] in a chaotic and dangerous exodus. Days of rainfall turned the roads into muddy streams. Families with children struggled through the terrain, and looting broke out.[12] Many of the wealthier residents packed up their volantes – large, wheeled carts drawn by a single horse – and loaded mule carts with their baggage, fleeing to the countryside.[13] The vast wealth of silver and gold from the city treasury was hidden in the backcountry. Evacuated Habaneros camped out in the countryside for months. Madariaga later wrote, "Despite the hardships in which many families live, hutted in houses, huts, tobacco houses, and other settlements, there are no robberies, fights, quarrels, deaths, injuries, or disturbances, which is admirable."[14]

The British barraged Morro from its one vulnerable point, a hill on the eastern side of the city. On the land side of the fortress, the Spanish had carved a huge moat into the solid rock that was over 50 feet wide and 60 feet deep. British strategists determined that the quickest path to victory was to sink a deep shaft into the rock, load the shaft with munitions, and then explode the moat. On July 27, Spanish sentries observed enemy soldiers excavating outside the fortress walls. The Spanish fired relentlessly but were unable to stop them. The British loaded the shaft with explosives, and on July 30, they lit the fuse. The city quaked and a storm of rocks and dust filled the huge moat, enabling the invaders to attack Morro on foot.[15] The battered fortress fell on July 31. Two weeks later, the Spanish and Cubans surrendered, sending shockwaves throughout the world.

The British occupied Havana for eleven months. They seized warehouses full of tobacco and sugar and the vast Spanish merchant fleet that was anchored in the harbor, a plunder worth millions of British pounds[16] and billions in today's dollars. The British harassed residents with random searches. As one angry citizen reported, "they made a show of searching all of the houses under the pretext of requesting a chest... they assumed that we had stolen."[17] Without Airbnb or hotels, British soldiers moved into the citizens' homes for an extended stay.

British officers threatened to seize the cathedral's bells and melt them down for artillery[18] and the British commander, the Earl of Albemarle, wrote to the Catholic bishop of Havana, Pedro Agustín Morell de Santa Cruz, demanding an astounding sum as a "donation" to the victorious Army of the Church of

England. Morell threatened to sue the commander in London and Albemarle accused the bishop of treason, since he was now technically a British subject and was disobeying authority. As punishment for his defiance, the British forcibly seized Morell and shipped him to the swamplands of Florida.[19] Albemarle spitefully used the bishop's beloved church as a stable.[20] To provide lodging for British soldiers, Albemarle seized the Hospital of San Juan de Dios, and British soldiers forced out sick patients, the homeless poor, and the brothers of the order.[21] In addition to seizing the riches to which he was entitled under British rules of war, Albemarle listed Havana's many religious institutions as "rich," "very rich" and "very, very rich" — hoping for more opportunities to seize Spanish wealth. He wrested control of the lucrative slave trade from the Havana cabildo trading company and appointed himself as the intermediary to import more enslaved people into Cuba, to further enrich himself.[22]

Angry disputes erupted among the city's elite merchants when several businessmen treacherously collaborated with Albemarle while others resisted. The import and export trade was heavily regulated under Spanish law, and some merchants viewed the less restricted trade under the British as a business opportunity. Several merchants expanded their import of enslaved Africans while exports of Cuban goods to Britain increased — including exports of Havana's famous tobacco snuff.* Two leading businessmen, Sebastián de Peñalver Angulo and Gonzalo Recio de Oquendo, were accused of collaboration and "vileness, thievery, wicked impostures, and other means, but all at the expense of this unfortunate town and the honor of both men, if they had any."[23] Both men were accused of conducting shake-downs of their fellow citizens, the Royal Havana Company, and religious organizations, demanding hundreds of thousands of pesos on behalf of Albemarle and themselves. They redirected trade of lucrative merchandise, including flour, iron, and tobacco, to benefit themselves at high profits. After Havana was liberated in 1763, both men were extradited to Spain, where they were tried and convicted. Peñalver died in disgrace in Spain, while Oquendo was eventually pardoned.[24]

---

*For Bridgerton fans, Queen Charlotte married King George III in 1761 before the invasion. Charlotte may have been one of the happy customers when Cuban snuff shipments arrived in 1763.

For Spain, the defeat of Havana marked a disastrous and humiliating entry to the Seven Years' War. Spanish leaders watched with growing alarm as their French allies steadily lost territory to Britain in the French and Indian War in North America, a theater uncomfortably close to Spain's own holdings in the American Southwest. Across continents and oceans, the globe was ablaze with warfare, a struggle later recognized by historians as the "first war of the world."

The First War of the World

When Carlos III was crowned King of Spain in 1759, the Seven Years' War was already raging, with the French fighting against the British, among other nations, in a multi-front war. Millions of people around the world were embroiled in this terrible conflict as European powers viciously fought for colonial conquests and domestic territories. The bloody struggle rattled the earth and most of its seas, through Latin America, the Caribbean, the Philippines, India, West Africa, the Ohio Valley, Pennsylvania, New York, New Jersey, Virginia, Canada, and most of Europe. Armies of hundreds of thousands marched through Europe, while forces of tens of thousands landed in North America. In India, the British and French battled for commercial power and trade. This rivalry continued for decades during the wars with the kingdoms of Mysore and Maratha. The global scale of the conflict was unprecedented. More than one million people died, including those in a ruinous skirmish in 1754 led by an inexperienced Virginia militia officer under the British Army — the young, ambitious, red-haired George Washington.

Starting in the 16th century, the ruthless fur trade raged through the immense forests, lakes, and rivers of North America. This far-flung ecological landscape would astonish us in the 21st century. Hundreds of millions of animals, including beavers, mink, sea otters, and wildcats, lived among the emerald cathedrals of trees and the crystal blue waters. Species were hunted almost to the point of extinction. This savage commerce ignited the French and Indian War in 1754.

The fur-hunting grounds were on the homelands of the Native American nations, through which British and French hunters and soldiers recklessly trampled. The Native Americans fought on both sides of the conflict, astutely concerned with safeguarding their sovereignty. The powerful Haudenosaunee, the Iroquois

League, had an important and unacknowledged influence over the outcome in eastern North America.[25] Tanaghrisson, a Haudenosaunee leader, was central in sparking the conflict in the Pennsylvania woodlands. The French had expanded their forts along the Ohio valley, and the Native Americans were angered by this invasion. Tanaghrisson delivered a stern, eloquent warning to the French camped near Lake Erie, Pennsylvania, as Washington later wrote in his journal. "Fathers, both You and the English are White. We live in a Country between, therefore the Land does not belong either to one of the other," Tanaghrisson said, insisting that the French withdraw. The French commander mocked his speech, and Tanaghrisson astutely waited for his chance to respond. He struck back in May 1754 as the French fought against the Virginia militia commanded by Washington, with their Haudenosaunee allies. After the French surrendered, Tanaghrisson killed Jumonville, an important French envoy. While Washington received the attention of the ethnocentric London press for the musket volley that "set the world on fire," Tanaghrisson himself struck the killer tomahawk blow. Washington was blamed for the "assassination," which he unknowingly conceded in the French language surrender agreement. As the French Governor wrote, "he [Washington] was stupid enough to admit in his capitulation".[26] (Ouch!)

Europe was irrevocably inflamed with the chain of events of the Prussian invasion of an ally of Austria in 1756, which then entangled France, also an Austrian ally. By 1762, Carlos III and his advisors made the fateful decision to enter the War. The two monarchies signed the Bourbon Family Compact in 1733, pledging cooperation and military alliances during the wars that frequently raged in Europe. The Spanish also had their own motivations for acting against the British, which included protecting their valuable mines and territories in Latin America and reclaiming Gibraltar, the small rocky territory at the southernmost tip of Spain held by the British since 1713.[27]

After declaring war on Spain, British forces rapidly invaded Spain's empire throughout the world. After Cuba, their next target was the rich Spanish trading center of Manila in the Philippines, which they attacked in late September 1762. The port was a cosmopolitan and lucrative FedEx-type warehouse hub for international trade. Merchants from all over the world congregated to buy and sell. A traveler reported as early as 1662 that the diversity of people in Manila was among the greatest in the world, including globetrotters from Italy, the Netherlands, Germany, Denmark, Sweden, Poland, Turkey, Greece, Persia,

Russia, China, Japan, and Africa.[28] Majestic Spanish galleons encircled the world during these centuries, calling on ports across Asia and the Pacific Island nations, trading aromatic spices, lustrous silk, rare woods, crafted pewter, elegant Chinese porcelain, glowing pearls, and sparkling gems.

The British East India Company funded the Manila attack. Chartered by Queen Elizabeth I in 1600, the Company became the most powerful commercial and military "broligarchy" in the world. The conglomerate instigated and impacted events throughout the globe — from conquering India to kindling the devastating opium pandemic in China to inciting the Boston Tea Party in 1773. For a modern comparison, imagine a combination of OpenAI, Meta and Apple, completely unregulated and dedicated to corporate violence,[29] with their own private military force of over 260,000 in the 19th century — a terrifying thought! The East India Company expedition sailed from Madras, India, with a thousand men. The Spanish recruited five hundred soldiers from Mexico, who fought with a small number of local volunteers to defend Manila. The battle was over quickly, and the Spanish surrendered Manila in October 1762. The economic loss for the Spanish was staggering. The largest Spanish galleon in the history of the Pacific trade was captured, with a cargo worth 3 million pesos,[30] or approximately $6.2 billion in today's dollars.*

This first war of the world was structured on an international economy that was globalized for the first time in our history as humans. All the continents of the world interacted in this economy, powered by the trade in precious metals.[31] At the center of this trade were Spain's colonies in Latin America, which had the richest silver and gold mines in the world. The Spanish held vast expanses of continents, millions of subjects, and dazzling mineral wealth. Spanish silver was the global currency from the 16th through the 19th centuries, just as the green US dollar is today. China, then the powerful Middle Kingdom, was known as "the silver graveyard," since so much of the world's silver was used to pay for Chinese goods and remained in China.[32]

---

*Calculation is based on the Economy Cost Comparator. Consumer Price Index (CPI) data is also available; based on my grocery bills over the past six months, I think the CPI drastically underestimates the change in value. Please see Bonus Feature: Money, Money, Money for details.

Discovering neither precious metals nor populous kingdoms in North America, the Spanish focused their attention on the southern hemisphere, which then held the balance of people and wealth in the Americas. By the mid-18th century, Mexico City – formerly Tenochtitlan, the elegant Mexica capital – had a population of 150,000, five times larger than Philadelphia, the most populous city in the US. "Silver kings" managed Latin America's mines, building huge operations from the mountains of Peru to the stark deserts of central Mexico to the jungles of Central America. Within one year, the British had captured Havana and Manila, two of the most important trading ports of the Spanish Empire.[33] Stunned by these developments, Carlos III and his government feared for Spain's silver and gold mines in Latin America.

As stipulated in the 1763 Peace Treaty, the British withdrew from Havana thirteen months after invading the city, and the new Spanish governor arrived on July 4, 1763.[34] The British lowered their flag, and the Spanish raised theirs. The Spanish and Cubans celebrated with 24-hour parties. The Afro-Cubans had more reasons to celebrate. At the time, more than half of Cuba's population was of African descent[35] and Spain had promised freedom to enslaved Afro-Cubans who enlisted to defend the country. These men were predominantly from the Mandingo, Fulani, Hausa, Ibo, and Yoruba civilizations, and many were trained warriors in their home countries. This promise was kept to a surprising degree.[36] In one instance, a formerly enslaved man escaped to Spain to pursue his case for freedom, which eventually escalated to Carlos III. The King instructed his officers to confirm the man's manumission, reimburse his former owner from the government treasury, and enforce the promise to enslaved Africans "as reward for their fidelity and honor."[37] The newly appointed Spanish governor held hearings for two weeks, then posted the names of the liberated men publicly to ensure that their *Carta de Libertad* status was protected.[38] This legislation, plus the Spanish law of coartación through which enslaved people could purchase their own freedom, resulted in a large, free, Afro-Cuban population in late 18th century Havana.[39]

Completely shaken by the outcome of the War, the Spanish government implemented an all-encompassing reorganization and restrengthening of its Empire through 1773. The Bourbon Reforms, as these programs were known, impacted almost all sectors of the Cuban economy, society, and military. The Cuban military forces were rebuilt under the leadership of Ambrosio Funes de Villalpando, conde de Ricla, and his close friend, General Alejandro O'Reilly, one of the many Irish officers serving in the Spanish Army.[40] Acknowledging that the number of Spanish and Cuban males was not sufficient to provide the needed military forces, Ricla also created two battalions of free Afro-Cubans and biracial Cubans, confidently predicting that they would become the best volunteers on the island.[41] The Spanish built a huge new fort on the hill near Morro. With the established trade between Cuba and the US, this massive fort was partially built with bricks produced in Virginia and New York.[42] When Carlos III learned that the new fortification overlooking Morro Castle was completed in 1774, he reportedly asked for his telescope. Certainly, as the story goes, with the immense cost and years of labor needed to construct the fortresses, the King could view them across the Atlantic from his palace in Madrid.[43]

During the peace negotiations in Paris in 1763, the Spanish were forced to give up their territory in southeastern America. At the time, the Spanish were long established in Florida; by 1675 they built a chain of more than thirty missions across the state. Thousands of Spaniards hastily packed their possessions and sailed from Florida to Cuba and Mexico at the start of the British occupation in 1763. To compensate the Spanish for these disastrous outcomes, the French gave Louisiana and New Orleans to Spain, as a buffer against further British expansion into Spanish territory in western North America and ultimately the priceless mines in Mexico and Latin America. The Spanish maintained their claims to territory west of the Mississippi. A map of 18th century North America shows the sweeping expanse of this empire, from the small outpost of San Francisco founded in the desolate wilderness of Alta California in 1776, to the province of Tejas with its Spanish cattle ranches to the fortress of San Augustín, Florida, the first continuous European settlement in North America, founded in 1565 decades before Jamestown, Virginia. Spanish explorers traveled up the Pacific Coast to Canada in 1774 and by the late 1700s had established a military post on Vancouver Island, 350 miles north of Seattle. The Spanish sailed up the Atlantic Coast through the Chesapeake Bay in 1526 – then called the Bahía de Santa María – about 80 years before the English encounter with Pocahontas. In the 1520s, Spanish navigators explored as far north as Cape Cod, Massachusetts, and the present site of Bangor, Maine.[44] The Spanish settled the southwest of America in the 16th century, battling with Native American nations, and officially founded Santa Fe, New Mexico, in 1610. The Palace of the Governors in Santa Fe is still open to visitors and remains the oldest continually occupied public structure in the US built by Europeans. Spain had dominated the Caribbean since 1492, and the sea was known as the "Spanish Lake." The massive fortress of Castillo San Felipe del Morro rises 140 feet along the coast of Puerto Rico, watching over the beautiful colonial city of San Juan. The fortress was so formidable that the British refrained from attacking it during the Seven Years' War and the American Revolutionary War.

The King and the Anti-King Revolution

The Spanish and French kingdoms were rivals with the British for their global empires and were related in an intricate lineage. Carlos III, who ruled Spain from 1759 to 1788 and during the years of the American Revolution, was the son of a Spanish King and an Italian duchess, the great-grandson of French King Louis XIV, and the uncle of the then-ruling French King Louis XVI.[45] Carlos III and Louis XVI were further united by a renewal of the third Bourbon Family Compact in 1762, which declared that the enemy of one of the two countries was the enemy of both — in other words, the British. This strong political and familial relationship between the French and Spanish kings united their actions during the American Revolution.

Carlos III had a decisive impact on the outcome of the American Revolution. He actively authorized Spain's financing of the extensive supply shipments and military campaigns, issuing orders from Madrid to his leadership throughout Latin America and the Caribbean. Carlos was a man of simple tastes, sharply contrasted to the showy opulence of monarchs of his time. His usual attire, described by a traveler in 1776, "seldom varies from a long hat, gray Segovian frock [named for the Spanish province], a buff waistcoat, a small dagger, black breeches, and worsted stockings; his pockets are always stuffed with knives, gloves, and shooting tackle."[46] He had to be patiently persuaded by his servants, with whom he had unusually cordial relationships, to wear new clothes. He wore wigs only on formal occasions, unlike his male contemporaries whose heads were constantly coiffed, curled and powdered.

His hobbies included carpentry, fishing and billiards, but hunting was his favorite sport. The report of a wolf sighting sent him rushing outdoors, regardless of the weather. His portrait by Francisco Goya, the headshot painter for the celebrity class, shows him standing in the countryside with one gloved hand gripping a long rifle and the other holding a hunting glove, with a sleeping retriever by his foot. He was not handsome; his face narrowed too sharply from a high wide forehead towards his small chin, accentuating his long, bulbous nose. His blue eyes were lively and warm; his expression one of seemingly bemused tolerance for the formality of a royal portrait.

Carlos III was viewed as a progressive man, genuinely concerned with public service. He was a supporter of the Enlightenment, the powerful intellectual and social movement sweeping Europe with electrifying, humanist ideas, which Carlos III viewed as a force for modernization. A man of his times, he supported revolts against *other* kings in *their* colonies, but certainly not in his own — 18th century NIMBY. In 1780, his regime brutally suppressed the revolt of Micaela Bastidas Puyucahua and Túpac Amaru II, the Incan power couple who tried to overthrow the Spanish Empire in Peru.

Although his marriage was an arranged affair of state, he fell deeply in love with his temperamental blue-eyed blonde Saxon queen, Maria Amalia. At their first meeting, Maria Amalia walked forward intending to kneel as was customary in formal presentations, but Carlos chivalrously picked her up, took her to his carriage, and they rode off into the sunset for as much happily ever after as royal life in the 18th century allowed. She died of tuberculosis at the age of 36, leaving him with a large family of 13 children, seven of whom reached adulthood. Carlos was inconsolable, refusing to remarry despite pressure from the politically inclined matchmakers at the Court. His projects to improve Madrid are the highlights of 21st century tours, including the Prado Museum and the Royal Botanical Gardens. His mission statement during his reign is worthy of modern democracies: to balance the budget, cut taxes and to devote all his attention to improving the welfare of his subjects.

"Everything that circumstances permit"

The Seven Years' War and the French and Indian War had dramatic and unforeseen impacts on the American colonists and their relationship with the British. The British national debt almost doubled, from £75 to £125 million, an increase of about $656 billion in today's currency.[47] To pay for the huge costs of the conflict and to maintain troops in the colonies, the British passed a series of laws restricting the economic power of the colonies, taxed personal income, and levied tariffs on trade. Taxes covered everything from liquor licenses to dice and cards. The British East India Company tried to take over the tea trade with higher prices, which infuriated Americans as much as doubling coffee prices would today. The Americans responded to these British efforts as "Taxation without Representation," and engaged in noisy protests, bloody street riots and determined boycotts, actions that led to the movement for American independence.[48] The Crown prohibited Americans from printing their own currency to retain control of the colonies' financial system. Parliament restricted domestic production of fundamental industrial commodities to ensure that Britain dominated the American economic infrastructure. These restrictions constrained production capacity as the Americans mobilized for war.

The Spanish carefully monitored the growing American rebellion. Two leading Spanish newspapers, *El Mercurio* and the *La Gaceta de Madrid*, printed regular reports on the ongoing rebellion, the 18th century equivalent of dooms crolling.[49] In March 1777, José Moñino y Redondo, the conde de Floridablanca and the powerful Spanish Secretary of State, wrote, "the fate of the colonies interests us very much, and we shall do for them everything that circumstances permit."[50]

Spain, with its Latin American empire, was a world power in the 18th century. Their kingdom possessed the financial strength, production capacity, armed forces, naval fleet, and economic might to influence the outcome of the American Revolution as victory or defeat. When the harsh discussions of war echoed in the elegant marble palaces of Madrid, Carlos III and his ministers remembered all too clearly the devastating losses of power, wealth and territories from their last conflict with the British during the first war of the world in 1762. The Spanish had much to lose and much to protect in the dangerous period of convulsing empires and global conflict that loomed before them. The silver and gold mines of Latin America and the strategic territories in Central America were as important as today's highly contested oil fields or rare earth mineral mines. They knew the British would retaliate if the Spanish openly aided the American rebels. This time, they carefully planned their response. From 1775 until the Spanish declared war against the British in 1779, Spanish assistance to the American rebels was provided with as much secrecy as possible. Before the ink had dried on the US Declaration of Independence, the Spanish and Latin Americans began their long, costly campaign to defeat the British — by helping the Americans to win the Revolutionary War.

Chapter 2

Days and Days without a "Mexican"

The General was in his labyrinth of deep despair. On a cold night in January 1776, far from the warm hearth fires of his comfortable plantation, Washington confided to a friend that while others were wrapped silently in sleep, he lay awake thinking, "Few people know the predicament we are in, on a thousand accounts.... I have often thought how much happier I should have been, if, instead of accepting a command under such circumstances, I had ... entered the ranks ... or had retired to the back country, and lived in a wigwam."[1]

These were discouraging words from the leader of the struggling US Army upon whom so much and so many depended. To understand the lonely despondency of Washington in his freezing tent on that winter night, transport yourself to the United States of America in 1776, to places and people both contentedly familiar and startlingly strange. You will recognize a distant reflection of yourself in those gathering and chatting in small shops or working on farms or in shipyards. You'll see familiar landmarks that still stand humbly among the skyscrapers and electric city lights — the Old North Church in Boston, the colonial courthouse in Williamsburg, the imposing Spanish fortress in San Augustín. But the economic landscape of the Revolutionary era is an almost unimaginable contrast to the 21st century nation of global power and affluence that has marked your lifetime.

Your 21st century United States of America would also have shocked the colonists, who never could have imagined their homeland rising to become a global power, stretching from coast to coast, laced with highways, railways, and airports and sparkling with telecommunications networks, data centers, and satellites. Could they foresee that their insolvent financial system would generate the currency that has been the world's standard for decades? Or that the US Army, which once could not afford to buy blankets for its soldiers, would become the most powerful military in the world, with fighter jets, hypersonic missiles, attack drones, and nuclear submarines?

Imagine yourself softly falling through time, into the 18th century that Washington and the Patriots faced. If you are fortunate enough to have hard cash in your pocket in an economy that so often relied on barter, your fingers would touch an odd assortment of coins and banknotes. You'd usually calculate and bargain in Spanish pesos, sometimes called "Mexicans," since so much of the silver that comprised the world currency of the late 18th century was mined in Mexico.[2] If you were a global merchant, you'd officially transact in English currency, but actually use a dizzying array of foreign coins – silver pesos and reales from Spain, cross dollars from Peru, ducats and ducatoons from Italy, shillings and guineas from England, and guilders and lions from the Netherlands – but none of your own.[3] Gold was not discovered in North America until after the Revolution, beginning with small mines in the Carolinas and bursting into the spectacular California gold rush in 1849. The colonies had little precious mineral wealth, unlike the vast silver and gold opulence of Latin America.

You'd probably work on a farm or have a job related to farming, since 95% of Americans in 1776 worked in agriculture, while only about 2% do today.[4] Family farms averaged 250 acres, with larger plantations in the southern colonies. Displaying the American penchant for entrepreneurship, many towns established workshops and mills that employed mechanics, craftsmen, and artisans. Americans also produced non-agricultural products such as deer and beaver pelts, hoops and wooden barrels, and rum and cider, but made few of the goods required to support an army at war.[5]

When the Revolutionary War erupted, the absence of a national currency and financial system meant that the Americans could not collectively finance an army payroll or pay for imported or domestic supplies and production facilities. The American Patriots, as the rebels called themselves, lacked facilities capable of producing sufficient gunpowder, blankets, shoes, tents, uniforms, muskets, rifles, and cannon. No national lending institutions or banking systems existed to underwrite the capital investment required to create them. These economic conditions and legislated restrictions both influenced the start of the war and made achieving victory so precarious. The colonies were regulated to benefit the British economy, forced to trade agricultural products and natural resources for refined British products. These financial conditions rippled through the entire rebellion, seriously threatening the viability of armed resistance, and decisively increasing the impact of silver currency and military supplies from Spain and Latin America.

Still traveling with your imagination, you reach the 18th century battlefield to stand with your fellow soldiers. This Revolutionary battlefield is devoid of tanks, helicopters, armored transport vehicles, and sophisticated communications equipment. A few weapons that have lobbed death for centuries, such as mortars, are still on this battlefield, then standing as stubby basic cylinders, distant relations of the computerized, high-tech mortars in current use. But the same emotions that haunt men and women on battlefields and in military camps are here: disorienting confusion, nauseating terror, wild elation, and dulling boredom.

Among their meager supplies in 1776, US soldiers carried a powder horn for rationed gunpowder, a musket or perhaps a homemade "Pennsylvania rifle," a flask for lead bullets, and a buckshot pouch for hunting game. The powder horns were soon replaced by paper cylinders filled with powder and balls, bound at either end with jack-thread, which were easier to load quickly or during rain or snow.[6] Another year passed before soldiers learned to fight with the terribly lethal combat weapon of these times, the cold steel blade of a seventeen-inch bayonet.

The critical need for weapons and equipment plagued the rebels throughout the long years of the War, but few shortages were as immediate or as frightening as the lack of gunpowder. By 1775, most of the stored gunpowder had gathered dust since the French and Indian War. The few gunpowder mills were out of production, and few Americans had the expertise to manufacture the valuable material in sufficient quantities to supply an army. The ingredients to produce black gunpowder included sulfur and potassium or sodium nitrate, which were not widely produced in the colonies. The US Army, also known as the Continental Army, faced an acute shortage of gunpowder throughout the entire Revolutionary War. In the words of the inimitable Benjamin Franklin, "The world wondered why we so seldom fired a cannon. We could not afford it." Historians estimate that 80% to 90% of all the gunpowder that fueled the Revolution during the first two and a half years was imported.[7] This imported powder was purchased on world markets in hard currency, usually silver pesos. While the US Army did not have the silver "Mexicans" to purchase the gunpowder, the Spanish did. When the British blockaded Boston in 1774, Spanish merchants began shipping larger quantities of gunpowder and weapons to the besieged Americans.

Los Mosquetes "heard 'round the world"

The irrevocable "shot heard 'round the world"* was fired on Lexington Green, Massachusetts, on a cool April morning in 1775, igniting the first armed clash between American colonists and British troops. The confrontation arose from Britain's threat to seize Patriot leaders who had fled Boston and from the urgent defense of precious stores of imported gunpowder. The Americans understood with chilling clarity that if those munitions were taken, they would stand defenseless before a disciplined and well-armed army. Rumors flew through Boston as swiftly as wild wraiths. As Ebenezer Fox, a soldier in the Massachusetts militia, wrote, "Great anxiety was manifested in the country in the vicinity of Boston to know what was going on there. People were out in all directions to hear 'the news from town.'"[8] One of the leaders of the resistance, Dr. Joseph Warren, was able to confirm the rumors of the planned British raid with an unnamed informant well-placed within the British command. The informant told Warren that the commander of the British Army was sending forces under cover of night to Concord to seize the gunpowder and weapons stored there.

The resistance groups had to be warned quickly before the Redcoats arrived. On April 18, rebel leader Paul Revere organized riders who raced through the countryside spreading word that the British were on the march.[9] As the day dawned in Lexington, British troops faced a ragtag volunteer militia of farmers and tradesmen — some of whom carried muskets marked as the property of the King of Spain.[10] The two groups faced off uncertainly across the town green. No one expected what happened next: a lone shot cracked the sky – to this day, no one is certain as to who fired first – and the battle began. When the last shot was fired late that day, 273 British soldiers and 95 Americans lay dead on the spring fields.[11]

---

*Ralph Waldo Emerson wrote this famous phrase in 1837. When you hear this phrase during the 250th celebration, please remember that some of the shots fired that day were from Spanish mosquetes, i.e., muskets.

The identity of Dr. Joseph Warren's unknown informant was never confirmed. As he promised, Dr. Warren took his secret to the grave, where he would soon be buried. Evidence indicates that it was Margaret Kemble Gage, a New Jersey woman married to British General Thomas Gage. Her 1771 portrait shows an attractive woman with calm dark eyes and an elegant profile, her long hair billowing over her shoulders. During the early days of the Revolution, all calm must have vanished from her mind as her heart was torn between her loyalty to her British husband and her beloved homeland. General Gage was shocked when he learned that his plans for Concord had been thwarted. Suspecting that Margaret had betrayed his confidence, he packed his shaken wife off to England. Their marriage reportedly never recovered[12] from that long tumultuous April day. Neither did the relationship between the British and the Americans.

DIY Gunpowder and Military Hardware

A portion of the gunpowder that was available during the first years of the rebellion was stolen or appropriated – depending on your point of view – from the British prior to the Declaration of Independence. In 1775, friends and neighbors from New Hampshire, Connecticut, Rhode Island, Georgia and South Carolina banded together to break down the doors of British storage depots, called magazines, and take the British gunpowder. This powder amounted to an estimated 80,000 pounds at the start of the war. The inexperienced soldiers quickly and inefficiently squandered the available powder, and when Washington arrived to take command, little remained. Washington was deeply concerned as the newly created army faced the powerful British, "without any money in our treasury, powder in our magazines, arms in our stores...and by and by, when we shall be called upon to take the field, shall not have a tent to lie in."[13]

State governments and entrepreneurs rallied and began to organize the financing of powder mills to increase domestic production. Milling operations comprised a basic system of waterwheel, shaft and gears. Mills were established in the colonies to produce consumer goods such as wheat flour and tobacco snuff. The Patriots began to convert these existing production facilities into gunpowder mills, but few were sustained over the years of the war. The Pennsylvania state government made several notable efforts. As of 1774, one of the significant powder mills in the colonies was located on Frankford Creek, north of Philadelphia. The ever-ready Paul Revere inspected this mill in 1775, when he traveled to the region for the Massachusetts Committee of Safety.[14] The Pennsylvania Committee of Safety worked frantically to establish more production facilities. The Committee scraped together the cash to finance the construction and conversion of several small mills. Most of these mills lapsed into disuse due to shortages of ingredients, rising costs, explosions in the inherently dangerous production environment, and targeted destruction by the British Army. The Continental Powder Mill, a relatively large-scale effort, burned to the ground in a horrible explosion in March 1777. The British seized the Frankford Creek Mill in September of that year, and the mill's operator scandalously cooperated with the invading force. When the US Army recovered Philadelphia, the miller was convicted as a traitor and had to hurriedly escape the city, leaving the mill without skilled management.[15] Some of the colonies started gunpowder manufacturing operations, but the goal of supplying the army through domestic production was never achieved.

While the struggle to establish factories for domestic production continued, independent merchant captains, state governments and the Congressional Committee of Secret Correspondence organized "powder cruises." Month after month their ships stealthily left the safety of colonial ports, carrying commodities to exchange for scarce gunpowder. The powder cruise organizers were encumbered by the harsh British blockade of the American coastline and the lack of a currency that was accepted in international markets. One of the first British military actions in the war was to initiate a blockade of the few port cities, a chillingly effective tactic. The deliberate strategy of the British Navy was to hold the struggling Americans "in irons," the naval term for a sailing ship stalled by winds or "dead in the water." The vast geographic expanse of the United States was then concentrated on the East coast, only touching the Appalachian Mountains and the shore of the Mississippi, the frontier of Spanish territory. The British used this geographic circumstance and the small size of the US Navy to weaken the colonies with a choking blockade that limited the importation of industrial and consumer goods.

Those ships that evaded the blockade sped to Havana and the Caribbean, Bilbao on the Spanish north coast, and Nantes on the French Atlantic coast. Saint Eustatius, the tiny island held by the Dutch, was an 18th century shipping hub in the Caribbean with warehouses lining its streets.[16] Upon outdistancing the

British navy, the Patriots faced the next hurdle of trading without hard currency, bartering tobacco, flour, lumber, tar, animal pelts, and other commodities for military supplies.

Earning hard currency to purchase imports on the world market was challenging. The wealthy merchants of Havana were one of the few bright opportunities for trade without a transatlantic crossing, and they paid cash in shining silver "Mexicans" for the Americans' goods. Benjamin Franklin, first scheduled as ambassador to Spain and later appointed to France, reported from Paris in March 1777 that the Spanish court had quietly granted the Patriots direct admission to the rich, previously restricted port of Havana under Most Favored Nation status. Franklin also noted in the same report that 3,000 barrels of gunpowder were waiting in New Orleans, and that the merchants in Bilbao "had orders to ship for us such necessaries as we might want."[17]

The US Army was in want of "necessaries" ranging from medical supplies to iron and steel for bayonets, heavy artillery, cannons, and mortars. While heavy iron balls hurtling towards a flesh-and-blood human defended only by homespun textile are dangerous in any era, the impact of these weapons was exacerbated by the ghastly medical treatment of the time. Sterilized surgical tools and operating rooms, antibiotics, and powerful anesthesia did not exist. Wounds that are readily treated today would have led to certain death or terrifying amputations, usually sedated with rum. The few medical implements or rudimentary medicines that existed to treat wounds, such as needles, forceps, lint bandages, and incision knives, were also scarce.[18]

Bullets were among the few supplies that were easily produced. Individual soldiers could quickly make bullets from lead, a soft and malleable metal that readily melts and can be shaped into small spheres. Lead deposits were discovered by the 18th century and mining operations were in production. The American rebels used whatever lead they could buy, borrow, and confiscate, to make bullets. They eagerly melted lead-lined church windows, lead ballasts from ships, rain spouts, and even a statue of King George III.

The steel that made the deadly bayonets that were standard in the British Army and the heavyweight iron for cannons and mortars were not so easily produced. In 1750, the British passed the Iron Act, which restricted the colonial production to "pig iron," a processed raw iron with a high carbon content that rendered it very brittle and useless for military purposes. The Rappahannock Forge in

Virginia was a rare exception. The Forge operated from 1778 to 1781 and was able to produce bayonets and musket parts.[19] In their writings, British officers noted the scarcity of iron foundries throughout the colonies and the British Army's destruction of any facilities they did encounter. The need for bayonets and gunpowder became terrifyingly clear in the first major battle of the War, known as the Battle of Bunker Hill. Immediately after the battles of Lexington and Concord, the friends and neighbors of the Massachusetts militia formed a siege line around Boston, which was occupied by the British. The British could only exit the city through the harbor and sea. To break the land siege, the British decided to attack the hills of Charlestown in June 1775. An outnumbered 1,400 Patriot soldiers faced 2,600 British Army Regulars, one of the best-trained and equipped armies in the world.

Abigail Adams, the wife of John Adams, who would one day be the second US President, and her young son, John Quincy, watched from the distance as the Patriots held the positions at the top of the hill, dug into smaller fortifications called "redoubts." Dr. Joseph Warren, a close family friend of the Adams, joined the fight. From the temporary safety of these fortifications, the US soldiers stared nervously as the advancing waves of red-coated British marched steadily up the hill in lines of formation and listened as drummers beat a staccato of disciplined signals.

Imagine you're among the American soldiers, crouching behind freshly dug fortifications, the smell of dirt in your nose. As the stomp of boots and the rattle of muskets and bayonets grow steadier and nearer, as you and your fellow troops anxiously wait. You've received orders to only fire at the British at the shortest range possible,[20] to preserve the small supplies of gunpowder. With a crackling roar and blaze, the US soldiers fire their first round at the steadily approaching Regulars. Many of the Redcoats crumple to the ground, but still the lines advance. A second wave of troops rise and with a crescendo of boots the Regulars again march up the hill, while the Patriots defend their position, breaking formation and firing furiously. The British officers shout orders and the drummers beat out the drills for a third assault on the hill. As the Patriots brace themselves, devastating news sweeps through the lines: their army is out of gunpowder.

The muskets in the soldiers' hands are useless, except to be frantically swung as clubs as British soldiers swarm over the fortifications. British bayonets gleam in the sunlight, seventeen inches of piercing steel fitted with sockets wrapped around the muzzle's edge, designed for use in close combat. Without domestically produced steel, the Americans do not have bayonets to defend themselves. The soldiers rush to retreat. The British have the decided advantage in terms of weapons and position, and slash through the Patriots. As the sun sets over the bloodied, trampled grass, the Redcoats capture Breed's Hill at a terrible cost of casualties: 226 British and 140 Americans were killed. Among the casualties is Dr. Warren. As he promised, the name of his mysterious informant of the planned Lexington and Concord raid was buried with him.

The Americans started domestic production of cannons and mortars, but as with gunpowder, they were stymied by shortages of equipment, credit, and hard currency. To obtain critical artillery during the Siege of Boston in 1775, a despairing Washington authorized one of the most iconic and bold adventures of the War, the raid on British Fort Ticonderoga in upstate New York. Henry Knox, who learned military strategy by reading the manuals he stocked on the shelves of his Boston bookstore, led the mission. Knox was a twenty-five-year-old US Army colonel and one of the many rebels with the heritage of the "born fighting" Scots Irish. He was a large man with almost 300 pounds on his six-foot frame. He adored his wife, Lucy Flucker, whose Loyalist parents opposed the war and fled to British lines, never to see their rebel daughter again. Knox and his men reached Fort Ticonderoga in upstate New York near the Canadian border in the cold winter of 1775. His mission was to transport captured British artillery pieces of mortars, cannons, cohorns (a light, portable mortar), and howitzers (short, barreled cannons) that collectively weighed over 60 tons across 300 miles. With no paved roads, the overland passage became a staggering feat of determination and courage. The epic journey began in early December 1775, with soldiers loading the armament on sleds that were pulled by 80 pairs of lumbering oxen.[21] After 56 grueling days, the triumphant, exhausted men arrived in Cambridge on January 24, 1776.

"Weak in numbers, dispirited, naked"

Returning to the battlefield of your imagination, you look at the men themselves, seeing their clothing, shoes, equipment and the general conditions of their camp. If your soldiers are fortunate enough to have uniforms, and these are not tattered and patched beyond recognition, they are dressed in an array of colors and patterns. The forests and fields are colored with the yellow-trimmed blue coats of the 13th Virginia regiment, dark brown jackets from the 1st Battalion Philadelphia Associates, deep green clothing of the Massachusetts militia and Vermont's Green Mountain Boys, and the more familiar, red-trimmed blue coats of the Delaware Regiments and the Virginia State Line Infantry.[22]

In 1779, the Continental Army standardized blue uniforms with the red, white, and beige trims that you see in Hollywood films. These colors were worn by Spanish militias in the Americas and were in the shipments of clothing sent by Spain.[23] Common articles of dress are deerskin breeches that stretch from the waist to just below the knee, and leggings, also of animal skin. A few well-tailored, GQ-type officers wear stockings of cotton or silk beneath leather boots.

Throughout the military dispatches, letters, newspaper articles, and diaries, the concern for the soldiers' clothing, including shoes, is a consistent, plaintive worry. Clothing was a treasured commodity, and the average colonial man or woman had only one or two complete outfits.[24] This step of the journey to your past may be challenging to imagine, as your closet of trendy fashions and sturdy garments vanishes. The 18th century Americans would view today's consignment shops and flea markets as specters of wondrous abundance. Even among the wealthy, textiles were highly prized, and the fabric of fashionable dresses was often re-cut and re-sewn for updated styles or sizes, rather than discarded. Most non-agricultural consumer goods in the colonies, including clothing, were imported. The silk of a plantation owner's dress was transported from China, linen underclothing from the Netherlands, linen for shirts and hats from the textile mills of England, and woolen hosiery from Scotland.[25] While colonial museums in Williamsburg and Boston display elaborate fashions of satins, brocaded silk taffeta and silver gilt lace, these luxuries were not within reach of the majority of colonial women. Most women in the colonies wore simple and functional layered clothing, starting with a basic loose shift with straight lines at mid-calf length. A straight, ankle-length skirt, topped by a laced-up bodice of cloth or leather, covered this shift. A short apron, or a longer version called a pinafore, was pinned to the gown or bodice, completed the outfit.[26]

Most men had only a few shirts of unbleached linen or coarse cotton, with a leather apron for workers, and breeches, which were knee-length, form-fitting trousers. Workers' breeches were made of wool, broadcloth, homespun cotton, linens, and deerskin. More formal embroidered breeches were made of silk velvet, silk twill or other expensive imported fabrics. Breeches were fitted below the knee, highlighting the 18th century man's hottest feature, his calf. Padding calves under stockings was a socially acceptable affectation of male vanity.[27] Frock coats and waistcoats completed the dress; the more elaborate embroidery, buttons, fabric and accessories were owned by the wealthy. As the war progressed and as the army recruited men with fewer personal resources, the clothing shortage became more acute.

The military leadership continued to plead for supplies through 1777. That July, a distraught General Philip John Schuyler wrote to Washington about the shortages as he tried to defend his home state of New York, fearing his troops could not stop the well-armed Redcoats. "They have an army flushed with victory, plentifully provided with provisions, cannon, and every warlike store," he wrote despairingly. "Our Army ... is weak in numbers, dispirited, naked, and in a manner, destitute of provisions, without camp equipage, with little ammunition, and not a single piece of cannon."[28] The British did advance, and Catherine Schuyler,* his brave wife and mom of the Schuyler sisters, rushed into the wheat fields on their family farm gripping flaming torches in her hands. She burnt her own fields to bare soil rather than allowing the enemy to consume the family's crops.[29]

The shortages continued, and the solution for them was complex and lengthy, while the situation was as immediate as bullets flying through battlefields. Fortunately for the Americans, material and military supplies from the Spanish were arriving through a complex and covert supply chain, financed with the silver pesos from their mines in Latin America and the power of the Spanish New World Empire.

---

*If her name sounds familiar, Catherine Schuyler is the mother of the Shuyler Sisters who star in Hamilton The Musical. Catherine was not a feature character in the play but she had that main character energy.

Chapter 3

GoFundUs a Revolution

As the sun set from the lush mountains of Peru to the beautiful central deserts of Mexico in 1776, thousands of miners emerged from their hard day's work in the silver mines. Their multi-hued skins of brown, black and white are dusted with dirt and streaked with sweat. Their faces are a blend of races that trace the story of almost three centuries of invasion and conquest in the collision of cultures[1] that had shattered the Native Americans' brilliant civilizations and devastated their ancient homelands since 1492. In their hands, the miners carry tools of iron and steel, the harsh metals that were part of the unholy trinity of guns, germs and steel that defeated powerful warriors and decimated nations. These advanced civilizations flourished for centuries, recording codices in intricate systems of pictograms and hieroglyphics, governing expansive realms with quipu knotted cords, raising monumental pyramids and complex urban centers, and measuring time and the movements of the stars with a remarkable command of mathematics and astronomy.

The Spanish conquistadors brought deadly diseases with them, and in an age before vaccines, tens of millions of people died. The total population in the Spanish territories of the Caribbean and Latin America in the 18th century was about 20 million, 13 million of whom were Native American.[2] In contrast, the colonial North American population in 1776 was 2.5 million, of which one-third were enslaved African Americans. Gold was the driving force during the first days of the Spanish conquest. The conquistadors greedily searched for the legendary golden cities of El Dorado, which astute Native Americans assured them was definitely farther away than their cities — across another desert or distant mountain range.

The rise of silver began in the early 1500s in the vast Viceroyalty of Peru, which included Peru, Ecuador, Bolivia, and parts of Colombia and Venezuela. Latin

American silver was the basis of the global currency from the 16th through 19th centuries. When traders in Russia sold their furs, merchants in Singapore and China shipped their delicate porcelain, or spice dealers in India and Vietnam exported their aromatic cinnamons and cardamoms, most transactions were in Latin American silver. Even Britain, a nation that was not a fan of Spain, purchased Spanish silver coins, countermarked them with the head of King George III and issued them as dollars.[3] At the center of this explosion of wealth was Potosí, a city founded by Peruvians and Bolivians, later christened as European in 1546.[4] Potosí was literally a mountain of silver ore and produced 60% of the world's silver in the 17th century.[5]

If you were European and wealthy, 17th century Potosí was the place to be. After the discovery of silver beneath it, Potosí's population reached 200,000 people, second only to Mexico City. Merchants shipped riches from all over the world, landing the goods in ports on the low Caribbean coastline and transporting the merchandise into the cloud-ringed mountains at elevations of over 13,000 feet. Richly woven tapestry from Naples, marble from India, Venetian crystal, Persian carpets, and Arabian perfumes were purchased with the gleaming ore. At the height of its wealth and glamour, Potosí hosted theaters, dance schools, gaming houses, and sex worker establishments, including one owned and operated by an entrepreneurial woman, Doña Clara. Fashionistas dazzled the dusty streets clothed in silks, brocades, velvet, and cloth woven with gold.[6]

If you were not one of the privileged, Posotí was "the mouth of hell" in the words of a 17th century observer. Under the Incan *mita* system of labor, communities paid with their labor for part of the year, instead of currency or barter. The Incan empire reciprocated with public infrastructure including roads, bridges, and agricultural terraces.* The Spanish exploited this system, and many native peoples were forced to work year round in the dangerous mines, where they choked on the poisonous mercury fumes and suffered cold, malnutrition, and deadly accidents. Over the centuries that Potosí operated, an estimated one million people perished while working the mines.[7]

---

*Think of the Incan mita as rotational gig work, in which citizens' labor funds useful public works, such as an agricultural system to produce affordable food.

From Silver Mines to Battlefields

In the central Mexican desert, the Chichimeca people mined silver for centuries prior to the arrival of the Spanish. The story of these people is part of the complex history of northwest Mexico, which experienced waves of migrations of different cultures and the rise and decline of vast cities and brilliant civilizations over thousands of years.[8] The Mexica, pronounced "Me-SHEE-ka" and misnamed as Aztecs,[9] and Spanish encountered the Chichimeca. Both the warrior Mexica and the brutal conquistadors agreed that the Chichimeca were fiercely independent people who passionately resisted conquest. According to desert rumors, a Chichimeca made the unfortunate decision to give a Spanish conquistador a piece of local silver, and the rush was on.

By the mid-1770s, the epicenter of silver production in the Spanish empire had shifted from the Viceroyalty of Peru to Mexico. With the astute management of the entrepreneurial "silver kings" and the expertise of highly skilled Mexican miners, silver production in Mexico skyrocketed in the 18th century. Production increased by estimates of 600% and higher and Mexico alone produced 70% of the world's silver.[10] The first mint established in the Americas was in Mexico City in 1536, and by 1732, machinery was introduced to manufacture the newly re-designed coins.[11] The coins were "milled" instead of hammered, with deliberate vertical grooves struck into a coin's edge to prevent chipping to steal silver. Mints were established in Peru, Bolivia, Guatemala, Colombia and Chile in the 1700s.

New discoveries of ore reserves, sound government policies for commodity prices and increased financial incentives for the silver miners fueled the rise. The workforce of native Mexicans, Afro-Mexicans, and Mexican-born Spanish migrated to wherever ore was discovered. After centuries of slavery in the mines and decades of labor unrest, many of the late 18th century silver miners in Mexico were well-paid, with most camps sharing a percentage of the ore in addition to a daily wage. The industry was financed by entrepreneurial merchant-capitalists and mine owners, with a chain of credit and supplies that connected bankers and merchants in the high plateaus of Mexico City to local traders, refiners and miners back in the busy desert camps that comprised a portion of the global Silver Road.

A string of elegant cities graced with colonial architecture stretched for hundreds of miles from Sonora in the north to Oaxaca in the south, sparkling through Mexico City, San Luis Potosí, San Miguel de Allende, Guanajuato, Zacatecas and Querétaro. Over 500 mining centers covered the territory in a busy industrial network.[12] Mining operations were lengthy and complex, and required skilled workers and technicians. The work began with the prospectors, fortune-hunting rogues who scoured the mountains and deserts at their own risk, hoping to strike the 18th century equivalent of the Powerball lottery. Once the silver reserve was found, the complex, arduous work of extracting it began. The foreman's role was to track the vein through the silent, obdurate earth. The mine was excavated to follow the vein ore by building massive tunnels or blasting through rock with gunpowder administered by specialists known as drillers or rocketers. The miners, named after the iron picks and shovels that they used, chipped out the ore to manageable sizes, assisted by basket carriers or mule trains.

The work was sometimes dangerous and deadly. Wood fires lit to burn the ore on site risked erupting into uncontrollable firestorms. The mine roofs could collapse without warning from the dryness and vibrations of the explosions. Unpredictable floods deluged the tunnels as the mines were dug deeper. Sluice box and waterwheel operators and other skilled workers managed the dangerous flows. Once the ore was extracted, the next steps were to draw pure silver into the sunlight. The two primary techniques were smelting through heat so intense that it would melt the glasses in your kitchen cabinet or a chemical process of amalgamation using mercury. Smelting relied on systems of furnaces, water baths, and strong blasts of air into the furnaces. The amalgamation process required grinding the ore into a powder, washing the amalgam and refining it with poisonous mercury.[13] As the final step, the refined pure silver was hammered into the bars and coins that fueled the world's financial system, including the economic and financial infrastructure of the desperately cash poor United States.

One of the largest enterprises was the Valenciana mine in Guanajuato, a city and state in the heart of Mexico with a central role in the country's history for centuries. The Valenciana mine employed over 3,000 miners working in an underground city with numerous tunnels lacing through the solid earth. The central octagonal stone-lined shaft was constructed with a circumference of 32 yards and a depth of over 600 yards. Eight mule-drawn vertical drums transported the ore from the depths.[14] Today, locals and tourists drive underground through brightly lit tunnels paved with cobblestones, whirling beneath charming tree-lined plazas and extravagant churches and cathedrals.

One of the most fabled and controversial silver kings in the late 18th century was Pedro Romero de Terreros, the first conde of Regla. Loathed and loved, feared and revered, some accounts excoriated Terreros for using slave labor and his persistent conflicts with free workers while others acknowledged his savvy business management and generous donations to religious charities, including sponsorship of the Santa Cruz de San Sabá mission near Menard, Texas.[15] His life story is a classic tale of a poor boy rising to stupendous riches, an American dream. Born in the small town of Cortegana, Spain, his fortunes were limited until he immigrated to Mexico in 1728. He began his career in Querétaro with the help of his uncle, becoming the wealthiest man in Mexico during the late 18th century. Most of his mining operations were in Pachuca, Real del Monte, and the Regla region, northwest of Mexico City.

His official portrait expresses the inner strength and forceful personality that propelled his success. His eyes gaze out unwaveringly from under heavy dark eyebrows. His expression is stern and confident; his mouth is drawn in a tight line. One of his large hands is held open near his chest, which Terreros ordered the artist to paint. In the iconography, or body language, of colonial Spanish painting, an open hand indicated a charitable man, for which his detractors must have rolled their eyes. Considering his wardrobe – he was a stylish dresser who spent extravagant sums on finely tailored clothing and expensive fabrics – he is dressed simply in a dark suit and subdued cravat. His hair is pulled tightly back into a small braid, giving him a modern appearance. This face could readily be placed in a 21st century business article featuring a hard-driving CEO outwitting regulators and competitors. Terreros' portrait is still visible in Mexico today: when customers pawn their valuables in exchange for a cash loan at the government sponsored Monte de Piedad, their exchange ticket is marked with Regla's unsmiling face.[16]

Ambitious and shrewd, Terreros often wrote of "sleepless nights" working on his business. He married into an aristocratic Mexican-born Spanish family and presented his new wife with a fortune in jewels and two dresses covered in diamonds.[17] When his first son was born, he reportedly showered the streets in Pachuca with silver. He sent his sons to Spain for their education, where they were warmly welcomed for their contributions to the Spanish Treasury. As coldly calculating as he was, he did not force arranged marriages on his four daughters and allowed them to follow their hearts — an unusually compassionate measure for a man of his times and position.

Terreros claimed that his initial investments in silver mining were driven by altruism to benefit religious charities and the Spanish Treasury.[18] Whatever his motives, Terreros was one of the most powerful and proactive of the silver kings, embarking on sometimes-risky ventures that helped to propel the Mexican mining industry to spectacular success. He died in 1781, the same year that the crucial silver coins arrived in faraway Virginia to assist the US Army at the Siege of Yorktown.

Querétaro, then the third largest city in Mexico, was a key location along the Silver Road. Located at the juncture of important trade routes, the city was a supply depot for the surrounding silver mining region, and a shopping hub for Asian goods shipped from Manila to Acapulco and European goods from the trade fairs at Jalapa, San Juan and Saltillo. Querétaro was a destination resort for 18th century residents in neighboring states. With small rivers and streams and adequate rainfall, agriculture flourished with crops of wheat, corn, and rye. The Spanish and Mexicans built grand mansions and cultivated verdant gardens. The city was home to Jesuit, Dominican, and Augustinian churches, and Santa Clara, one of the wealthiest convents in the Americas. The convent occupied four city blocks with streets, gardens, fountains, and houses for the nuns and their servants, with the nuns somehow squaring these arrangements with their vow of poverty.[19]

Further north along the Silver Road, the mines at Zacatecas were also leading sources of silver during this period. Zacatecas, now designated as a UNESCO world heritage site for its impressive cultural monuments, was founded in 1546. The silver kings built an impressive Mexican baroque cathedral of intricately carved pink desert stone in 1752. The Eden mine, worked from 1586 until the 1950s, is meticulously restored. Visitors descend by elevator or small train into the cool depths of the hillside of Cerro del Grillo where the mine is located. The cruel days of the mining operations in the 16th century are recounted, when the Spanish conquistadors punished the Chichimeca people for their valiant resistance by forcing men, women and children to work in the mines.

Pesos, Dollars, and Pieces of Eight

As the American colonies struggled to establish an independent financial system, Congress pegged the unsteady Continental dollar to the Spanish peso at a one-to-one ratio, which increased dramatically as hyperinflation ravaged the US economy. The peso, also known as the Spanish milled dollar, Mexican dollar, or peso fuerte were divided into smaller pieces, the famed pieces of eight or eight silver reales and "bits" (silver, not digital). When Alexander Hamilton established the first American silver dollar coin in 1794, the specifications closely replicated the peso in dimension, purity and weight.[20] The Spanish peso remained legal US currency until 1857, and still marks our bills: the government adopted the dollar symbol ($) from an invoice sent to Congress during the war with an abbreviation for ps (pesos).[21]

Latin American silver was so widespread that even the British paid their troops in the colonies with Spanish currency. The money was remitted from the British Treasury and converted to Spanish coins for distribution to their soldiers by contractors with deputy paymasters and agents in North America and the Caribbean.[22] This silver currency also circulated through the Bank of Amsterdam, an important network in the international finance system where Spain deposited secret funds for the Americans. Spain also channeled substantial sums for the Americans through Spain's diplomatic representatives in Paris, and through Havana and Nueva Orleáns. Military supplies were shipped to the colonies through various routes across the Atlantic Ocean, through the Caribbean Sea, and up the Mississippi River, completing the links from the Latin American mines. This complex supply chain was initially set in motion from northern Spain, in the heart of the Basque province.

The Basque Connection | Euskal Konexioa

When Carlos III and his ministers in Madrid plotted to smuggle more supplies to the embattled US Army, when Abigail Adams needed assistance with her textile import business to evade the British blockade,[23] and when the Massachusetts Committee of Supplies worried as to how to replace their dwindling stocks of gunpowder, these Americans turned to the Spanish Basque trading company of La Casa Gardoqui e Hijos. The company's business operations were based in Bilbao, a city near the northeastern Spanish coast. The Basques have a rich cultural heritage, delicious cuisine, and a unique Pre-Indo-European language, Euskara. Seafarers, fishermen and explorers, the Basques traveled across the Atlantic Ocean for over two centuries before 1776 in pursuit of the huge codfish that once swarmed in great schools in the cold currents of the northern Atlantic seas.[24] When, exactly, the Basques reached North America is still a subject of speculation. Centuries old manuscripts testify to lengthy voyages across the Atlantic by the Basques, who were famously secretive about the locations of their fisheries.

Diego María de Gardoqui y Arriguibar, the central figure at this crucial time, was born in Bilbao and grew up in the family trading business started by his father in 1724. He apprenticed in England at the house of Lord Hayley, a prominent commercial trader. He and his family were well-regarded and well-connected in the power circles of Madrid. Gardoqui was of slight stature and dressed stylishly. For his formal portrait he wore a powdered and curled wig that framed his high forehead, prominent eyebrows, and an elegant straight nose. His large eyes exude a quiet determined confidence. Gardoqui was an understated presence and soft power throughout the Revolutionary War and in the founding of the United States, beginning with covertly supplying weapons to the Americans in 1775 to marching in President Washington's Inaugural Parade in 1789.

Gardoqui e Hijos was authorized to trade with the colonies in 1736, and the company extended their merchant trade to Boston, Salem, and Beverly in Massachusetts. The multi-lingual Gardoquis dealt in a wide variety of goods, including the codfish that made the fortunes of many New England families. The Gardoquis had close connections with the influential trading and financial firm of Willing and Morris in Philadelphia owned by Robert Morris, the chief financier of the American Revolution.[25] During these decades, Massachusetts merchants established trading links with Spain. Ships from ports in Boston, Gloucester, and Newburyport regularly sailed to Cádiz and Bilbao, trading codfish, rice, tobacco, and indigo (a prized blue dye and cleaning agent).[26] The firm was known to American leaders, including Benjamin Franklin, in the years before the war.[27]

Diego de Gardoqui began assisting the rebels in early 1774, as the British began their blockade of the eastern seaboard. The Massachusetts Committee of Supplies wrote to Gardoqui in December 1774, requesting assistance in purchasing gunpowder. In his response to Jeremiah Lee on the Committee in February 1775, Gardoqui explained the difficulty in purchasing muskets, bayonets, and gunpowder, which were strictly regulated and controlled by the Spanish government. While Gardoqui said that his firm could secretly procure some munitions from Spain, he also offered to smuggle gunpowder from the Netherlands. Another risk, Gardoqui cautioned, was that the British on the European side of the Atlantic could seize ships carrying the munitions. Stealthy British spies seemed to be snooping everywhere.[28] But Gardoqui was loyal and persistent, as he wrote to Jeremiah Lee, "Altho of a very difficulty nature, we were determined at all events to assist you accordingly..."

The Massachusetts Committee wrote to Gardoqui later in 1775, pleading that he purchase gunpowder from other countries in Europe, suggesting that France, Holland, Denmark, and Sweden had supplies of the precious product. Elbridge Gerry, a member of the Committee, wrote that, "The Ministry in Britain have been endeavoring to keep a Supply of powder from the colonies, well knowing that they cannot enslave them by any other means."[29] Two letters from Gerry written later in August 1775 attest to the arrival of the needed supplies from Gardoqui. In addition to his work on the Massachusetts Safety Committee, Gerry was a leader of the famed men of Marblehead, Massachusetts, and the fifth Vice President of the United States.*

Gardoqui was often the intermediary between the Patriots and the Court in Madrid, where he maintained a residence. He analyzed the political, diplomatic, and economic aspects of the War, and mentored novice diplomats who sought to bargain with the sophisticated Spanish Court, including the inexperienced Arthur Lee.[30] Lee was a native Virginian educated at Eton in England and the University of Edinburgh in Scotland. He was a difficult man to deal with, prone to suspicions, and managed to irritate the Spanish and the French and his fellow Americans during his service in Madrid and Paris. Lee wrote to Congress after meeting with Gardoqui in Spain that, "I am authorized to assure you that supplies for the army will be sent to you by every opportunity from Bilbao. I can say with certainty, that a merchant there has orders for that purpose. He is now here with me to have a list from me and to contract for blankets.... I am also desired to inform you of ammunition and clothing being deposited at New Orleans and the Havana, with directions to lend them to such American vessels as may call there for that purpose. "[31]

---

*Gerry is the namesake of the word "gerrymander," a popular term in 2026.

In 1776, Carlos III and Floridablanca, the Spanish Secretary of State who had promised "to do everything that circumstances permit" for the Americans, instructed Gardoqui to begin smuggling operations directly funded by the government. Gardoqui was an excellent and discreet manager who administered the covert, complex international trading operations on an unofficial basis, shipping on both American and Spanish vessels. In 1777 and 1778 alone, twelve ships left Bilbao to race against the British naval patrol with supplies of cannons, mortars, bombs, guns, bullets, powder, lead, clothing, and military equipment valued at approximately 225,000 silver pesos, about $468 million today.[32]

In 1792, Gardoqui proudly recalled that, "I can assure your excellency that the Americans were given very important assistance from Spain by the Spanish Government during the years 1776, 1777, and 1778 to the enormous extent of 7,944,906 reales ... besides 30,000 blankets sent to them when blankets were an absolute necessity, or their soldiers would have perished."[33] These 7.9 million reales were equivalent to 1.0 million pesos, or about $2.1 billion in today's dollars. Gardoqui sent orders for woolen blankets to the Province of Palencia, then the center of the country's wool-weaving industry. Men and women hurriedly worked to weave the warm blankets and woolen articles, which were bundled into tall bales collected in plazas throughout the province. These blankets and clothing were packed into waiting ships with military supplies, and departed from Barcelona, Cádiz, and Bilbao to outmaneuver the blockade and reach the rebels.[34]

Gardoqui himself summarized the commercial and personal relationship that so benefited the Americans in a letter to Arthur Lee, "My person and trading house are well known in the colonies, not only due to our long-standing commercial relations of thirty to forty years, but also for the sincere affection with which we have endeavored to serve them." A bronze statue of Gardoqui, elegantly dressed holding a scrolled paper in his hands, now stands in Logan Square in Philadelphia. In 1977, King Juan Carlos I of Spain gifted the statue to the City of Philadelphia in commemoration of the Bicentennial of the United States. *

---

* Ironically, the Spanish government paid for this merchandise as well. My guess is that the document in Gardoqui's hand is an overdue loan.

The Bourbons Go Shopping

Two hundred bronze cannons, 27 mortars, 30,000 guns with bayonets, over 50,000 bullets, 13,000 cannon balls, 300,000 rounds of gunpowder, 30,000 complete military uniforms...quite a shopping list from the Spanish and French Kings. Pedro Pablo Abarca y Bolea, the conde de Aranda and Spanish Ambassador to Paris, carefully listed this extensive catalog of supplies in his dispatch to Madrid. These supplies were shipped to the US Army[35] beginning in 1776 and 1777 through Roderigue Hortalez y Compañía, the covert ops trading company established by the Spanish and French. The three men who set this supply chain in motion in Europe were Aranda, Vergennes, and Grimaldi.

Aranda was one of the men who actively worked to fund the company, along with French Foreign Minister Charles Gravier, the comte de Vergennes, and the Spanish Prime Minister, Pablo-Jerónimo de Grimaldi y Pallavicini. Aranda was a supremely confident and talented diplomat with one of the best-stocked wine cellars in Paris. He was 58 at the start of the American Revolution and was a battle-tested disabled veteran. Aranda was impressed with the Enlightenment and met with philosophical luminaries including Denis Diderot and the often-scandalous François-Marie Arouet Voltaire. He negotiated directly with Benjamin Franklin and American diplomats throughout the war. His portrait is interesting for his choice of setting. Although Aranda is dressed handsomely in a deep blue suit trimmed with gold braid, in the background, chaos reigns. Books are strewn on the floor and sketches of fortresses are crumpled next to a large cannon haphazardly resting behind his feet. He stands near a table holding a casually tossed red fabric, with a grey round cannon ball directly underneath. From this mayhem, Aranda placidly gazes out in an almost bored expression that could be interpreted as 'Nothing that you could do will surprise me.'

Vergennes was a Jesuit-educated career ambassador deeply versed in the diplomatic machinations behind France's relationships with the Portuguese, Russians, Swedes, and Prussians, among other cantankerous world players. He was appointed Ambassador to the Ottoman (Turkish) Empire in 1755. A portrait of Vergennes richly dressed in a red and white turban and the traditional flowing robes of the Ottoman Court is in the Pera Museum in Istanbul, Turkey. The court in Paris ostensibly recalled him home in 1768 for an affair of the heart. Despite his calculating and worldly nature, he married a widow, Anne Duvivier, without the permission of the King, which was required of ambassadors. Madame Duvivier was not approved of by the haughty Parisian society. By 1774, all was forgiven, and Vergennes was appointed to the powerful position of Foreign Minister when Louis XVI ascended to the French throne.

Grimaldi was another career diplomat who served at Spanish posts throughout Europe while working for the court of Madrid. Italian by birth and shrewdly calculating by nature, Grimaldi wasn't always popular. His house was ransacked during the riots that shook the Spanish aristocracy in 1766. An experienced policy wonk, Grimaldi was highly influential in shaping Spain's programs for the American Rebellion. He continually strategized how to advance Spain's interests while covertly weakening the British, calculating the timing of the declaration of war against Britain for Spain's greatest advantage.

In 1774, these three men were already planning to undermine Britain by taking advantage of Britain's conflicts with the Americans.[36] In March 1775, Aranda wrote to the Spanish Court that the British were struggling with their colonies and experiencing disruptions to their lucrative trade. Aranda proposed that if France and Spain combined forces to continue these disruptions, they could weaken British forces, enabling an attack on their mutual enemy.[37] Vergennes and Grimaldi were in discussions by March 1776, outlining how they could supply the rebellion with massive amounts of equipment while concealing the flow of aid from the British. The two men agreed that France was the choice location for the operations, since French ships could more easily evade British scrutiny by shipping directly into French territorial waters in the Caribbean. Early in June, Aranda sent Grimaldi a secret dispatch telling him that the French were funding the operations with one million livres tornesas, a unit of French currency with a ratio of about 5 to 5.5 livres to the Spanish peso. Grimaldi promptly replied that Carlos III was sending "the adjoining credit of a million livres tornesas .... We cannot do it directly and maintain the indispensable secrecy, but your Excellency [Aranda] will settle the matter with the Count de Vergennes as to the sort of assistance on which this amount is better to be invested."[38]

These were huge sums of money and amounts of supplies compared to the size and resources of the US Army. While hundreds of thousands of Patriots volunteered in the army and state militias throughout the years of war, the numbers that were under command and on the battlefields at a single point in time were much smaller. Many men served their enlistments and then returned to civilian life. During the early years of the rebellion, Congress and Washington planned for an army of 20,000 men but they could not recruit enough volunteers.[39] The estimated number of US soldiers early in 1776 was 19,000, declining to 5,000 by autumn of that year, rising to about 11,000 at the Battle of Yorktown in 178 1.[40] The Spanish shipments of uniforms, muskets, and supplies were a massive contribution to the poorly equipped US Army. The cannons and mortars were a gamechanger and were immediately deployed to the crucial Battles of Saratoga, in upstate New York, in 1777.

As might be expected of a covert enterprise, Roderigue Hortalez y Compañía has a complicated origin story. According to a Spanish account, the firm was established with the assistance of Luis de Unzaga y Amézaga, the Governor of Nueva Orleáns and a relative of Diego de Gardoqui.[41] Unzaga was a career military man who enlisted as a Spanish cadet at age 14 and fought for Spain in several global wars. During the Seven Years' War, he initiated a network of spies to report on British troop movements in America. He was well-positioned to leverage this network again in the early 1770's to monitor the progress and setbacks of the Patriots.[42] He was also one of the first military leaders to use the term "United States of America" in a letter that he wrote to General Charles Lee in 1776. Lee reported that, "I have just receiv'd a most flattering letter from Don Louis Venzaga [Unzaga, creatively misspelled] ... He gives me the title of General de *los estados unidos Americanos.*"[43]

According to the French, Vergennes recommended the appointment of a French playwright and watchmaker, Pierre-Augustin Caron de Beaumarchais to manage Roderigue Hortalez. Beaumarchais wrote the bestsellers *The Barber of Seville* and *The Marriage of Figaro* and traveled to Spain for a lengthy stay. He was recognized as a thought leader in the Enlightenment and was enthralled with the American Revolution. A confidential agent of Louis XVI, Beaumarchais assisted the king by resolving a troublesome matter of blackmail. He delighted the king's mistress with an exquisite miniature watch that fitted in a finger ring. This finger ring was a unique novelty in the 18th century; imagine owning the first and only Apple Hermès watch. Beaumarchais was reportedly a spy in Unzaga's network.[44] British spies kept him under watchful surveillance and monitored his extensive travel between London and France in 1775 and 1776. The British suspected, correctly, that Beaumarchais was working to arrange funding for weapons and military supplies. Beaumarchais met with Aranda in Paris as an *"hombre de confi-*

anza" to receive orders from Aranda to administer the program.[45] Beaumarchais and his staff spent months assembling the extensive military supplies and fleets to transport them. Beaumarchais worked with a French merchant who met with Congress. The Congressmen gave the merchant a shopping list of needed items. The merchant was based in Saint Domingue, a leading French colony initially settled by pirates of the Caribbean.[46]

According to the Spanish version, Unzaga and Gardoqui, who were also connected with Beaumarchais, shipped the first supplies through Roderigue Hortalez y Compañía, from Cadíz to Nueva Orleáns in December 1776.[47] Meanwhile in France, Beaumarchais chartered a fleet of nine merchant ships that launched from different French ports at staggered intervals beginning in March 1777. To elude the British, the route passed near the Bermudas, whose inhabitants were rumored to be sympathetic to the Americans and trusted to keep secret any sightings of French ships. The *Amphitrite* carried the first covert shipment from France, sailing into Philadelphia in May 1777. The cargo comprised 216 bronze cannons, 12,282 bombs with fuses, 30,000 rifles with bayonets, 20,000 uniforms, 27 mortars and 4,000 tents.[48] Eight of the ships dodged the Brits to arrive at the Caribbean islands of Saint Domingue, Saint Eustatius, and Martinique.[49] Robert Morris anxiously awaited confirmation of their arrival and arranged for vessels to travel to the Caribbean to retrieve the supplies.[50]

The Spanish and French continued the operations with great secrecy and succeeded in keeping the shipments from discovery by the British. Aranda was deeply concerned about retaliation by the British. Rumors circulated through Paris about the covert shipments, possibly from the French soldiers who had prepared the munitions and supplies and were now visiting their families in the city. Perhaps while sipping on a steadying glass of wine from his expansive collection, Aranda wrote to Grimaldi that the British "were already exaggerating the extent of the aid" to the rebels.

Given the secrecy of the operations and the extensive network of agents involved, the Spanish themselves could not calculate their assistance to the Patriots. Shipments were routed through multiple traders to conceal their origin, and it was difficult for Spanish officials to maintain a complete accounting of the armaments and supplies that they dispatched. The funds comprised loans, subsidies, gifts, and payments in various currencies.[51] In a report to the French court in 1777, a Spanish official noted, "...the total amount we, ourselves, are scarcely able to appraise owing to the variety of hands, and places, through which they passed making it impossible; and considering that this aid is a generous donation, this surely may be acknowledged to be already of great importance."[52]

Silver miners, merchant bankers, and sailors were among the many hands that made these achievements possible. The list stretches far longer, encompassing weavers, warehousemen, ship's carpenters, bargemen, craftsmen, gunsmiths, mill workers, seamstresses, and blacksmiths. As Joseph Plumb Martin, a 16-year-old enlistee who wrote a lively account of the war from 1776 to 1781, later reflected, "Great men get great praise. Little men, nothing." History remembers its famous names, yet those figures accomplished nothing without the labor of countless others whose names survive, if at all, unacknowledged in dusty archives. For some, such as the American sailors racing supply ships through the British blockade, the stakes were brutally high. Capture with cargo destined for the colonies often led to confinement in the floating hell of a British prison ship. For many others, their contribution was through the routines of ordinary days and seemingly ordinary lives. A Spanish weaver, exhausted after hours at her wooden loom, finishes a blanket. A cold soldier in a tattered shirt wraps it around his shoulders and finds the strength to continue his march. A Mexican silver miner, his arms aching from a day underground, studies the raw ore that he has wrested from the earth, soon to be minted into coins that purchase an American soldier's gunpowder and bread. From such uncelebrated labor, performed by unnamed people in forgotten stories, the improbable American Revolution was won.

Chapter 4

The Spies Who Loved Us

Under the luminous tropical sun in May 1776, the ship *Santa Barbara* glided out of the busy harbor of Havana, heading towards the Caribbean Sea. The *Santa Barbara* appeared to be one of the many merchant ships ferrying cargo along this well-traveled highway of waves. The crew was instructed by their VIP passenger, Miguel Antonio Eduardo, to travel to Santo Domingo, a Spanish colony west of Havana. Unknown to the crew, the ship had a secret mission to an unnamed destination far away from their stated port.

The sailors did know that Eduardo was Spain's official English interpreter in Havana who conducted sensitive negotiations for the Spanish government. As the days passed and the ship navigated the clear azure waters, the crew noticed that the vessel was increasingly difficult to handle. The sailors swore as their rough, calloused hands pulled at the ropes and sails, and they tried to determine the cause. They made an alarming discovery: the towering timber mainmast was damaged at its base. The sailors were puzzled since the vessel had passed inspection before its departure. They rushed to inform the ship's captain, Rafael Gonzalez, who inspected the main mast and announced they would sail north to Philadelphia for repairs. The crew were shocked: why Philadelphia? It was a small port in the American colonies patrolled by the British Navy. Gonzalez confirmed his orders, and the *Santa Barbara* rounded the coast of Florida and reached Delaware Bay on May 23rd.[1]

Philadelphia was Eduardo's unnamed destination from the start of the voyage, which was a spy mission. Eduardo was among the "unofficial" Spanish agents and diplomats that Carlos III and the Havana leadership selected to travel to the American colonies for intelligence gathering. Captain General Diego José de Navarro supervised Eduardo's mission, including secretly sabotaging the *Santa Barbara's* main mast before it left port. The ploy of a "damaged" ship was a cover story to land him in Philadelphia. Eduardo planned to reside in the rebel capital and establish a wheat flour trading business. Bread was preferred by Spanish and Cuban foodies, but the island's climate was too warm to grow wheat, and flour had to be imported. From there, Eduardo planned to smuggle reports back to Cuba in sacks of flour on the state of the growing rebellion and the movements of the British Army and Navy.[2]

As the ship continued sailing into the bay and the Delaware River, warning shouts from the crew sounded on the deck. The crew spotted a British warship in the distance, its sails billowing as it turned to close in on the *Santa Barbara*. The warship's cannons glinted ominously in the spring sun. British warships were cruising coastal seas to enforce the blockade of the New England colonies.[3] The warship *Liverpool* gained on the *Santa Barbara*, and the frightened crew saw armed British marines on deck, readying to board. Eduardo knew that the British would search their ship and find the large cache of 12,000 silver pesos concealed below deck,[4] destined to finance his trading operations. He heard the dull thuds of metal grappling hooks scraping against the wooden railings as the British sailors of the *Liverpool* pulled the *Santa Barbara* alongside their vessel, and the British marines boarded the ship. Eduardo and Captain González protested the boarding, arguing that they were a neutral merchant ship. British marines searched the ship and discovered the cache of silver coins. The British officers did not believe their well-planned story. The Spanish had not been off course, the officers charged but "had the audacity to carry money to the Americans," as Eduardo wrote later in his diary.[5]

The *Santa Barbara* sailed down the coast and surrendered to the Royal Navy in Virginia in late May. The British Admiralty initiated proceedings against Eduardo and the crew to prove that they were aiding the Americans. A captive of the British, Eduardo's mission appeared to be doomed, but he refused to give up. His English fluency and charm made him a favored dinner guest of British naval officers, including Lord Dunmore, the Royal Governor of Virginia. Dunmore had evacuated to a British warship after receiving threats from the rebels, who were enraged that he promised to free enslaved African American men if they joined the British Army.[6] Over dinner, the men discussed the colonial rebellion, the British war aims, and the dismal British view of those insolent insurgents.

Fortunately for Eduardo, the Patriots persisted in their attacks along the coastline, and the British Navy withdrew from the Chesapeake Bay in late August.

The admiralty dropped the case against the *Santa Barbara* crew. Eduardo posted a promissory note for the ship, and he and the crew were allowed to travel south to Havana. The Cuban sailors unfurled the sails to return home on October 1, after spending almost three months as prisoners of the British.[7] When Eduardo returned to Havana, he provided a detailed account of his time with the British in a journal that he presented to Navarro. Although he never established himself as a merchant in Philadelphia, the information he gathered made his mission a partial success. The following year, he departed for another covert assignment in Nueva Orleáns, continuing the mission to support the American rebels.

Team Carlos III in Havana

The Spanish leadership in the Americas were a remarkable team of men, and their expertise and commitment to defeating the British had a profound impact on the American Revolutionary War. These men oversaw the smuggling operations of critical weapons and supplies, established a network of intelligence gathering and espionage, fought directly in battles against the British in the southern and western regions bordering the American colonies, and led the financing throughout the war to the final Battle of Yorktown.

The Gálvez family was prominent within this team. The family's rise from poor shepherds in a village of 300 people to powerful advisors to the king was a stunning example of the rise in social mobility in 18th century Spain.[8] When he was a young student, the oldest son, José, so impressed a visiting bishop with his scholarship that the bishop arranged for him to attend the seminary in Malaga. José decided that the church was not his calling and switched to study law at the prestigious University of Salamanca. He moved to Madrid, and through his French wife's family connections, landed a post as the French Embassy Counsel. José was introduced to the Marqués de Grimaldi, and as his law clerk continued advancing his career.[9] From 1776 to 1787, Carlos III appointed him to the influential post of Minister of the Indies, where he promoted his family's interests.

His brother, Matías de Gálvez was appointed to the colonial administration in Guatemala in 1778. With his talent for political administration and military strategy, Matías soon rose to the governor of the Captaincy of Guatemala, where he later led fighting against the British in Central America. Matías disliked both the British and the Americans and hoped that the war would damage both sides. The two brothers' portraits are a study in contrast. José stands regally, directly facing the audience, elegantly dressed with a large blue sash crossing from his shoulder to his waistline. He holds papers in his left hand and points to a large map of Spanish holdings along the northern Gulf of Mexico. Matías is stylishly dressed in an elaborately brocaded coat and waistcoat. His half-turned face sternly stares across time under a sharply arched eyebrow. In his left hand, he grips a document, while his right hand is curled into a loose fist.

Both brothers promoted the career of Matías' son, Bernardo de Gálvez. Bernardo had a remarkable military and political career, an adventurous life and – unusual in the 18th century – a happy marriage based on love. He was a guitar player, a fan of bullfighting, and actively studied new military technologies, including hot air balloons. A seasoned combat veteran, he enlisted at age 16 with an appointment as a lieutenant in the French Army, arranged by Tío José. Since France was an ally of Spain, Spanish soldiers served in the French Army. Bernardo fought against Native American militias in the American southwest when he deployed to "New Spain" in 1769. In 1772, he returned to Europe and continued his education at the Royal Military Academy of Avila, which educated the best and the brightest young military technocrats. He gained more military experience in Portugal and Algiers, where he was seriously wounded. Bernardo served as the Governor of Nueva Orleáns in 1777, managing the smuggling operations to ship military supplies and provisions to the US Army. He led the critical military campaign against the British that ended in the triumphant Battle of Pensacola in 1779.

The wider circle of leadership based in Havana included men who were essential to the Spanish support of the Revolutionary War. Luis de Unzaga y Amézaga, Diego José de Navarro y Valladares, the Captain General of Havana, Juan de Cagigal y Montserrat, the Governor of Cuba, and José de Gálvez managed the Spanish network of espionage agents. José de Ezpeleta, a friend of Bernardo's from their student days in Avila, also battled the British during the American Revolution. Ezpeleta fought in the Battle of Pensacola and coordinated the army's efforts against the British in the southern and western regions that bordered the colonies. Juan Ignacio de Urriza, the Intendant of Havana and Agent of the Crown, managed the financial operations on the island.[10] These men offered what the Continental Army and American leadership did not possess: experienced military and administrative skills, vast resources of cash and equipment, and a stable base to direct smuggling operations and military campaigns. "Team Carlos" received frequent and direct orders from Carlos III in Spain.

Carlos III, the Court in Madrid, and this leadership in Havana understood the importance of establishing relationships with the Patriots early in the war. They determined that their best strategy for intelligence gathering was to place agents close to the inner circles of rebel political power and military activity. With planning and strategizing at the highest levels of leadership, the Spanish deployed trusted agents throughout Nueva Orleáns, San Augustín and further north in Philadelphia. These Spanish agents operated in the colonies throughout the rebellion, sending detailed military, economic, and political reports to Team Carlos in Havana. They developed friendships and close relationships in the highest circles of American leadership, including George Washington, members of Congress and leading businessmen.

In the autumn of 1777, Carlos ordered Havana to send two secret agents to the rebel colonies. One agent was to report from the war zone and the second to establish connections with the Continental Congress. Their mission, as described by José de Gálvez, was "to investigate the state of the war and its progress, the principal advantages of each party, their respective forces, the disposition which one or both of the parties may have either to continue the war or to abandon it, and any design prejudicial to Spain and her American possessions which can be detected."[11] This information was needed to determine the extent of Madrid's commitment to the American Patriots. Supporting the Americans was an expensive and risky business for Spain. To European observers, the Americans appeared conflicted and uncertain, as Patriots and Loyalists fought viciously against each other on city streets and battlefields. The Spanish leadership had to ascertain the Patriots' level of commitment: would they remain steady to their cause through years of hardship, or falter and negotiate a peace settlement with the British?

The two agents selected were Juan José Eligio de la Puente and Juan de Miralles de Trailhón. De la Puente had lived in Florida before Spain had lost it to the British in the Seven Years' War and was bilingual in English and Spanish, an asset in the days before Google Translate. Puente was well-regarded by the Uchize Native Americans in Florida (at least according to Spanish reports), who regularly sent trade delegations to Havana.[12]

Miralles was an established merchant based in Havana with connections throughout the Atlantic trading world, and was fluent in English, Spanish and French. Miralles and Puente had a personal connection: Puente was a first cousin of Miralles' Cuban wife.[13] Miralles was born in Petrel, a small town in eastern Spain, and the son of immigrants from France. His father, an entrepreneur merchant who traded with the British in the early 1700s, had earned a huge fortune. Miralles immigrated to Havana in 1740 at age twenty-seven to expand the family business. In 1762 at the start of the disastrous Seven Years' War, he reported to the Spanish command about the British preparations for war by monitoring their ship movements in the Caribbean.[14] He met British Lord Albemarle during the siege of Havana, when the British captured him and his ship as he returned to Cuba from a slave-trading mission.[15] Miralles married María Joséfa de la Puente, a woman from a prominent Cuban family and became a girl-dad, with seven daughters and one son. Miralles had conducted business in the northern ports of Charleston, Philadelphia, New York and Boston for over a decade.

Fishing on the Florida Coast

Puente's mission was to infiltrate the British command center in the southeastern colonies. His initial instructions were to proceed to San Augustín, Florida. Puente was aided by Luciano de Herrera, a Spanish merchant residing in San Augustín who carefully monitored the British troop movements and tracked the often uncertain reports of battles. In a letter smuggled on a vessel piloted by Cuban fishermen, Herrera wrote that he was willing to undertake the dangers of spying on the British. Navarro asked Herrera for information on British troop numbers, their estimated destination in the colonies, and the state of the American rebellion. Herrera's activities soon raised the suspicion of British commanders occupying Florida.[16]

Puente sailed from Havana to Florida in December 1777. If captured by the British, he planned to say he was collecting the rare, colorful flora and fauna in East Florida and that Herrera was an old family friend. He arrived safely in San Augustín and spent the next few months gathering intelligence and preparing to cross the border into the British-held southern colonies. Meanwhile, British authorities were busily rustling through message sacks and opening correspondence in and out of San Augustín, making it very difficult for Puente or Herrera to communicate with Havana. In May 1777, they succeeded in smuggling out a report through a Cuban fisherman, Miguel Chapuz, who shadowed them from the coastal waters. Chapuz, also working for Navarro, was fishing near the stormy Florida coast, waiting to assist the men if needed. He intended to bring their correspondence directly to Havana, but bad weather prevented his voyage for three months, and their letters were delayed in reaching Navarro.

As the weeks passed, Navarro was concerned that he did not receive messages or reports of sightings of Puente or Herrera. While Puente and Herrera were trying unsuccessfully to reach him, Navarro sent another agent to San Augustín, Lorenzo Rodriguez, to track down the missing men. Rodriguez sailed his fishing vessel to New Smyrna, Florida, and traveled the 70 miles north to San Augustín by canoe hidden by night. When Rodriguez surprised the two men playing cards* in the candlelit parlor of Herrera's home,[17] the men ended their game and spent the night hastily writing a report for Rodriguez to take to Havana. Their quill feathers scratched hurriedly over papers, providing a comprehensive overview of the political and military situation. They included an analysis of the Carlisle Commission, the British attempt to reconcile with the colonies that had arrived in April 1778 to a storm of protest from the Patriots. They reported on the rumors of battles sweeping through the towns and countryside of Florida.

Puente stayed in San Augustín through the summer, to monitor whether Continental troops were moving further south into British-held Florida. (They didn't, Patriot troops were busy being defeated by the British in the southern colonies.) Later that year, Puente made several attempts to cross the border into Georgia. The British had him under such heavy surveillance that he could not travel northward or send reports to Havana.[18] Back in Havana, Navarro realized that Puente's intelligence-gathering mission had accomplished all that was possible, and with the approval of the Court in Madrid, he offered Puente the choice of moving closer to the British operations in the South or to return to Havana. Puente decided to sail to Havana. As Puente's mission ended, Miralles' mission was underway.

---

*If you're a 21st century gamer and not familiar with 'cards', these are paper handheld devices with various symbols that were very popular with 18th century gamers.

The Payas Identity

While Puente was departing for Florida, Team Carlos sent another secret agent to establish relations with the US Congress, also on an "unofficial" basis. On December 31, 1777, the *Nuestra Señora del Carmen* discreetly sailed from the harbor of Havana, carrying a passenger on a secret mission to a destination that differed from the port told to the unsuspecting crew. José de Gálvez and Navarro carefully planned Miralles' assignment and the ruse by which he landed in the rebel colonies. To maintain his secrecy, the Spanish used the same cover story as for Eduardo's earlier mission to Philadelphia in 1776. Miralles publicly announced that he was traveling to Spain to lobby for a lucrative international trade concession based in Havana. Under this ruse, the vessel was sabotaged and forced to make an "emergency" landing in Charleston, South Carolina. Once in Charleston, Miralles traveled to Philadelphia, to establish a flour export business and send reports to Havana. Miralles devised a code name for himself, "Pedro Payas," in case he needed to send covert messages back to Havana.[19] Navarro arranged a detailed disguise for Miralles, specifying the content of the ship's cargo and the amount of money that Miralles carried, and personally selected the captain and ship.[20] Navarro detailed the alibi for Miralles if stopped by the British Navy.[21]

While Team Carlos intended for Miralles' arrival to appear accidental to British spies, they ensured that Miralles was welcomed by the Patriots and perceived as more than a "private citizen." As the French Minister to the Americas, Conrad Gérard, later informed his ministers in Paris, the Spanish secretly shipped military supplies to support Miralles' arrival. The supplies included five vessels loaded with gunpowder for the US Army, smuggled through Nueva Orleáns.[22] When he arrived in Charleston in January 1778, Miralles established relationships with local political leaders. His first letter to José de Gálvez reported on the sentiments of the South Carolinians towards the British and noted that people favorably viewed Spain and France as potential allies in their struggle. In March 1778, he wrote to José de Gálvez, "All the people here long for the day when they will hear that France and Spain have declared war against England, and for that day toasts are proposed at the tables of the most prominent citizens of this city."[23]

The South Carolina state government was in financial difficulty – no surprise, all the state governments were in financial difficulty – and relied on silver pesos for their state finances. Miralles "lent" the state government a small fortune of 36,000 pesos from his personal account, about $75 million today. In 1786, Robert Morris investigated this loan on behalf of Miralles' family estate, and learned the sum still had not been repaid.[24]

Through his family's business Miralles had an established network of trading and mercantile connections in the colonies, including a partnership with Robert Morris. Most 18th century trading companies trafficked in human beings, and Miralles and Morris also profited from the horrific exchange of stolen lives. The company managed by Morris was the trade factor, or financial broker, for the Spanish firm of Aguirre and Aristeguí, a trading company based in Cádiz, Spain. Aguirre and Aristeguí held the monopoly to import enslaved Africans into Cuba and traded the produce and provisions from North America preferred by Spanish foodies. Miralles was central to this business in Havana, and Morris and Miralles became leading investment and shipping partners to build the trade between the embattled colonists and the moneyed merchants in Havana. The two men engaged in numerous business deals to provide war supplies to the US Army and later the French forces. This trade expanded through 1781 and onwards, becoming so extensive that Robert Morris added a line item in the official Treasury Report of 1785, listing "Bills of exchange sold, including Havana bills and bills for flour."[25]

On March 11, 1778, Navarro wrote to George Washington from Havana, explaining Miralles' "misfortune," that diverted the ship to Charleston, adding that Miralles planned to stay in the colonies until he could safely return to Cuba. Navarro requested that Washington extend his protection to Miralles during his stay. Miralles traveled to North Carolina in May 1778 and was introduced to the local Congressman.[26] He continued north to Williamsburg, visiting with the famously outspoken Governor of Virginia, Patrick Henry, or Patricio Enrique as the Spanish called him. He wrote to Gálvez of rumors that the British were soon to evacuate Philadelphia, which they had held since September 1777.

Miralles settled in Philadelphia in July 1778 and resided in a house that still stands at 242 South Third Street, which was honored with a historic marker in 1967. With his introductions in place, Miralles became a friend and confidant of many people in Congress and the military, including George Washington.

Miralles was a true fan of Washington and ordered eleven copies of Washington's portrait painted by Charles Wilson Peale,[27] two of which he shipped to Team Carlos in Havana.[28] Washington wrote that Miralles was in Philadelphia to report back to the Spanish Court,[29] and understood that Miralles' analysis influenced Spain's decisions as to the extent of its aid to the Patriots.

Miralles was a charming, sociable man, and his voluminous letters and reports, preserved in the Library of Congress, detail the many political and social meetups that he hosted for the American leaders and their wives. His soirees were attended by top military brass, including Washington's most trusted generals.[30] The political leaders included John Jay, the envoy to Spain and first Chief Justice of the Supreme Court. Always a generous and congenial host, Miralles sent baskets of chocolate, sugar, and pink guava fruit jelly from Havana to Martha Washington, the wife of George Washington, and Caty Greene, the wife of General Nathaniel Greene. Miralles' home was well-stocked with imported Cuban cigars, Spanish brandy and wines, chocolates, almonds, olives, and other rare gourmet selections, to which he treated his many guests. The Cuban cigars were a grand favorite of General Washington, affording the stressed-out Commander-in-Chief the rich joy of an aromatic, hand-rolled Havana cigar.*

Miralles met regularly with Conrad Alexandre Gérard de Rayneval, the first diplomat appointed by the French Court to the US. The two men hosted a glamorous New Year's Eve Ball in January 1779 that was the highlight of the social season in a city demoralized by war and mocked by occupation. Seventy guests gathered for the ball, including George and Martha Washington, prominent military leaders, and members of Congress with their wives. The revelers danced long past midnight, enjoying a few bright hours during the long shadow of war.[31]

During the following months, Miralles sent Gálvez and Navarro detailed accounts of British troop movements, battles between the Americans and the British, and the assistance of the French Navy in the rebellion. Understanding the movements of the British navy was a priority for the Spanish, who were concerned about an attack in the Caribbean from British naval bases in the southern colonies.[32]

---

*Warning: For professional use only. As of 2020, if you bring Cuban cigars into the US, your crime will be punished with civil fines of up to $55,000 per violation and criminal prosecution. Worse, your cigars will be confiscated.

From his base in Philadelphia, Miralles expanded the shipments of clothing, gunpowder, weapons, medicines, and other critical supplies through Nueva Orléans. Bernardo de Gálvez and Francisco Bouligny, a secret agent assigned from Havana to assist the Patriots, coordinated with these operations.[33] In Miralles' letters, he frequently discussed a proposed joint action with the Spanish and US armies in the southern colonies and Florida. The Spanish wanted to retake their territory in Florida and the Americans wanted to push the British out of the Carolinas and Georgia. Navarro instructed Miralles to encourage the American conquest of San Augustín to divert British troops from reinforcing Pensacola. Miralles wrote to Congress asking it to authorize the expedition.[34] In October of 1778, Miralles wrote to Navarro that he thought a plan was in place for a campaign against the British in San Augustín with a joint force of French and American troops. This proved to be incorrect, though discussions on joint operations between the Spanish and US Army continued into 1781.

Miralles pressed on with his mission gathering intelligence on the state of the colonies and the British military. He watched for any suggestion that the British intended to invade Spanish territories west of the Mississippi. Washington and his officers thundered into Philadelphia on horseback in late December 1778, to confer with Congress and to lobby for money and supplies for their army surviving in the dismal cold and unrelenting hunger at Valley Forge. Washington and Miralles became more acquainted during the wintry evenings while the General stayed in the city. Miralles wrote that Washington visited him in January to brief him on the movements of a British navy squadron that was heading towards the Caribbean. Miralles relayed this information to Gálvez, expressing his concern for the security of Puerto Rico and other Spanish colonies.

Washington left Philadelphia to return to his winter camp at Valley Forge and invited Miralles and the French minister Gérard to visit in the spring. Miralles and Gérard departed for Valley Forge on April 27 in a carriage escorted by twenty-five of the leading citizens of Philadelphia and cavalrymen riding with their sabers unsheathed and glinting in the sun. A boisterous band of musicians marched alongside the procession through the streets of Philadelphia. The group camped in New Jersey that night, and as they approached within twenty miles of the camp headquarters, an escort of twenty dragoons commanded by General Johann de Kalb greeted them. The dragoons were named for their weapons, a short musket known as "the dragon," since the guns flared with so much smoke when fired. De

Kalb, a highly effective general who later died on the battlefield, was a self-made man who had worked as a waiter in Europe.

Washington designated the passwords to enter the camp to honor the nationalities of his guests. As Miralles and Gérard approached the checkpoints, the soldiers called out the names of Spanish and French leaders, including "Carlos III" and "Aranda."[35] To the beating of drums and shouted orders, three thousand men performed precise military maneuvers while Miralles and Gérard watched from a nearby hilltop. The day concluded with a dinner party hosted by Baron Von Steuben and attended by Martha Washington and the officers' wives. Miralles and Gérard returned to Philadelphia on May 2nd. As they departed camp, Washington and his officers rode with them for the first part of their journey.[36]

Throughout the military inspections, the hushed diplomatic discussions, the business dealings, and the evenings spent dining and conversing, Miralles continued to send reports to Havana and to lobby for Spanish and Continental forces to cooperate in joint military action against the British. His warm admiration for Washington and many Americans is evident in his letters. The admiration was mutual, as evidenced in a letter Washington sent to Miralles thanking him for his hospitality. "All that I can send you from these quarters, in fair reciprocity, is my sincere friendship which you, Sir, have had for some time."[37] Miralles persisted in his heartfelt goal for Spain to declare war on Britain, which he knew would greatly assist the struggling Americans. While sending covert reports to Madrid, he built up his local business empire. Miralles had extensive business dealings in Philadelphia that supported the American economy, leasing buildings, financing ships and cargoes, and lending money to friends, businessmen and public officials. When funding from the Spanish Treasury was delayed or insufficient, Miralles advanced his personal funds for the cause.[38]

Miralles' mission ended when he died of a sudden illness in Morristown, New Jersey, on April 28, 1780. Alexander Hamilton and Baron von Steuben were with him at his bedside as he completed his will. Fashionable to the end, Miralles was buried in a scarlet suit embroidered with gold lace and a profusion of diamond jewelry. George Washington was among the mourners at his funeral, which was conducted with military honors. Washington wrote directly to Navarro on April 30, assuring him that "no care or attention, in our power, was omitted towards his [Miralles] comfort or restoration."[39]

"His sincere love for the Spanish nation"

Francisco Rendón arrived in the US in 1779 to serve as Miralles' executive assistant and assumed Miralles' position after his death. Rendón successfully expanded American trade with Cuba and worked with Morris to support American merchants. Rendón became a close associate of Morris, and the two collaborated on joint trade deals. Building on Miralles' work, Rendón provided desperately needed economic support to the struggling rebellion, both through his business investments and by providing Americans with the opportunity to earn hard currency. The commodities trade was very lucrative for the Americans, and Rendón negotiated deals that ensured large profits for them. He expanded the flour trade with Havana. Spanish troops stationed in Havana had increased by over 12,000 soldiers as preparations for their war with the British expanded, and the city needed more food imports. Rendón contracted with American merchants, underwrote shipping costs, and managed the paperwork for the extensive trade. He attempted to initiate other business sectors for the Americans, including a ship-building industry.[40]He financed ships and expeditions for American privateers. Rendón actively supported Morris' attempts to establish an American central bank that – surprise, surprise – the US planned to finance with loans from Spain. The country was in a vicious spiral of inflation, which Morris and Rendón hoped to resolve with Spanish financing. Unfortunately, given the Patriots' record of continually requesting loans with what the Spanish viewed as unrealistic expectations, their government declined Morris' request.[41]

Navarro instructed Rendón to focus on three geographic areas for military intelligence: British-held New York, the southern colonies, and the Caribbean. Navarro was concerned that these areas could be launch points for a British invasion of Spanish territories.[42] Rendón and Miralles both thought that the Spanish would initiate a joint campaign with the American forces against the British in Florida and the Gulf Coast. In October 1781, during the battles between the British and Americans and French at Yorktown, Rendón wrote to Bernardo de Gálvez that Congress had authorized US forces to cooperate with Gálvez in a campaign against the British in Florida, "... those instructions have not been revoked by Congress it is clear that General Greene will agree gladly to whatever

[Gálvez] proposes."[43] That month, George Washington wrote to Rendón, "In the meantime, you can assure General Gálvez that there cannot be any operation more advantageous to the states of the South than one in which the armed forces he commands are employed against East Florida."[44]

Building on the extensive network that Miralles had initiated, Rendón cultivated relationships with American political and business leaders. Washington and Rendón became close colleagues, and Rendón hosted Washington and his entourage for Christmas in 1781. Washington invited Rendón to visit West Point in the winter chill of early 1782, where he was greeted with the pomp and formality of a distinguished diplomat.[45] He returned that July for a longer visit to the army's headquarters at West Point, where he was treated to full military honors and diplomatic protocols.[46] Washington organized a banquet in his honor and Von Steuben presented a two-hour display of the Army's crisp military maneuvers and drills.[47] As Rendón wrote to Jose de Gálvez of the visit, "Surely because he wished to convince me of his sincere love for the Spanish nation ... General Washington took great pains to shower distinctions upon me."[48]

In August 1783, Rendón completed an extensive and detailed economic analysis of the US economy which he researched for over a year. In the first part of the analysis, he reviewed the economies of each state. The second part was "a very extensive plan in which the United States will be considered as an independent Power trading with the nations of Europe."[49] His comments on the transformation in US culture are insightful: "The customs of America are beginning little by little to differ from those of Great Britain .... Before the war, the customs of the cities resembled those of the mother country." But the long presence of French and Germans and the upheaval of the war, "in this country have introduced into it a spirit of society and even of luxury which was unknown eight years ago."[50] We were becoming, as our Spanish observer carefully noted, Americans.

Throughout the war, the Spanish Court in Madrid and Team Carlos persisted in their intelligence operations, dispatching agents and spies across the colonies and the Caribbean. Some worked at the margins of the conflict, such as the Cuban fishermen who quietly carried messages to Havana. Others, operating at the heart of events, including Miralles and Rendón, were steadfast supporters committed to advancing the American cause. These men forged bonds of friendship that still resonate across centuries in their letters and reports.

Chapter 5

The American Crisis

From her sturdy farmhouse near Dedham, Massachusetts, a determined farmer intently watched the nearby road and fields. Mary Draper was waiting and formulating her plans. Her husband and son had left earlier to join the newly formed Continental Army. She was certain that more volunteers would arrive soon on their way to Boston, twenty miles away. She turned to her daughter, and said, "You and I, Kate, have also a service to do. Food must be prepared for the hungry; before tomorrow night, hundreds, I hope thousands, will be on their way to join the continental forces. Some who have traveled far will need refreshment, and you and I, with Molly [a farmworker], must feed as many as we can." Their farm's granaries were full, and their thriving dairy was Mary's proud achievement.[1] The three women spent two days and nights baking brown bread, then placed tables and benches along the roadside to hold pans of bread and cheese, and tubs of cider that were ladled out by volunteers from the neighborhood. The hungry men did arrive, walking many miles on foot, and stopped for food on their way to join the American Revolution.

This scene of women working long hours to provide food and beverages made with their own roughened, unmanicured hands was repeated hundreds of times across the country. While historical plaques map the movements of the army through the towns and countryside, no markers commemorate the women who provided the men with what they needed to continue their march: food and drink. These "ordinary" Working Moms provided logistical support to the army; the war could not have been fought without them. While the army commissaries struggled to provide meals to soldiers on the march and in camp, many Patriot women provided sustenance from their own pantries and kitchens. Throughout the colonies they wrote in their journals and letters with understated and valiant endurance as they recounted their aid to the many famished, dirty, exhausted men who arrived at their doorsteps for a decent meal. No modern infrastructure supported them: no A-rations or B-rations or Door Dash, no refrigerators or microwaves. None. Instead, American women kneaded dough, milked cows, pressed apples into cider, butchered pigs, dug up vegetables from the dirt, plucked feathers from wild turkeys and chickens, harvested wheat, hunted geese and ducks, curdled cheese, stirred porridge, fermented liquor, picked fruit, hauled water buckets, and chopped wood to fire stoves and ovens.

"Turning me out of house and home in the middle of winter"

As American men marched out of their homes into the war, the war marched into the homes of American women. Who were these women, who lived and endured during these hard times? Their experiences of the war were formed by their politics, social status, ethnicities, and the decisions made by the men in their lives. The usual focus, if women are noted at all, is on white Euro-Americans. But three other groups of women were part of these times: African Americans, Native Americans, and Latinas and Hispanics. Many African American women, including Ona Judge, an enslaved woman who worked for the Washingtons, did not have a choice as to which side to support. Others chose the desperate pursuit of life, liberty and some semblance of happiness, as with the women who answered the British call to service in exchange for freedom, including Judith Jackson, who escaped from slavery and spent years serving the British Army. Tekonwatonti, "She Who Stands Alone," also known as Molly Brant, was a diplomat and war chief who battled for the sovereignty of her Mohawk nation as the Patriots seized her homeland. Tekonwatonti was the sister of Mohawk military and political leader Joseph Brant. The Latinas and Hispanics,* saw the war from glimpses of the battles that the Spanish military fought from Nueva Orleáns to Pensacola, Florida and the collection of silver pesos throughout California, New Mexico, Arizona and the entire Spanish empire that Carlos III ordered in 1780 to fund the war.

---

*Hispanic refers to people from Spain and their descendants while Latina/o includes South Americans who may not speak Spanish, such as in Brazil and Haiti. And of course, Latina/o/x/e people in El Norte.

For most women in the colonies, the war was an invasion that dramatically uprooted their once normal lives. Their letters and journals preserve stories of the famous and the forgotten, recounting personal tales of ingenuity, courage, and perseverance. Sarah Franklin Bache, the daughter of Benjamin Franklin born in Pennsylvania in 1743, was forced from her home by the invading British Army on two occasions. As she wrote while shivering in February 1777, "I never shall forget nor forgive [the British] for turning me out of house and home in the middle of winter...." Bache and her family were on the run again in September 1777, as the British marched to Philadelphia after their victory at Brandywine. Packing up her baby daughter, whom she had delivered just four days earlier – without anesthesia or sanitized instruments – Bache fled for a second time. She returned to Philadelphia in July 1778, writing to her famous father that, "they stole and carried off with them some of your musical instruments" and "some of your electric apparatus is missing also."

Although she was the daughter of a wealthy entrepreneur and the wife of a successful businessman, Bache's purchasing power was decimated by the rampant inflation of US currency, and like most women, she had few silver pesos to serve as a hedge against economic collapse. In October 1778, she wrote her father, "If I was to mention the prices of common necessaries of life it would astonish you. I have been all amazement since my return; such an odds have two years made, that I can scarcely believe I am in Philadelphia."[2] She was shocked by the price of gloves — up to $6.00! For a basic comparison, the average salary of a US Continental soldier was $6 to 8 dollars per month[3] so the price of gloves was certainly a sticker shock. The currency hyper-inflation continued, and Bache and her domestic employee were soon taking two shopping bags to market: one full bag to carry the wads of Continental dollars for purchasing and one empty bag to carry home their goods. By the time that winter approached in 1779, she wrote to her father of the continued "amazing" depreciation of the currency. She planned a staycation that winter, since "I cannot get a common winter cloak and hat ... under two hundred pounds."[4] Prices for different food and commodities fluctuated wildly. From October to November 1779, during the most extreme month for this commodity in the Revolutionary War, the price of wheat doubled, and wheat flour doubled over three months.[5] The British understood the impact of hyperinflation and worked to exacerbate the currency crisis. As Miralles reported, a British ship captured in 1779 carried "a cargo of cloth and a box of prepared paper, plates, a printing press, and all the rest needed for counterfeiting Continental money."[6]

Thomas Paine, the celebrated writer and influencer described the staggering challenges that the Americans confronted this way: "Truly may we say, that never did men grow old in so short a time!" To paraphrase Tom, never did *women* age in so short a time. Years later, Lucy Knox remarked that she lived more in one year in this intense and frightening period than in a dozen years of ordinary life. Joseph Plumb Martin also remarked on the bravery of women on the battlefield including one who "would be unpardonable not to mention" as she manned – or womanned – the artillery at her husband's side during a battle. While stepping out with one leg to reach for an artillery cartridge, a speeding British cannon ball passed directly between her legs, tearing off the lower part of her dress. "Looking at it with apparent unconcern, she observed that it was lucky it did not pass a little higher, for in that case it might have carried away something else, and continued her occupation." The woman, Mary Ludwig Hayes, was the wife of a Pennsylvania private whom she had joined in the war. Another woman, Deborah Sampson, dressed herself as a man and served for 18 months in the Fourth Massachusetts Regiment.[7] Sampson somehow kept her disguise through ragged clothing, long marches, close quarters, and shared latrines, without even the privacy of a Porta-Potty. Her gender was only revealed when a high fever rendered her unconscious and a shocked doctor treated her.

The Enemy at Your Gate

The far more fearful scenario was when the unknown "guests" were the enemy. This was a war of invasion and occupation of their home country that lasted for years. A day that began as a normal day was shattered when soldiers' boots tromped into homes. In a century without a developed infrastructure of motels or hotels, where and how to house soldiers was a challenge. The invading and occupying British Army camped out in the front yards of farmhouses and yards, while officers expected to be housed in homes. A very unsettling thought — the very men who were determined to kill your family and friends expected you to feed and lodge them.

American women met these unsettling occasions with audacious fortitude and wit; not as shrieking, helpless damsels in distress. On a cool spring morning in March of 1781, Banastre Tarleton, a British officer of the dragoons, arrived at a farmhouse in North Carolina. He was grandly dressed in a forest green uniform gleaming with burnished buttons and a leather hat with a vain fur plume on his head. Accompanied by two aides, with twenty dragoons in guard, Tarleton announced himself to Mary Slocumb as she sat on her front porch. The discussion quickly turned political as Tarleton inquired whether the man of the house was a rebel. The words that Slocumb spoke next still echo centuries later: "No sir. He is in the army of his country, and fighting against our invaders; therefore, not a rebel."[8]

The unabashed Tarleton tried for a second round in this verbal duel. Tarleton and one of his British companions began a discussion of their vision of the ultimate rebel defeat, and that the conquered farms and plantations such as the Slocumbs' would be divided as rewards to the victorious British officers. Slocumb retorted sharply, "Allow me to observe and prophesy, the only land in these United States which will ever remain in possession of a British officer, will measure but six feet by two." Almost on cue, a volley of shots was heard within distance of the house, beginning a desperate chase and skirmish between Tarleton's forces and the Patriots, including Slocumb's husband. Colonel Slocumb escaped, to which Tarleton noted that "Your husband made us a short visit, Madam. I should have been happy to make his acquaintance." Through the entire evening, with armed British officers and a near miss at widowhood, Slocumb retained her calm composure and biting wit. On this singular visit, Tarleton* behaved as an officer and a gentleman, taking only what was necessary for his troops' support and offering remuneration.

Slocumb was fortunate. Many accounts by Patriot women accused British soldiers of threat, assault, rape, and theft. A young South Carolina woman named Jane Morrow wrote of Tarleton's attempt to assault her, and Marrow fought back with ferocity and managed to knock over Tarleton. Hearing the noise, a neighbor rushed into her house and found Tarleton lying on his back with Morrows' knee jammed into his chest as she tried to choke him.

––––––––––––––––––

*For Outlander fans, Tarleton makes a few appearances in the book series, initially as an acquaintance of William ("Willie") Ransom.

The Morrow family never forgave their neighbor for interrupting Morrow's assault on Tarleton, and for the rest of his life, the neighbor had to avoid them at social gatherings.[9] Other women and girls were not so fortunate, and the Patriots recorded gang rapes of girls as young as thirteen.[10]

As the British and American Loyalist soldiers marched through homes and farms, all private possessions were in danger of seizure. While women of means buried their valuables and silverware in fields, farmers' wives hid crops and live-stock in swamps and forests. One woman creatively hid a calf under her bed, muzzling the frightened creature to prevent it from revealing its presence.[11] Eliza Wilkinson of Charleston recalled that her friend's wedding ring was snatched from finger at gunpoint, earrings were ripped from her sister's ears, and buckles were seized from their shoes.[12] The theft of wedding bands was a common cruelty. Clothing, boots, shoes, liquor, food, and kitchenware were stolen and loaded into carts or stuffed into soldiers' pockets and shirts. Many families wrote of their hard-earned homes and furnishings being stripped down to bare wood.

Families struggled in the wake of these devastating losses, without insurance or FEMA. Mrs. Potter, who lived near Cowpens, site of a victorious rebel battle in 1781, recalled how a detachment of about 250 American Loyalists thoroughly trashed her farm. The men fed her family's corn crop to their horses and ripped up the railed fences for firewood. At that point, the family was surviving largely on roasted corn, without bread, meat or salt, and had replaced their leather shoes with woolen rags sewn around their feet. Little was left of their beds as their mattresses were ripped open, the feathers scattered throughout the pastures and the mattress cover was stolen to make tents for the soldiers.[13]

Thomas Paine knew the importance of American women in the war and called on them to revive the fading hopes of a young anxious nation, comparing America's distress to France's fight against England hundreds of years earlier. The French were saved as they rallied under the leadership of "a woman, Joan of Arc," he wrote. "Would that heaven might inspire some [New] Jersey maid to spirit up her countrymen, and save her fair fellow sufferers...." Whether the inspiration came from heaven or from love, loyalty, and dedication, American women and men did "spirit up" to fight the war, year after discouraging year.

Meanwhile, on the Other Battlefield

Moving silently and quickly, thousands of exhausted US soldiers evacuated under the cover of an inexplicably thick fog after their defeat at the Battle of Long Island in August 1776. The men struggled through the muck and mud after two days of torrential rain that preceded the evacuation. Their orders to abandon their camp were kept secret until the very last hour so they didn't realize the perilous danger that they were in. The British had pressed forward by land and blocked a rear escape by sea. As described by one American officer, the fog "... began to rise, and settle in a peculiar manner over both [British and American] encampments." Vision was almost impossible; the officer wrote that he was "scarcely able to discern a man at six yards' distance."[14] As night fell, with their troop strength at 22,000 and the Continentals at about 10,000, the British commanders were confident of a total victory and a quick end to the rebellion the next morning. But by the dawn's early light, the British were stunned to discover that the US Army had vanished under cover of the fog.

The Battle of Long Island was one of several frightening losses in 1776. After their remarkable success at the Siege of Boston in April of 1775, the army began to lose battle after bloody battle: Kip's Bay, White Plains and Fort Washington, followed by the loss of Fort Lee and another hurried evacuation. The numbers of the Army were dwindling. Thousands of enlistees returned to their homes; only an estimated 5,000 soldiers remained by the autumn of 1776. Fewer citizens along the route supported the weary troops in their painful retreat across New Jersey and the Delaware River into what Washington hoped was the safety of Pennsylvania. In a disheartening contrast, the British Army continued to amass more troops and supplies. By mid-August of 1776, nearly 32,000 British soldiers camped on Staten Island, New York, which was the largest single military force in America during the Revolutionary War.[15]

After this string of losses, Washington and his commanders knew that the dispirited troops needed encouragement. Along with the silver coins that were awarded as bonuses for reenlistments,[16] the leadership turned to a powerful force: words. Thomas Paine galvanized Americans with his pamphlet "Common Sense," published in January 1776. While the largest newspapers had 2,000 sub-scribers, Paine's 84-page pamphlet sold over 100,000 copies in the first month and over 500,000 copies total.[17] In the true spirit of public service, Paine donated his proceeds to the Continental Army. He wrote his series, "The American Crisis" to encourage the demoralized Patriots in the dark December days of 1776, when he marched with the retreating army as an embedded journalist. "These are the times that try men's souls: The summer soldier and the sunshine patriot will, in this crisis, shrink from the service of his country; but he that stands it now, deserves the love and thanks of man and woman."[18] These words were so inspirational that the Army used them as watchwords in camp and soldiers shouted them as battle cries as they ran into the fight.[19]

Toward the end of 1776, Philadelphia, the capital of the new republic, was evacuated as members of the new Congress hurriedly escaped to Baltimore in fear of capture and hanging by the approaching British Army. A victory was urgently needed to rally the dispirited Patriot soldiers and citizens, which was won at the Battle of Trenton in December 1776. The hardy boatmen of Marblehead, Massachusetts, rowed Washington, around 2,400 soldiers, dozens of horses and 18 artillery pieces across the frozen Delaware River. You may have seen the famous picture of the Delaware Crossing painted by Emanuel Leutze later in 1851. Leutze shows a calm, dignified Washington standing stoically in a boat with the American flag waving in the wind. Rays of soft sunlight in the distance shine on an organized fleet of boats moving imperturbably through ice crags on the river, ferrying a well-dressed cross-section of troops, including an African American and a Native American.

The limited diversity of the troops was one of the few accurate features of that picture. The event was chaotic and precarious, with frightening time delays and missed communications that divided the army on opposite banks of the river. The Stars and Stripes Flag did not yet exist. The sun was not basking the men in glorious rays. Night had fallen by the time they embarked, and cold rain, hail and snow dampened some gunpowder. An exasperated Washington climbed into his designated boat and nudged Henry Knox, the officer managing the transport of artillery. According to a long-cherished meme, Washington told Knox, "Shift that fat ass, Harry, but slowly or you'll swamp the damned boat,"[20] to the great amusement of his troops.

The Hessians were camped in Trenton. The presence of the Hessian officers angered the Patriot leadership and Washington in particular. The Hessian soldiers themselves were forcibly pressed into service from six small states in modern Germany. About 30,000 to 34,000 German troops fought for the British against the Americans during the war. The British Army needed additional troops, since the availability of military forces for the American campaign was limited.[21] British military resources were also challenged by the conflicts in Europe with the Spanish and French and in India with the Mysore and Maratha kingdoms.

The Hessian commanders were not expecting an attack. What army, after nearly losing their entire force a few months earlier, would row across an icy river into enemy territory on the day after Christmas? The American Army, that's who. The Americans surprised the Hessians and defeated them in a forty-five-minute gun battle in the streets of Trenton. Immediately after the troops surrendered, the ragged American soldiers commandeered the winter coats of their prisoners.* The US Army soldiers were in tattered uniforms, and the warm European clothing was eagerly snatched.[22] Since Washington and his men were the only contingent that managed to cross the river, they were a small force in enemy territory with a large number of prisoners. The Marblehead men, exhausted from struggling across the river, had to row the troops back to the other side. Washington conferred with their leader, John Glover, requesting another heroic effort of transport, which must have been an interesting conversation. The Marblehead men, whose members included African Americans, Native Americans, and Hispanics, rallied to save the army.[23] The risky triumph at Trenton was exactly the victory that the country needed.

Exacerbating the challenges of the struggling army, a deadly smallpox epidemic raged from 1775 through 1782, terrorizing people from the Hudson Bay in the north to Mexico City in the south. In 1777, Congress authorized the inoculation of the Army to prevent its spread, but inoculations in the Revolutionary era were hazardous. Bacteria-laden discharge was painfully scraped from the pustules of the sick to inoculate the healthy by producing a milder bout of the disease and immunity. Even Martha Washington, who bravely traveled to join her husband at his various encampments throughout the War, chose inoculation. The soldiers undergoing inoculation were too ill to fight and had to be quarantined, some for weeks. Washington ordered the program to be kept as secret as possible from British spies, fearing that the British would move against the weakened force.[24]

---

* Please remember this point for later in our story; a 'borrowed' Hessian coat would play an unexpected and fateful role in averting a near disaster for the Revolution.

In October of 1777, the Continental Army achieved a stellar victory at the Battles of Saratoga in New York. For the first time in a major battle, cannons, artillery, muskets, and gunpowder provided by the Spanish and French arrived in time to support the Americans. These metal allies propelled the army's success. British General John Burgoyne lost this crucial series of eleven battles over the five-month campaign. Burgoyne seriously overestimated his strength on the battlefields. The 17,000 Patriot soldiers heavily outnumbered Burgoyne, and he surrendered his force of 5,728 to General Horatio Gates, an immigrant and former British officer who had switched to the Patriot side. The news shocked European and British policy wonks betting against the rebels. The startling possibility emerged that the Americans could defeat the British. Based on this dramatic turn of events, the French Court made the history-altering decision to put boots on the ground to help their American allies.

Team George III

General John Burgoyne, who surrendered at Saratoga, was one of several top generals and naval officers assembled by George III and the British government. Team George III was a formidable challenge to Washington and his inexperienced officer corps. Burgoyne, known as "Gentleman Johnny" for his fashionista couture, fought in the Seven Years' War, raided the coast of France, and battled with the Spanish during their invasion of Portugal. General William Howe arrived in 1775 and served as Commander-in-Chief of the British Army through 1778, fighting the Americans at Bunker Hill. Howe captured the key cities of New York and Philadelphia, the Patriot capital. General Charles Cornwallis arrived as the Declaration of Independence was being written. After difficult campaigns in America, including the loss at Yorktown, he joined the East India Company and battled the Indian military leader, Tipu Sultan, in the wars with the Mysore Kingdom. Major General Guy Carleton was dispatched to America in 1775 and fought in Canada and at Saratoga. Carleton organized the evacuation of Loyalists and African Americans in 1783, during which he made the astonishing decision to countermand orders and transport African Americans who had fought for the British to safety and freedom in Canada.

British General Sir Henry Clinton was a complex man who had an outsized impact on the Revolutionary War, from initiating the Black Pioneers regiment of freed African Americans to organizing the espionage network that almost defeated the Revolution. Clinton commanded the British Army throughout the war, starting at the bloody disaster at Bunker Hill in 1775 and finally departing five months after the defeat at Yorktown in 1781.[25] Clinton had a lifelong connection with America. His father was appointed as the British Governor of New York and moved there with his family in 1743, including Henry. The family returned to England in 1751, and Clinton continued his military service on the battlefields of Europe in the Seven Years' War. A few years after returning home, in 1767, Clinton married Harriet Carter. The happy marriage ended far too soon. In an 18th century without sanitized obstetric care, pregnancies were high risk for women. Harriet endured five pregnancies in five years and died eight days after the birth of their fifth child. Her death devastated Clinton, and he lapsed into what is now recognized as a major depressive disorder (MDD). About four months later, he received a caring, stern letter from one of his best friends, "I will endeavor ... to assist you ... But it is absolutely [necessary] for you to fix on a system, or your life will pass in continual anxiety and endless suffering." After a lengthy sabbatical in Europe to ease his depression, Clinton returned to England and was ordered – as he noted later, he did not volunteer – to sail to Boston to quell the upstart agitators. His notes on his voyage reflect a man of surprising candor and self-awareness, "At first (for you know I am a shy bitch) I kept my distance, [and] seldom spoke till my two colleagues forced me out."[26]

"Fatigue and thirst, joined with hunger, made me almost desperate."

As the cold winds began to blow in 1777, the US Army marched into winter camp at Valley Forge twenty miles northwest of Philadelphia. Imagine yourself among the weary army of 12,000 ragged men and 400 women,[27] walking through the forests and fields.[28] Among the soldiers is Joseph Plumb Martin who despaired on their arrival that, "The army was now not only starved but naked. The greatest part were not only shirtless and barefoot, but destitute of all clothing, especially blankets."[29]

As you gaze around the camp, you see men whose feet are frostbitten and bleeding bright red into the snow. You peer into the smoky, dark, windowless huts to see men who don't have adequate clothing to venture outside. You smell the stomach-churning stench of bodies devastated by typhoid, jaundice, pneumonia, while the unrelenting odor of blood-laced diarrhea from dysentery in open trench sewers burdens the air. The bloated bodies of dead horses add to the putrid mix. Without hay or grain, over 200 horses starved to death. Each evening, officers read the somber count of the day's tally of the dead. That winter, an estimated one in four men would die, almost 2,500 men of the 12,000 who arrived in December. Throughout the War, historians estimate that twice as many men died from disease, exposure, and exhaustion than from combat deaths, marching silently and no less heroically into the finality of cold earth.[30]

Now, step into the two-story stone house that was used as the army head-quarters, still standing among the trees in the National Park. You can rest your hand on the same smooth, worn wooden banister that was held by Washington, the senior officer staff, and many more men and a few women who once held it eagerly, wearily, hopefully in their hands. You watch young Alexander Hamilton, looking far different from his stuffy portrait on the American ten-dollar bill, hurrying with sheets of impeccable handwritten orders. He is in his early twenties, an immigrant from the Caribbean Island of St. Kitts, showing the flashes of brilliance and unwavering determination that would resound later in his career as he worked to establish the nation's banking system. During this cold winter, Hamilton's heart was kindled by the start of his romance with Elizabeth Schuyler. General Nathanael Greene, the fighting, dancing Quaker, limps slightly and assuredly throughout the scene. The Quaker religion did not approve of dancing or fighting, so Greene was quite a maverick. He was burdened by the almost impossible task of Quartermaster General in charge of supplies. You listen to phrases in French language and bright discussions of French literature from Caty Greene, his wife, who shared his hardships at camp.[31] Quietly present around Washington is Billy Lee, the biracial slave owned by Washington, a tall, elegant man whom Washington always referred to as "my fella." Billy Lee served as Washington's personal valet, his coffee-colored hands brushed and braided Washington's graying hair throughout the long years of war.[32]

At the center of activity is Washington, "the indispensable man," working late into the night, his eyes straining as he reviews order after order and dispatch after dispatch, trying to relieve the distressing and deadly circumstances of his men. He was a complicated human being, balancing the image of a freedom fighter against the tyranny of owning enslaved human beings that enabled his wealth and political aspirations. With his preference for the few carefully chosen words, his troubled teeth and thin lips, his mouth was habitually pressed into a straight line. A graceful man, he was known for mastering the arts of being a gentleman: he was a true pleasure to watch on the dance floor, men openly admired his superb horsemanship, and his scrupulous attention to etiquette rivaled that of White House protocol of any era. His height, at six feet, two inches, was tall for the times. He accentuated his image by meticulously dressing in his blue-coated commander's uniform with rows of gleaming buttons and selecting a striking white horse as the ultimate 18th century gentleman's accessory. He had not attended college or traveled widely and his self-improvement was a continual preoccupation. He was a scrupulously caring stepdad and step-grandad for Martha's family, occasionally shaking his head over the difficulties of keeping young adult children out of trouble. Forty-three at the start of the Revolution, his once auburn hair grayed completely by the end of the war. In December 1777, the indispensable, discouraged Washington wrote, "I am now convinced, beyond a doubt that unless some great and capital change suddenly takes place in that line, this Army must inevitably be reduced to one or other of these three things. Starve, dissolve, or disperse, in order to obtain subsistence in the best manner they can."

The men who gather around low campfires with you, still not dispersing or dissolving, are on average about 24 years old. Their ages range widely compared to present day armies. The flecks of gray hair in older men and the freckles of under-aged boys gleam in the firelight. Valley Forge hosts soldiers from eleven of the thirteen colonies, and you hear a cheerful hum of regional accents, from the genteel drawl of Tidewater Virginia to the distinctive staccato of Massachusetts. Many soldiers speak with foreign accents: different cadences of English and brogues spoken by recent immigrants from Ireland, who comprised a large portion of the army, and the accents of soldiers from Scotland, England, and other European countries.[33] Tuscarora, Oneida, Mohican and Wampanoag are spoken by the Native Americans.[34]

The jobs that the assembled troops left to heed this uncertain call to adventure were overwhelmingly in agriculture, and included urban occupations such as brewer, bookbinder, butcher, tobacco spinner, gunsmith, coppersmith, rope maker, and bricklayer.[35] Some women accompanied their men — wives, friends, sisters, daughters, lovers, mothers. The Army compensated many of the women, who worked as seamstresses, nurses, laundresses, albeit at lower wages than the men.[36] Laundering in the 18th century was a far more essential and arduous task than you may think. The soldiers' clothing and bedding were infested with lice, ticks and bedbugs. Manual washing was a labor-intensive process; the women boiled soiled linens over campfires using a harsh mix of lye-heavy soap, borax, and water.*

In the background are the sounds of hammering and sawing as trees are built into small log cabins with earthen floors. A shortage of axes hampered construction, but the troops' houses were still built in a remarkably brief time. Food is in short supply; often the only meal is "fire cake," a dough made from water and flour and baked on heated rocks. Martin wrote about these difficult times. The food shortage was so severe that, "Fatigue and thirst, joined with hunger, made me almost desperate. I felt at that instant as if I would have taken victuals or drink from the best friend I had on earth by force. I am not writing fiction, all are sober realities."[37]

Arriving in February 1778 is the man indelibly linked to the history of Valley Forge, the charming, brilliant Prussian immigrant, Friedrich Wilhelm Ludolf Gerhard Augustin Von Steuben. His travel expenses were paid by the Spanish and French through Roderigue Hortalez y Compañía.[38] A self-educated, voracious reader whose favorite book was the Spanish novel *Don Quixote*, Von Steuben was influenced by the Enlightenment and was a political progressive.[39] He was from the poor, lesser nobility of Brandenburg-Prussia, and had served in the Prussian Army where he gained valuable experience, including fighting with distinction in the Seven Years' War. His military career in Europe was marred by accusations of "familiarity with young men,"[40] a very serious charge in an era that stigmatized and punished gays in the military. Forty-seven years old, with a limited command of English, he dressed impeccably in full military uniform with an imposing hat, polished buttons, and epaulets (decorative shoulder pieces).

---

* I attended a reenactment of 19th century camp life, including a live demonstration of laundering. When I returned home, I hugged my electric washing machine.

Von Steuben confidently strode into the camp of threadbare men with such flair that one soldier described him as dazzling as Mars, the god of war.[41] Von Steuben began the challenge of remaking the US Army that made him a legend. He created a model company of 120 men that he drilled, scolded, guided, and encouraged. He paced on the drill fields at all hours, sometimes with his gloved hands on his hips in a stance of unwavering determination, intently watching the company's maneuvers, occasionally throwing his large hat to the ground in enraged frustration. He cursed the undisciplined men loudly in French and German, the scalding words mingling with his puffs of warm breath visible in the frigid winter air. When he felt that French and German obscenities were failing him, he instructed his aide-de-camp to curse the men in English. Von Steuben's dedication and devotion were clear. He never gave up on the men or on his quixotic vision of what and whom they could become. Martin would later categorize his time with Von Steuben as a "continual drill."

Word of Von Steuben's programs spread among the discouraged supporters of the Revolution, and Patriots gathered to watch the men practicing adroit formations, fierce bayonet thrusts, and rapid maneuvers. Their concern and fear turned to awe and astonishment as the farmers, shopkeepers, artisans and laborers who had arrived in December were transformed into disciplined battalions of soldiers in the warming air. With all the obstacles and shortages, there is the presence of hope and possibility throughout the camp, as subtle and ever present as smoke from campfires. You gaze around Valley Forge once more before returning to your 21st century comforts, as the men begin their daily drills. You cannot imagine as you watch these thousands of dirty, ragged, hungry men that an Army that is far more powerful, competent and confident will rise from these cold muddy grounds, and rise they did.

Chapter 6

Two Tales of Two Cities

While the US Army fought Redcoats from the woods of New York through the swamps of South Carolina, American politicians understood that the victory also depended on winning in the diplomatic arenas in Madrid and Paris, the two courts of the Bourbon Kings. Madrid was the center of the Spanish Empire across North and South America, where reports from Spanish explorers from as far north as Alaska and as far south as Tierra del Fuego on the tip of Argentina were dutifully sent to the capital. In the 18th century, Madrid was a sophisticated metropolis with a population of 150,000 Madrileños, more than three times the size of Philadelphia. Madrid was under construction, as Carlos III implemented his ambitious projects to revitalize the capital with the parks, boulevards, museums and public buildings that still enchant visitors today. Paris in the mid-18th century was a city of winding, narrow streets and alleyways, reflecting its medieval past. The inviting wide boulevards lined with cafes and trees were built later in the mid-19th century, when entire districts were leveled to create a luminous new vision of urban planning for the City of Lights. The French court was then located outside of Paris at the magnificent gardens and palaces of Versailles, with its famed hall of 357 arched, sparkling mirrors. In these two capitals, Spanish and French diplomats hosted, counseled, and negotiated with the inexperienced American diplomats and envoys, who often aggravated, annoyed and confounded them.

William Carmichael, assigned to Madrid, seemed to happily acclimate to Spain, learning Castilian Spanish and marrying a Madrileña. John Jay, the future first Chief Justice of the Supreme Court, also stationed in Madrid, grumbled continually and disparaged every effort of his gracious Spanish hosts. When John Adams traveled through Spain to France, he wrote that of the warm reception that he received, with support given by Spanish government officials and merchants. Most American diplomats appeared clumsy and cumbersome to both courts and particularly irritated the powerful Spanish minister Floridablanca. Only Benjamin Franklin seemed to be truly at ease in diplomatic circles, given his years spent in London and the reputation of his scientific studies in Europe, where he was treated like a rock star.

Crossing an ocean patrolled by the British Navy was a courageous act, and once the voyage was underway, there was little choice of turning back. While the American Patriots viewed themselves as diplomats and emissaries, the British viewed them as traitors and outlaws, and when captured, treated them as enemy combatants without any rights to fair or decent treatment. When the Americans reached Madrid and Paris, they began their work to borrow money to finance the perilous venture of rebellion. Intense personality clashes, charges of corruption and embezzlement, and spying and lying soon began. Rumors of inappropriate conduct with the opposite sex buzzed back home to Philadelphia. In certain respects, it was politics as usual, but in a far more precarious time, and with far higher stakes — the survival of the nation itself. Some diplomats were recalled by Congress in disgrace, and some were dazzlingly successful.

Discordant Musical Notes in Madrid

The ethereal music drifted through the marble corridors of a palace in Madrid, echoing a novel musical instrument invented by the highly talented Benjamin Franklin. Among his repertoire as politician, globetrotter, editor, scientist, and entrepreneur, Franklin was also a musician. His invention, the armonica, consisted of 37 glass bowls of varying sizes, placed on a horizontal spindle and rotated by a fly wheel and foot pedal. The armonica is played with moistened fingers — think of rubbing your fingers around the top of a crystal glass. In 1774, while he was stationed in London, Franklin sent an armonica to Don Gabriel de Bourbon, Carlos III's youngest son. The grateful Prince sent Franklin a book that he had personally translated. Franklin wrote back stating, "It seems therefore prudent on both sides to cultivate a good understanding that may hereafter be so useful to both; towards which a fair foundation is already laid in our Minds by the well-founded popular opinion entertained here of Spanish Integrity and Honor."[1]

Unfortunately, a "good understanding" was not cultivated, and discordant diplomatic tones were soon struck in Madrid. Franklin was originally appointed as ambassador to Spain, but he was advised of this assignment when he had already reached Paris in 1776. Considering his very difficult journey across the Atlantic and overland in France, the seventy-year-old Franklin felt that his health would not allow him to travel by coach to Madrid. In his place, the official US envoys were Arthur Lee and John Jay, accompanied by William Carmichael. The disharmony began on a few scattered notes and quickly reached a crescendo.

In 1775, Arthur Lee was appointed as an official Secret Agent by Congress, with instructions to "know the disposition of foreign powers towards us." Congress added that: "We need not hint that great circumspection and impenetrable secrecy are necessary."[2] Unfortunately, since he unknowingly hired a British spy as his personal secretary (oops) and made several other blunders, "great circumspection and impenetrable secrecy" were almost impossible.[3] Arthur Lee landed in Spain in 1777 and quickly succeeded in exasperating experienced diplomats, including Grimaldi. He journeyed to Burgos, in northern Spain, where British spies discovered his presence and reported him to their ambassador. The British ambassador immediately lodged a formal protest to the Spanish court against receiving Lee. From the British point of view, Lee was a scurrilous traitor against his lawful king, not an emissary to be received by a powerful court.

The Spanish were in an awkward diplomatic position. The court requested that Lee remain in Burgos, where he corresponded with Floridablanca. Lee also wrote several letters to Grimaldi, asking to be officially received at the Spanish court, which would have further provoked the British. Grimaldi replied with a lesson in realpolitik for Lee: "You have considered your own situation, and not ours. The moment is not yet come for us. The war with Portugal – France being unprepared, and our treasure ships from South America not being arrived – makes it improper for us to declare immediately." Grimaldi was referring to the ships loaded with silver that were crossing the Atlantic from the mines in Mexico and South America.[4] If war was provoked, the British Navy could legally seize the Spanish treasure fleet as a privateering prize — potentially capturing the annual revenue for the Spanish Treasury. (This almost unbelievable scenario actually occurred in 1628, when an ambitious Dutch pirate captured the entire Spanish silver fleet.) Meanwhile, Grimaldi reassured Lee, stores of clothing and powder were deposited at Nueva Orleáns and Havana for the Americans, and further shipments of blankets were collected at Bilbao.[5]

Lee was eventually permitted to travel to Madrid, where he established contracts for military supplies with Spanish merchants. In December 1777, he wrote Congress, "I have directed all the naval stores that are collected at Bilbao to be shipped forthwith the moment the court of Spain agrees to furnish the money," referring to his meetings with Gardoqui. Lee soon moved on to Berlin to seek aid from the Prussians, only to learn that they were aligned with the British. While traveling in Berlin, the servant of the British ambassador stole Lee's personal papers, compounding his disappointment and failure to keep secret his mission. He then returned to Paris, where he began his nitpicking quarrels with Benjamin Franklin and Silas Deane, leveling accusations against them.

Americans in Paris: Spies and Lies

In Paris, Lee continued to correspond with Floridablanca, with the intent of alarming the Spanish with reports of British successes in the South. The US Army struggled against American Loyalists, British troops, Native Americans, and with rebellions by freedom-fighting enslaved African Americans — in other words, everyone. Lee wrote of the British victory at the Battle of Savannah in December 1778, and of British plans to invade Charleston, South Carolina. "These acquisitions ... with their contiguous possessions, will give them such a command upon that coast and in the Gulf ... and seconding their enterprises against the neighboring territories of Spain, as may be difficult to resist, if they are not prevented."[6] He tried to persuade Floridablanca to send Spanish troops from Havana. Floridablanca sent Lee a cordial decline, and the Spanish continued to monitor the unsteady progress of the Continental Army in the southern colonies.

Silas Deane arrived in Paris earlier in July 1776, to begin negotiations for aid for the rebels. The son of a blacksmith, a Yale graduate, and teacher turned lawyer turned merchant, Deane became a controversial, tragic figure, suspected of treason and embezzlement. He soon linked up with Louis XVI's spy, Beaumarchais, and worked with procurement and shipping operations for Roderigue Hortalez y Compañía. Subtle and diplomatic, Deane was not. He quickly overstepped his orders from Congress, handed out commissions as major general in the US

Army to French officers, became mired in a plot to replace George Washington as Commander-in-Chief with a French count, and collaborated with a Scottish pyromaniac to burn British naval yards.[7] Most damaging to the American cause, he was suspected of embezzlement and corruption, suspicions that greatly worried the courts in Madrid and Paris. Mercy Otis Warren, a famous writer who wrote a three-volume history of the American Revolution, noted that, "His weakness and ostentation, his duplicity, extravagance and total want of principle, were soon discovered."[8]

During his brief career as a schoolmaster, Deane taught Edward Bancroft, Massachusetts native and a double-dealing double agent who covertly worked for the British. Bancroft traveled to South America and worked as a medic on a plantation in British Guiana (now Guyana) and published a book on the country's natural history in 1769. Bancroft also studied natural poisons, including curare, a highly toxic poison that slowly asphyxiates its victims. Through his contacts with Franklin, Bancroft obtained a position as secretary to the American Commission in Paris, where he spied on the British for Benjamin Franklin.

Or, that's what Bancroft tried to make Franklin believe. Bancroft was actually recruited by the ever-vigilant British espionage networks to spy on Franklin, the Americans and the French. He was motivated by greed; he wanted extra income to play the stock market in London. George III understood his motives and sourly complained that Bancroft was a waste of money.[9] In true secret agent form, Bancroft used special ink to write his reports, which he stashed in a glass bottle tied with a string, lowering the bottle into a hole in a designated tree. He managed to steal valuable information for the British, alerting them to the Franco-American treaty of alliance, providing information on Roderigue Hortalez y Compañía and on the departures of ships carrying French and Spanish supplies to the American revolutionaries. Franklin guessed that Bancroft was spying on him, writing "If ... my *valet de place* was a spy, as he probably is." His view of this scenario was philosophical; he wrote that, "what spies may see and welcome when a man's actions are just and honorable, the more they are known, the more his reputation is increased."[10]

Deane and Arthur Lee bitterly quarreled over just about everything: from Deane occupying the suite that Lee planned to live in at the mansion in Paris to receipts and expenses for the extensive shipments of supplies from France. Deane was recalled by Congress and arrived in Philadelphia in July 1778. He was unable to produce sufficient receipts or explanations of his financial dealings, given his sloppy bookkeeping and accounting, and that most of his papers were in Europe. Some believed he was unwilling to produce accounting statements due to his embezzlement and corruption.

In 1781, Deane returned to Paris ostensibly to collect these records and instead spent his time bickering with French officials. Another scandal erupted when his private letters to his brother criticizing the Revolution were published in mainstream media, an early leak to the press. Mercy Otis Warren wrote that, "He afterwards wandered from court to court, and from city to city, for several years: at last reduced to the extreme of poverty and wretchedness, he died miserably in England."[11]

Or that's what Edward Bancroft may have tried to have history believe. Deane's scandals followed him to the grave, and rumors still swirl as silent, unrevealing ghosts around his final demise. Deane planned to travel back home to America in 1789 to clear his name but died shortly before sailing. Was he poisoned by Bancroft, who feared that Deane's revelations would incriminate him, as some historians suspect? Bancroft had admitted to bringing a quantity of poisonous curare powder back with him to Britain.[12] Did he commit suicide with a self-administered dose of laudanum, a medicinal drug comprised primarily of opium, or die of natural causes, plagued by tuberculosis? To this day, the ghosts have not revealed their secrets.

Arthur Lee's animosity towards his colleagues continued to grow. He accused Deane, Beaumarchais, and Franklin of corruption, convinced that Franklin's "frauds and wickedness" were kept from the public domain by "hush money." Lee was recalled to the colonies at about the same time as Deane. Lee was replaced by John Adams, who was later joined by his wife, Abigail, who braved the French aristocratic social scene at the final height of its vanity.

The Americans in Madrid and Paris faced the growing impatience and distrust of the Spanish and French courts. The French ministers were concerned that British spies were too close to the Americans, and felt that they could no longer share sensitive information, even to Franklin. The American Commission verged dangerously close to bankruptcy and was saved from embarrassment by Vergennes. Spanish diplomats in Paris and Madrid were deeply worried about the political acumen of the Americans. When John Jay arrived in Madrid as envoy, the Spanish decided to keep many of their sensitive state secrets safely from the Americans.

Whose Truth was True?

Reading the journals of John Jay and John Adams is a study of perception and point of view, with uncertain and contradictory images flaring among their letters and reports. Both men traveled to Spain on diplomatic missions. Jay was in Spain for about two years and Adams was in Spain for about two months. Both men wrote detailed accounts of their experiences, sometimes with similar observations and sometimes directly contradicting each other. For a modern comparison, think of the coverage of the same events by Fox News and MS NOW. To Jay, the Spanish were arrogant, uncompromising, and ignorant of America. To Adams, the Spanish were well-informed, supportive, and eager to be best friends. To the Spanish, Jay was grindingly difficult and best managed through his strong and intelligent wife, Sarah Livingston Jay. Adams was viewed as an interesting man with a good character.

In many aspects, John Jay was a brilliant and remarkable man; in his attitude towards Catholics, he was not. His political career was long and illustrious. Although he owned enslaved people, he was one of the few Founding Fathers supporting emancipation. His grandparents were Huguenot Protestant refugees from France, where these perceived religious heretics were sanctimoniously persecuted, tortured and executed. These horrific events certainly chilled his feelings towards Catholicism, and Jay's open-mindedness towards emancipation did not extend to Catholics. When the British Parliament passed the Quebec Act in 1774 that allowed Catholics in North America to have freedom of worship and a bishop, he vehemently protested. After the Revolution, he attempted to pass a law in New York that prohibited Catholics from holding political office. Even with these public prejudices, Congress selected Jay as diplomatic representative for the Catholic nations of Spain and later France. With his wife and entourage, he departed for Europe in December 1779.

After a few misadventures at sea, the Jays arrived in the port of Cádiz on the southwestern coast of Spain. The port was a safe harbor for American privateers outrunning the British and for American prisoners of war, who sought refuge there after escaping from British prisons. Upon their arrival, Sarah Livingston Jay wrote that Matías de Gálvez graciously sent a boat to transport them from the port of Cádiz across the bay to Puerta de Santa Maria. The boat "was ornamented by a crimson damask canopy handsomely fringed and the benches covered with cushions of the same, the rowers were 16 to 20 in number, in a uniform that was after a fanciful taste...."[13] When they landed at Puerta de Santa Maria, they were greeted by servants of Captain-General Alejandro O'Reilly. The Jays boarded O'Reilly's coach and were entertained that evening with an elaborate dinner hosted by O'Reilly and his Cuban wife, Rosa de las Casas. The O'Reillys invited their acquaintances to a reception for the Jays. In brief, the Spanish gave the Jays a celebrity welcome that included some of the most prestigious members of the court and Spain's empire in America.

The Jays then traveled by bumpy coaches north to Madrid, complaining about their accommodation in letters. Sarah was six months pregnant when she arrived in Spain, and the journey was especially difficult for her. They stopped in Córdoba, where Sarah declared that she "never saw anything more enchanting" and admired the marble columns and architecture of the Moorish-mosque-turned-Catholic-cathedral. They met up with hospitable Irish living in southern Spain and reached Madrid in April 1780. After some house-hunting, they settled in the residence of another former diplomat, with a fountain in the enclosed courtyard in traditional Spanish Moorish architecture. Sarah enjoyed the "very beautiful walks and publick gardens"[14] and admired the landscaping that was in progress, noting that "the trees alone with which he [Carlos III] has adorned the roads and walks" were representative of the King's excellent taste.

Their stay in Madrid soon became troubled and problematic. On the personal side, Sarah's infant daughter died within three weeks. The Jays were heartbroken. Infant death and pregnancy complications were crushingly common in the 18th century. On the public side, Congress had neglected to allocate funds for Jay's mission, assuming that he could quickly borrow money from the Spanish government for his living expenses and purchases of military equipment. Jay was very low on personal funds — picture traveling to Europe without credit cards or smart wallets, with your only financial plan being to borrow money from hosts whom you had never met.[15]

The Spanish Court, which had recently incurred huge budget expenditures for an unsuccessful invasion of England, was monitoring its own budget. Congress and merchants continued to send bills drawn on Jay's supposed lines of credit. While the Spanish paid many of Jay's bills and provided direct funds, Jay never seemed to think that Spain adequately catered to his unauthorized spending. Finally, the Spanish Court, which quickly developed a negative view of Jay and his exorbitant spending, decided not to continue their loans. Jay then turned to Franklin in Paris to request funds from him. Jay's spending became an embarrassment to Franklin. The always resourceful Gardoqui, the Basque agent and merchant, finally stepped in with more cash to settle Jay's reckless bills.

In May 1780, four months after his arrival in Spain, Jay had his first meeting with Floridablanca, beginning a series of mismatched expectations, stalled negotiations, and increasingly rigid demands from Jay. The money chase began in earnest, with Jay attempting to deal with various brokers and bankers to continue to purchase supplies for the war and writing to Franklin in Paris requesting financial reinforcements. Jay's letters home and his negotiating positions in Spain became increasingly demanding, which exasperated the French Ambassador in Madrid. Jay wrote, "I am still much inclined to think it advisable to push this Court by a demand of a categorical answer. The French Ambassador thinks it would be rash, and opposes it."[16] He arrogantly referred to his continued requests for money and credit as, "the Court indeed owes me."[17] He correctly guessed the gossip in Madrid and Paris, "the public might have had room to conjecture, or individuals to insinuate, that I had imprudently run into such rash and expensive engagements as to render it improper for Spain or France to afford me the necessary supplies."[18]

Jay made surprise purchases without informing the Spanish in advance. In his dispatch to Floridablanca in February 1781, Jay accepted a bill for a shipment of clothing in Cádiz, adding that "I had no opportunity of giving your Excellency previous notice of it." Jay did not want to "lose the opportunities of sending the Cloathing to America, where it is much wanted and will be extremely welcome."[19] Jay was certain that the Spanish and French Courts were to be blamed for all of his financial difficulties. The Spanish continued to view Jay as an extremely difficult man. Gardoqui felt that the best way to deal with him was through his wife, Sarah, whom the Spanish perceived as having a strong influence over her husband. Gardoqui reported that Sarah was fond of gifts, particularly excellent wine, and he astutely pursued this path of diplomacy.

Jay rejected invitations to Court, and most undiplomatically refused an invitation to meet with Carlos III, again stating categorically that the United States had to be recognized before he deigned to accept an invitation. The Spanish had demanded American independence as part of their pre-war negotiations with the British in 1779, but unsurprisingly, the British refused this demand. According to John Adams, favorable rumors were circulating that a treaty and recognition would soon be concluded, but John Jay had a different point of view.

"Although offense and disrespect are very far from my thoughts," Jay wrote Congress in April 1782, "I fear that the Count [Floridablanca] will be a little hurt at my declining the invitation in question."[20] Jay further acknowledged that he had declined other invitations,* "Reasons similar to those assigned for this refusal have induced me ever since my arrival to decline going to Court, where I might also have been presented as a stranger of distinction, but as Mr. Carmichael had been presented in that character previous to my coming to Madrid, I never objected to his making subsequent visits."[21] Jay's animosity towards the Spanish continued through his negotiations at the peace table in Paris in 1783, when he made several outrageous proposals to undercut both Spain and France in the peace settlement.

A Matter of Titles: William and Carlos

William Carmichael was the son of Scottish immigrants from a wealthy family in Maryland who traveled and lived in Edinburgh, Ireland, and London. He joined the American staff in Paris as an unpaid volunteer.[22] Later in his career, he gained a measure of respect, and Washington appointed him to lead sensitive negotiations with Spain over the Mississippi navigation rights. Franklin referred to Carmichael as his "very much and esteemed friend."[23] Thomas Jefferson was not a fan, but he understood that Carmichael was well-liked by the Spanish.

---

* Let's take a minute to review this scenario: Jay represented a nation that was so broke that their soldiers marched without shoes, but Jay refused to meet with one of the most powerful men in the world who had financed, supplied, and supported the Americans for years?

Jefferson wrote in 1787 that he thought Carmichael was "vain and more attentive to ceremony and etiquette than we suppose men of sense should be. Many persons of different nations coming from Madrid to Paris, all speak of him as in high esteem and I think it certain that he has more of the Count de Florida Blanca's friendship than any diplomatic character at that court." Carmichael was suspected by some of treason, given his friendship with a fellow Marylander named Hynson, a courier who delivered secret documents from the American Commissioners in Paris to waiting British spies.

Carmichael was sent by the Commissioners to Holland and Prussia on a secret mission in late 1776. By January 1777, he was supervising the loading of munitions and cannons onto French ships at Le Havre, a port on the northern French coast. After briefly serving in Congress, he was elected to the position of Secretary to John Jay in September 1779. He dodged British warships in the Mediterranean and landed in Cádiz in January 1780.

Carmichael had a long, enjoyable stay in Spain. He married a Spanish woman, Antonia Reynon, and they had one daughter, Alphonsa. Although Jay refused the King's invitation, Carmichael was delighted to accept it, and he was the first United States citizen to meet a Spanish monarch. Carlos III and his children hosted him with a warm and gracious reception in keeping with the friendship and high esteem in which he was held. The king was a popular and powerful celebrity to meet, and Floridablanca was pursued by ambassadors throughout Europe for presentations to the king. Floridablanca promised Carmichael that he would keep his word to arrange the meeting, and the date was finally confirmed in August 1783. Floridablanca coached Carmichael for the meeting, noting that the king did not appreciate long speeches and harangues. Carlos III seems to be the type of executive who in today's meetings would affably but firmly shut down a long Power Point presentation and politely ask the speaker to get to the point.

Carmichael and Floridablanca met at the King's apartments, where Carmichael was presented as the Chargé d'Affaires of the United States, an official of a sovereign nation. Jay, determined to claim that the Spanish Court insulted him, scornfully and erroneously predicted that he would be received as an individual of no national standing. Mindful of his instructions to keep it brief, Carmichael "contented myself with expressing to his Majesty my happiness in being the first of my countrymen who had the good fortune to assure him of their desire to cultivate his amity." Carlos responded graciously, "that he hoped I should have frequent occasions of making him the same assurances."[24]

The meetings continued for several days, for visits of about forty-five minutes. Carlos' family joined in the meetings, and "[the] Prince of Asturias spoke of me during the dinner as of a person he had long known, and when I was presented he told me so." One of Carlos' daughters was also present, and charmed Carmichael. "The Princess... spoke to me six or seven minutes in French and Spanish, and among other things said to me, that I ought to like Spain, because, she had been told, that I was much liked by the Spaniards."[25] Carmichael reported that the "other branches of the family received me equally well."

BFFs and Best Friends in Spain

In December 1779, John Adams arrived in "the magnificent Spanish port of Ferrol,"[26] in the province of Galicia. Adams was on his way to France, traveling with two of his sons, aged ten and twelve, and several other officials. Their ship sprang a serious leak, and despite two pumps manned by both the crew and passengers, the captain had to stop in the nearest safe harbor. Ferrol was and remains a major shipbuilding port, now home to the northern department of the Spanish Navy. Adams traveled through "the ancient kingdoms of Galicia, Leon, Old Castile, and Biscay [the Basque countryside]." Galicia has its own rich history, with a distinct language close to medieval Portuguese with hints of Celtic. The famed Santiago de Compostela is its capital and the final destination of the lengthy pilgrimage of The Way of Saint James, traveled since the 9th century by believers and sinners and more recently by those on a spiritual or personal quest. Gardoqui accompanied him. Lagoanere y Compañía, based in the port city of La Coruña in northwestern Spain, was one of Adams' hosts when he arrived in Spain. Lagoanere gave Adams thousands in cash for his expenses.

Adams reported that he was "treated with the utmost attention and politeness since my arrival in this place, both the Spanish and French officers... who have all obligingly offered me every assistance in their power."[27] Adams traveled farther up the Spanish Atlantic coast to La Coruña, where he made influential friendships. He wrote that the provincial Governor of Galicia assured him that "he was not only disposed personally to render me every hospitality and assistance in his power, but that he had received express orders from his Court to treat all Americans who should arrive here like their best friends."[28]

Unlike Jay's reports of the ignorance of the Spanish of the Americans – Jay apparently didn't read or acknowledge the coverage by leading Spanish newspapers – Adams noted that his hosts were "very inquisitive about American affairs, particularly the progress of our arms." The Galicians also respectfully inquired about "the appointment of a Minister Plenipotentiary to the Court of Madrid," who was actually the ungracious John Jay. "They requested his name, character, nativity, age," wrote Adams, "whether he was a member of Congress, and whether he had been President, with many other particulars." At this point, before Jay's diplomatic mission began, Adams' hosts assured him that "It is the prevailing opinion here that the Court of Madrid is well disposed to enter into a treaty with the United States, and that the Minister from Congress will be immediately received, American independence acknowledged and a treaty concluded."[29] Obviously, events did not unfold as "well disposed" once Jay arrived and began his mission of questionable diplomacy.

While Adams was negotiating in Paris, he relied on Gardoqui to safely send his famous love letters to his wife Abigail in Massachusetts. Adams wrote that their personal correspondence was best trusted to the Gardoquis, for "Bilbao was the most secure means of transport that I know."[30] He thought about stopping in Madrid. Unlike Jay or Lee, Adams realized that "the political situation that I might be in, my country not being yet acknowledged as a sovereign State by any formal act of that Court, [and] it being known, that another gentleman had a commission for that Court." Adams concluded that, "I thought it upon the whole the least hazardous to the public interest to avoid that route."

Adams felt that after independence, "a commerce extremely advantageous to both countries may be opened between us and Spain" and he sent detailed notes of the economy, cities, ports, and civil government back to Congress. He observed "the numerous blocks of sheep" in Leon and Castile, "with the most beautiful fleeces in the world." He envisioned an international trade of American resources for Spanish "wine, oil, fruits, some silks, some linens ... and with any quantity of wool... but above all with silver and gold." He reached Bilbao by mid-January 1780, where he met up with Gardoqui, who helped finance his journey to France. Adams continued his connection with the House of Gardoqui when he reached Paris in February. Once in Paris, Adams soon began quarrelling with Franklin over diplomatic policies and pushed the limits of the French court, to the dismay of both Franklin and his French supporters.

Adams, Carmichael, Jay, and Lee recorded markedly different and often contradictory accounts of their time in Spain and their dealings with the Spanish. With Jay acting as lead negotiator at the 1783 Paris Peace Treaty, the historical narrative that endures today overwhelmingly reflects his perspective. Jay moved to Paris to join Franklin in negotiations with the British, Spanish, and French. While there, despite the amiable and generous treatment that he had received from the Spanish, and with the knowledge of the aid and support Spain provided throughout the War, Jay worked to undermine Spain in the peace settlement.

Adams foresaw the emerging conflicts, and he worried that British negotiators would try to convince the US to make a separate peace treaty without Spain and France. The British, he wrote, will attempt to "persuade her [America] to join them against the House of Bourbon. One would think it impossible, that one man of sense in the world could seriously believe, that we could thus basely violate our truth, thus unreasonably quarrel with our best friends, thus madly attach ourselves to our belligerent enemies. But thus it is."[31] And, unfortunately, at the final peace negotiations in Paris 1783 with John Jay as a lead negotiator, thus it was.

Chapter 7

Pirates of the Caribbean, Atlantic and Pacific

With the outbreak of the Revolutionary War, the seas were transformed into battlefronts and ruthless privateering rampaged across the globe, from the inlets of Puerto Rico in the Caribbean to the coast of Mauritius in the Indian Ocean. Privateering was a lucrative "Grand Theft Shipping," the state-sanctioned practice of authorizing private ship owners to attack and capture enemy merchant vessels during wartime. Governments encouraged the practice and issued legal documents granting civilian captains the right to seize enemy ships and cargo for profit.

As expected, this licensed piracy created havoc, particularly in an era without sophisticated communications equipment or visual technology. Acrimonious disputes as to whether pursuing ships were privateers, corsairs or pirates rattled diplomatic relations throughout the European courts, as zealous captains – including Americans – seized vessels from neutral countries. Commercial merchant ships and military transport vessels loaded with cargo were chased relentlessly across the seas. Many were captured, sometimes with a quiet surrender, other times with the clang of metal grappling hooks and cutlasses, the thunder of cannons and the crack of musket fire. Congress passed a resolution in the spring of 1776 that authorized privateering, and the games began. Some American privateers were fortunate and returned with their sea chests jingling with coins; others were captured by the British navy and imprisoned as criminal pirates, either dying slowly on dreaded prison ships or engineering daring escapes.

The Spanish and Latin Americans actively assisted American privateers, who often aggrieved them with illegal seizures of their own national ships. The Spanish military provided safe havens from British warships pursuing American privateers, Spanish shipwrights repaired American ships in their ports, and Spanish businessmen funded their frequent cash shortfalls. In Philadelphia, Miralles and

Rendón financed privateer ships and expeditions.[1] The crucial last step in privateering was to sell the loot, known as "prizes," for silver and gold, which Spanish merchants transacted on their behalf. In the unfortunate event that American privateers were captured, those who managed to escape fled to sanctuary cities in Spain and Cuba, where they were sheltered and aided. Privateering was essential to a nation with few resources and under a choking blockade by the most powerful navy in the world. The cash earned from the sale of prizes was used to purchase supplies and armaments needed by the US Army. When Franklin arrived in Paris, he carried a stack of blank privateering authorizations to appoint Americans ship captains in Europe and soon ran out of the papers.[2]

The small but spirited US Navy was founded in October 1775, with 57 ships deployed during the entire war. Several states, including Pennsylvania and South Carolina, also formed their own navies. A ship's size determined its number of guns. The largest ships of the line, which the US Navy could not afford, carried hundreds of guns on three decks and fought in line formations. Two-deck ships carried 74 or fewer guns. The huge ships were slow on the seas, with a top speed of six knots,[3] about 7 MPH or 11 KM/H. Of the US ships, only 27 of the 57 were classified as warships and only one, the *America*, was large enough to classify as a ship of the line, but it was not launched until 1782 after the major battles were over.[4] The British Navy fleet numbered 270, of which 117 were formidable ships of the line.

The British Navy was superior in terms of critical technology. The British sheathed the hulls of their ships with copper sheets, a decisive advantage that the Americans could not afford. The copper sheathing protected against corrosion and extreme weather and prevented the growth of barnacles and algae that enabled greater speed and durability. The American domestic economy did not produce the copper needed and had to import it. American ships were often rushed into production with unseasoned timber and defective masts and spars.[5] Despite being outsailed and outgunned, the Americans did manage a few extraordinary victories, including daring raids on the coast of England.

The American privateer ships far outnumbered US military ships. Americans launched over 2,000 privateer ships throughout the War, armed with 18,000 guns and crewed by 70,000 men.[6] The long list of Americans who participated in privateering by either financing ships or sailing them included George Washington, Paul Revere, and John Hancock.

"Not on earth a more disorderly set"

The American privateers' legal and financial dealings on land were often as contentious and chaotic as those on the seas, as Patriot privateers chased, harassed and captured merchant ships, sometimes mistakenly (or deliberately) plundered ships of neutral countries, and occasionally fired on the ships of their Spanish allies. British privateers swarmed the seas around the globe, focusing on the Atlantic trade routes. Adams wrote to Jay in Madrid that "we find it almost impossible to get a letter across the Bay of Biscay from France in a merchant vessel, there are so many privateers in the route."[7] On the other side of the world in the Indian Ocean, where the French and the British battled over India, French and Mauritian corsairs – privateers with a fancier title – successfully attacked many of their enemy's merchant ships, with the French navy occasionally joining in the profitable adventures.[8]

George Washington was one of the first American leaders to sponsor privateering. During the Siege of Boston in 1775, he decided that since "we were not likely to do much in the land way, I fitted out several privateers, or rather armed vessels, in behalf of the Continent."[9] Bickering and squabbles prevailed, with many high-profile accusations of questionable actions. John Glover, one of the Marblehead, Massachusetts men, incited criticism when he charged the colonial government premium rates to lease his sixty-foot boat, the *Hannah*, named after his wife. Privateer ships were named after prominent Patriot leaders, including *Lady Washington, General Gates,* and *Franklin* or more poetically christened *Hope, Freedom,* and *Fortune.* The Pennsylvania state navy had a global perspective, and named one of their warships the *Hyder-Ally,* after the ruler of the Mysore kingdom, Hyder Ali, who was battling the British in India. With no international laws or dispute resolution, the privateering business was a chaotic brawl across the waves. Prizes were sometimes recaptured after their initial capture as fighting broke out between the captive crews and the capturing crews, and the captives succeeded in capturing their captors. One nation's ships could be seized by a second country, then attacked and captured again by a third.

Ships often flew under false colors, meaning that they deceitfully flew the flags and banners of their enemies or neutral countries to lure targeted ships into a sense of false security before launching their attacks. Washington sighed that, "I do believe there is not on earth, a more disorderly Set."[10] American privateers occasionally seized Spanish ships. In July 1779, three commercial merchant ships from Spain carrying hundreds of thousands of pesos in clothing, grain, and indigo[11] were attacked by American privateers. And in 1781, American privateers fired on a Spanish ship as it sailed along the Spanish coast from La Coruña to Bilbao. The Americans hailed the ship as it approached and ordered the crew to send out a launch boat for boarding. The Spanish replied in English that their launch boat was being repaired. The Americans, shocked that the Spanish sailors spoke English, decided that the ship must be British, and opened fire. According to John Jay, this incident was entirely the fault of the Spanish; the conduct of the American captain was impeccable. Floridablanca was angered by Jay's letter and stated that his [Floridablanca's] reports of the incident were "received from persons of respectability and entirely worthy of credit [for] very accurate statements."[12] Jay continued to grumble about the Spanish for holding the American captain accountable. Finally, Carlos III stepped in to resolve the conflict, given that the American captain paid for the damages to the Spanish ship. We can only imagine what Carlos III thought of this behavior by the country to which he was generously supplying military assistance and financing. Despite the difficulties, the Spanish continued to assist the American privateers. Cádiz, Bilbao, and other Spanish ports sheltered American ships. Americans also docked at Havana, San Juan in Puerto Rico, and other Spanish ports in the Caribbean. John Jay reported that Cádiz was also a sanctuary city for "our distressed seamen, who, escaping from captivity ... daily arrive here."[13]

As usual, British informants were watching. Late in 1776, a Massachusetts privateer landed with his ships in Bilbao. Its captain, John Lee (no relation to Arthur Lee), wanted to put his captives onshore, in hopes of avoiding a re-capture attempt at sea. British spies soon reported John Lee's presence to their ambassador, and Britain formally requested John Lee's extradition as a pirate. The legal judgement was crucial. If Spain decided to protect John Lee, they were implicitly recognizing US sovereignty, since their action would acknowledge Lee as a privateer appointed by a recognized foreign nation, not a lowly, stateless pirate. Vergennes and Silas Deane managed the negotiations from Paris. The Spanish court decided to defend Lee from the furious British, keeping him safe from prison and hanging — and tacitly recognized the United States.[14]

The 'Dunkirk Pirate' & Friends

The well-known John Paul Jones and the less famous Alexander Gillon and Gustavus Conyngham were appointed as privateers in service of the hopelessly outnumbered US Navy as it challenged the numerically and technologically superior British. Their bold privateering adventures on the seas were directly aided by the Spanish and Latin Americans. Although they were outnumbered and underequipped, Jones and Conyngham terrified British civilians with their bold, almost recklessly courageous attacks that struck directly at the English home shores. All three men were immigrants: Jones was from Scotland, Conyngham from Ireland, and Gillon from the Netherlands. The three men experienced widely differing fates: Jones' murky position in history was rescued later by a President who unofficially named him as the Father of the US Navy, Conyngham remained unappreciated and unrewarded, and Gillon became a successful politician and businessman in South Carolina after the war.

The son of a Scottish gardener and former housekeeper, John Paul Jones started his career at thirteen when he first left to work on a sea voyage. After a brief assignment on a slave ship, he joined the US Navy as a First Lieutenant in December 1775. He already had a tarnished reputation, given the death of one of his sailors for which he was perceived to be responsible, and several other altercations. Discord and disagreements plagued him throughout his naval career, but his courage and daring were beyond dispute. He insisted on attacking the English on their home turf, an almost unthinkable strategy given the overpowering British Navy, and was described as the "extraordinary character who kept the coasts of the United Kingdom in a constant state of alarm for a considerable time."[15]

In April 1778, he succeeded in attacking Whitehaven Harbor, a seaport on the northwest coast of England. Jones landed on shore with his party, disabled the defending artillery, and hurled "candles" (explosive firebombs of canvas dipped in sulfur) into one of the docked ships. Although no blood was spilled on either side and little material damage done, the British were horrified by this raid on their homeland. The news sent shockwaves throughout the country. A British seaport had not been successfully attacked in more than two hundred years.[16] Jones was portrayed in British media as a pirate, drawn with a skull and crossbones on his hat and clothing. He overcame tremendous odds to capture the British naval ship *Drake*, again a profound psychological victory against the mighty Royal Navy that was feared by its enemies and revered by its citizens.

During his eighteen months of naval service and privateering, Jones collected about $3,000 in prize money, a huge sum compared to a Continental Navy Captain's wage of $32.00 a month.[17] Jones was also famed for his difficult personality and he quarreled with both allies and enemies.[18] The reliable companies of Gardoqui e Hijos and Lagoanere y Compañía assisted Jones in transacting his prizes, which Jones contacted on the recommendation of Benjamin Franklin.[19] Jones was deeply concerned over the recruitment disadvantage that the navy had compared to the lucrative lure of privateering. He stated that the navy compensation was "paltry," and he felt that the tension between the privateers and the navy was a "woeful predicament, of which there were many during the Revolution."

Born the same year in Ireland as Jones, Gustavus Conyngham emigrated with his father to the colonies in his early youth. He apprenticed to a ship's captain for trade runs to Antigua in the Caribbean. His first venture on behalf of the American cause was a powder cruise from Philadelphia to the Netherlands to obtain needed military supplies. The trip home was thwarted by the British, who complained to the Dutch that Conyngham's ship was carrying military supplies to the rebels — an illegal act from the British point of view. In March 1777 while in Europe, he received a privateering commission from Benjamin Franklin, and his new career began.

Feared as the "Dunkirk Pirate" by the British, he was soon snatching enemy merchant ships throughout Europe. The *Revenge*, his warship, was refitted and resupplied at Ferrol, Spain. The ship's extensive upgrades included a large mast, planks, iron nails, tar, grease, and the services of carpenters and workmen which were financed by Gardoqui and Miguel Lagoanere.[20] In its 22 months of operation, the *Revenge* captured or destroyed 60 British ships, an incredible record. Conyngham relied on the Spanish for support, docking in Spanish ports to release his prisoners, sell his prizes, and repair his ships. His financial transactions, including the refurbishment of the *Revenge*, were managed by Lagoanere and Gardoqui. In early 1777, Lagoanere wrote to their office in Cádiz, noting that Conygham was arriving in the *Revenge* "belonging to the Congress of ... America" and requesting that the Cádiz office "render to him every service within your power."[21] These relationships proceeded amicably, until Arthur Lee insisted on involving himself. Lee began to accuse both Conyngham and the Spanish merchants of corruption and mismanagement — surprise, surprise. Lee constantly peppered Silas Deane with questions about the transactions in Spain. In 1797, still faced with lawsuits and disputes over his privateering, Conyngham angrily wrote that, "Every difficulty was thrown in my way by Arthur Lee."

Deane described Conyngham as "the terror of all of the eastern coast of England and Scotland. But though it distresses our enemies, it embarrasses us."[22] The embarrassment was due to Conyngham's aggressive and occasional deliberate illegal seizures. He began privateering before the French were prepared diplomatically, putting Vergennes in an awkward position. He seized a Spanish transport on the grounds that it carried British cargo, to which the exasperated Spanish objected. He also ransacked a Swedish ship, knowing that ships from this neutral country should not be attacked. His men signed a document declaring that this cargo must also be British, and that they would take the ship to America to sell its cargo. European diplomats across the continent were furious, and Benjamin Franklin rushed in for damage control.

Conyngham sailed briefly with John Paul Jones, who was in Holland with what was left of the *Serapis*. He parted with Jones and changed ships at La Coruña, hoping to sail home to prize money and his family. With another twist of bad luck, the ship that he was traveling on was apprehended, and Conyngham was taken prisoner in March 1780. He was incarcerated at Mill Prison in southwestern England, where he endured a year of brutal treatment, eating rats, cats, dogs and grass with the other prisoners. He managed to escape again, accompanied by his resourceful wife who had traveled to Europe to be near him, and returned to Philadelphia.

The 'Beautiful' *South Carolina*

Alexander Gillon was the leading commander in the very small but stalwart South Carolina Navy and had close ties in Havana. Gillon began his service in the Revolutionary War as a politician in 1775 and joined the fighting with his appointment as Commodore of the South Carolina Navy in 1779. A successful, multilingual businessman, Gillon was able to gather the resources and financial backing that eluded Jones and Conyngham.[23] He received direct aid from the Spanish early in March 1778, with funds sent "in greatest secrecy" from Miralles to repair the much-admired warship *South Carolina*.[24] In August of that year, Gillon sailed into the Havana harbor with three ships from South Carolina, flying distress flags. The ships needed repairs and provisions, and Gillon did not have cash on hand. As he explained to Navarro, "My dear Governor, please heed what cruel necessity compels me to beg of you, and consent to supply to me the sum of ten to eleven thousand dollars for my bills of exchange."[25] Gillon promised to repay the loan when he sold his cargo of indigo in Havana. Navarro provided Gillon and his men with lodging, lent Gillon money to repair the ships, and offered a warehouse to store his cargo. In 18th century flowery prose, Navarro assured Gillon that, "you cannot have retained the slightest doubt of our willingness to try to reconcile the orders of our Sovereign with proofs of our affection for your admirable person and for the state which adorns you with its confidence."[26]

Gillon frequently docked in Havana to sell his prizes, repair his ship, and meet with Team Carlos, including Cagigal, Solano, Navarro, and Urriza. During his visit in 1782, he discussed the new US Articles of Confederation with Francisco Saavedra de Sangronis, the King's Special Agent who played a critical role in funding the Battle of Yorktown. He partied at the home of Bernardo de Gálvez and Marie Felicitas, who were visiting Havana, and dined with Urriza at his home.[27] He joined the Spanish and Cubans in one of the last battles of the Revolutionary War, the invasion of the British Bahamas in 1782, the only time in the Revolution that the Americans and Spanish fought in a direct joint campaign.

Gillon commanded the *South Carolina*, the largest ship under US command during the war. With a mast over 100 feet tall, and the capacity to fire 40 cannons and carry 500 men, the ship was admired by Spanish military officials. José Solano y Bote, the Captain General of the Spanish Armada, visited the ship in Havana, and was a fan, as was Cagigal. Bernardo de Gálvez also boarded the *South Carolina*, declaring it as a "beautiful" vessel.[28] You may be wondering how a financially strapped nation that relied on a hyper-inflated Continental dollar could possibly have afforded this superb vessel? Great question! As usual with American international finances in the late 18th century, the answer is complicated. Gillon was the driving force behind the ship's success and clearly possessed unique and formidable skills as a businessman, state politician, and naval officer. The fabled ship was built in the Netherlands and financed by the French, originally christened as *L'Indien*. Various owners squabbled over its title before Gillon sailed it out of the Dutch harbor in 1781.[29] Louis XVI "lent" the ship to the Prince of Luxembourg, and somehow – the path is still not clear – the prince contracted with Gillon to use the ship for privateering, with the prince receiving a portion of the prize money. Gillon also pledged money from his personal wealth and the financially unstable South Carolina government as compensation if the ship was confiscated or lost. At least, that was the deal on paper. The complexities of the arrangement were, in the words of one historian, "a contract that would warm the hearts of lawyers on both sides of the Atlantic for years to come."[30]

Gillon's privateering mission soon encountered troubled waters. The crew mutinied over lack of pay as the ship sailed out of Amsterdam.[31] During its first six weeks at sea, the ship was low on food and water, in need of repairs, and overloaded with cargo, including trunks for Washington. Gillon determined that he could not sail across the Atlantic and instead turned to A Coruña, Spain. The Spanish aided him by selling his prizes, repairing his ship, and providing the provisions that he needed. As he departed for his voyage back to the US, Gillon sailed into another Spanish port in the Canary Islands, where he was welcomed by the Spanish commander.[32] Gillon continued to raid and seize ships throughout the war, until the British commandeered the *South Carolina* in December 1782 after its joint military campaign with the Spanish military in the Bahamas. Then, the mighty ship quietly disappeared into history.[33]

"This floating Pandemonium filled us with horror"

The British Parliament passed the "Pirate Act" in 1777, essentially designating the American privateers as enemy combatants, without the legal rights usually granted to prisoners of war, including trials and exchanges. The Act was controversial in Britain among both war hawks and liberal doves who argued in Parliament and in heated discussions in taverns and meeting houses. Captured rebel pirates were usually incarcerated at either Forton Prison near the Royal Navy dockyard at Portsmouth, or at Mill Prison in Plymouth. The conditions at these prisons were not as bleak as the deadly prison ships, though overcrowding, corrupt management of rations, and disease took the lives of many Americans. Local Brits, including community organizers who opposed the war, sympathetically provided clothing and food to the foreign prisoners. Franklin, deeply aggrieved by the appalling treatment of his countrymen, also assisted them.

Several prison ships were anchored near American shores. Prisoners were crowded into the dark holds of the ships, with no provisions for sanitation or comfort. Among the prisoners was Ebenezer Fox, a militia soldier and sailor who ran away from his home in Boston at age 12 to work on a ship. After his time at sea, Fox returned home and at 15 was apprenticed to a barber, making wigs and cushions. He described himself as a lousy barber, "being occasionally allowed to scrape the face of some transient customer, who might reasonably be expected never to call again for a repetition of the operation." In September 1779, a few months short of the legal enlistment age of sixteen, he joined the army. He marched to Albany, but then Washington decided not to attack New York. By then Fox was at the end of his enlistment — short enlistments and a high turnover of soldiers were a continual problem for the Continental Army. He began the journey home to Roxbury, his clothing "much worn and damaged." One pair of his shoes were stolen, "leaving me with no other alternative but to go barefoot or secure the remaining ones to my feet by winding rope yarn around them." His feet were "covered with blisters while I marched over frozen ground and snow" until he finally arrived "almost crippled" at his father's home.[34]

Most people would have decided that this painful experience was enough of an adventure, but Ebenezer Fox was not most people. Although he did not wish to be a soldier again, at 17 his restless spirit prompted him to sign up for duty on the *Protector*, a twenty-gun ship funded by the Massachusetts state government. "Our coast was lined with British cruisers," Fox wrote, "which almost annihilated our commerce."[35] Decidedly outnumbered, the Massachusetts men of the lone *Protector* joined the battle against the powerful British navy.

The ship cruised to the Caribbean where they captured a British merchant ship. The men then sailed this ship to San Juan, Puerto Rico, where the Spanish obligingly paid them for its prize cargo, which included fourteen enslaved human beings. The *Protector* turned to travel north past the Carolinas and towards Boston, continuing to seize prizes and annoy the British. They met up with a ship commanded by Conyngham that was traveling from Havana to Boston, carrying a large quantity of silver. Conyngham thought that the cash would be safer on board an armed vessel and asked that it be transferred to the *Protector*. Unfortunately, given the treachery of the local Loyalists, all was soon lost.

As they sailed farther north, two warships flying French flags started to pursue them. Worried that the ships were British in disguise, the ship's captain turned the *Protector* and tried to outrun the British. Meanwhile, Fox and a few friends, thinking that they may not be eating well in the event of capture, went below deck to quickly eat and drink a quantity of captured gourmet provisions and returned to the top deck "without our absence having been noticed." Their pursuers were British warships, tipped off by local Loyalists that the *Protector* was soon scheduled to return to Boston. Faced with far superior British firepower, the American privateers had to surrender, and Fox's high-spirited dreams of adventure turned to a nightmare on a British prison ship. The Americans were quickly loaded onto the British ships, prodded, kicked and cursed as "damned rebels." Some of the Americans were forced into British service, but Fox was among those taken to the prison ship *Jersey*. "The idea of being incarcerated in this floating Pandemonium filled us with horror," Fox later wrote, "but the idea we had formed of its horrors fell far short of the realities which we afterwards experienced."

The *Jersey* was unfit for sea and was used as a storage ship until someone had the cruel idea of turning it into a floating prison. The ship was close to shore, a huge dark hulk, with its port holes closed and secured to prevent escape. Two tiers of holes were cut through her sides, about two feet square and ten feet apart, which were covered by an iron grating. These holes were the air supply for the hundreds of men trapped below deck. Fox stumbled down the ladder to the gloomy interior and gasped at the stench and the "collection of the most wretched and disgusting looking objects that I ever beheld in human form." His fellow prisoners were "covered with rags and filth, visages pallid with disease, emaciated with hunger and anxiety, and retaining hardly a trace of their original appearances." Fox was terrified and fearful that he would die, "I could hardly realize my situation." The food was disgusting. The biscuits crawled with worms, so the men banged them against the wooden hull to dislodge the pests before eating the crumbs. The meat was colored with "motley hues" with the "appearance of variegated fancy soap." The flour and oatmeal were so sour that the stench of these provisions could be smelled across the ship. To worsen matters, the water in which the meals were cooked was taken from the muddy salt water alongside the ship — the same water in which the men dumped their buckets of urine and feces.[36] The men were allowed on the deck during the day, and each morning climbed up the ladder to the open sky, carrying the decaying bodies of those who had died during the night for burial. As the sun set, the men were ordered down below again, "and we were left to pass the night amid the accumulated horrors of sighs and groans, of foul vapor, a nauseous and putrid atmosphere, in a stifled and almost suffocating heat."

The British sent emissaries of temptation into this inferno to recruit the men who were at their breaking points. Duty in Jamaica in the British Army was one of the options. After an unsuccessful escape attempt, with his health deteriorating daily, Fox and several men made the difficult decision to enlist in the British Army. Their goal was to escape from Jamaica, and with the help of the Spanish and Cubans, they succeeded. Once he had landed in Jamaica, Fox pursued his career as a barber for British officers with better results than his earlier attempts in Boston, fortunately for all involved. He slowly gained the confidence of his captors. With increasing privileges to spend time outside of the armed camp, he began to plot his escape with several of his fellow prisoners. On the appointed day, Fox and his compadres began their desperate race through the Jamaican jungles, pursued by the British Army and local bounty hunters.

After five days of panicked running with little to eat or drink, the fugitives reached the sea. They captured a small boat and sailed for the sanctuary of Cuba and soon neared the island. After several days, they were sighted by the Cubans, who boarded their boat. Fox and his crew did not speak Spanish, but "by a variety of gesticulations and by repeating the words America, Jamaica, and Kingston… we made them comprehend, in some degree, our circumstances."[37] The Cubans recognized the distressful condition of these refugees and cared for the ragged, hungry men, carrying them to a hut and feeding them a meal of pork, peas, and beans, and standing guard while they slept. Fox wrote that, "I think that I have never since enjoyed a more satisfactory meal or more refreshing sleep than I did that day."

The Cubans arranged for the men to sail on board a Spanish vessel departing for Santo Domingo, where they met up with an American ship, the *Flora*. Fox spent a final night celebrating with his companions, and then sailed to France on the *Flora*, departing in mid-May 1782. They secured passage home from France. In 1783, the fortunate Ebenezer Fox arrived home in Boston.

World of Warships

Until the Spanish declared war on the British in 1779, the British Navy were the masters and commanders from the coastal seas on the American colonies to the oceans across the world. The British fought with a total of 117 ships of the line, far outnumbering the French fleet of 70. This British dominance impacted the American war effort, impeding privateer runs, blockading ports, and challenging the small US Navy in its home waters. Washington and his leadership knew that unless the Spanish joined forces with the French, Britain would continue to rule the waves. As Washington wrote to Henry Laurens in November 1778, "The English are now greatly superior to the French by Sea in America; and will from every appearance continue so, unless Spain interpose — an event, which I do not know, we are authorised to count upon."[38] Fortunately for the struggling Americans, they were able to count on Spain. The Bourbon Kings opened their long planned joint naval operations in 1779. The 59 ships of the line of the Spanish navy began operations with the French, creating a combined fleet of 129 ships of the line. Finally, the British navy was outnumbered.[39] The British still maintained an advantage since all its ships of the line were fitted with copper sheaths, while only a percentage of the Spanish and French ships were powered with this technology.

The massive wooden warships of the 18th century, driven by capricious winds and constrained by rudimentary communications, made coordinated naval operations extraordinarily difficult. After their painful losses in the Seven Years' War, Spain and France initiated a comprehensive program to standardize and align their fleets. Shipbuilders, naval architects, and engineers from both kingdoms labored together for years to create a powerful joint naval force. British officials watched the effort with growing unease, as their spies dutifully reported on the Bourbons' progress. Years of planning, restructuring, and rebuilding produced a decisive result: during the critical three years preceding the Battle of Yorktown, the British Navy no longer dominated the seas.[40] The naval clashes that erupted only weeks before Yorktown made clear the impacts of the redesigned Bourbon navies — control of the seas, not only the battlefields, decided the war.

Chapter 8

Friendship, Love and War on the Western Front

Under cover of a humid dark night in Nueva Orleáns in August 1776, Luis de Unzaga y Amézaga, the Spanish governor of Louisiana, met with several unusual visitors: US Army officers disguised as merchants who had quietly sailed into the Spanish port city from the northern battlefields. The rebels carried a letter from General Charles Lee, a leading commander of the army. General Lee appealed to the governor to send supplies with the Patriots through barge transport up the Mississippi to the river ports in western Pennsylvania. Lee's letter sketched an appealing vision of the future, predicting a powerful alliance between the new United States of America and the Spanish empire in the southeast and west of North America.

General Lee is remembered today for his disastrous command of the Battle of Monmouth and his personal eccentricities that included a large collection of smelly dogs. Early in the War he had an excellent international reputation as a former officer in the British, Portuguese, and Polish armies, in contrast to the many earnest amateurs in the US Army. Lee's letter was translated from English to Spanish by Oliver Pollock, an Irish immigrant and international businessman who was the leading financier of the Revolution in the West.[1] Pollock arranged the meeting between the two US Army officers, Captain George Gibson and Lieutenant William Linn, and Unzaga. Pollock was well known by the Spanish in Louisiana and his business network extended to Havana. Pollock and his wife, Margaret O'Brien Pollock, had lived in Havana during the British occupation in 1762.[2] He leveraged his business funds to finance the Revolution, spinning him from prominence and wealth to the bleak cells of debtors' prison. Pollock was a friend of the influential General Alejandro O'Reilly in Havana[3] and of Bernardo de Gálvez, riding with Gálvez as aide-de-camp during his successful campaign against the British in Pensacola in 1779.

Governor Unzaga had served in both North and South America for over 40 years. At the time that he served in North America, the Spanish Empire ranged from the Presidio of San Francisco, California to Nueva Orleáns on the Gulf Coast of Mexico. Despite the armed resistance by Native Americans who had inhabited the vast region for thousands of years, the Spanish proclaimed the territory as theirs. During the Revolutionary War, the conflicts with the British, Spanish and Americans heavily impacted their lives and national politics. Native American alliances and military forces were prized and feared, and each of the powers devoted substantial resources to managing these relationships. After the peace negotiations in 1763, France quietly transferred Nueva Orleáns and the surrounding region to Spain.*

Unzaga was concerned about the consequences of assisting the American rebels in defiance of the British. Earlier in 1776 he stealthily sent a ship to Philadelphia on the pretext of importing flour but his goal was to discern the strength of the British. Unzaga's dilemma was that Spain was still officially neutral in the conflict. Thus, as he replied to the officers, any assistance would have to be covert, with ploys to prevent the ever-present British spies from proving any connection of shipments of supplies to the Spanish. Unzaga promised to assist the rebels and fulfilled his commitment with 10,000 pounds of gunpowder that were smuggled to the US Army during the autumn of 1776 and later in the spring of 1777. The bulk of the powder – 9,000 pounds – was sent with Lieutenant Linn, who managed the transport barges under the protection of the Spanish military. Working feverishly on day and night shifts to speed their valuable cargo out of Nueva Orleáns, the crew arrived at the Spanish fort on the Arkansas River as their travel on the river was stalled by winter weather. The crew spent the winter with the Spanish soldiers at their command post, presumably enjoying the selection of brandies and wines that were usually offered in established Spanish military encampments. The American crew continued east along the Ohio River as spring thawed the river ice. The remaining 1,000 pounds of powder was sent to Robert Morris in Philadelphia with Gibson, on a vessel purchased by Pollock.[4]

-----

* When you're in Nueva Orleáns, please visit the Cabildo, or *Casa Capitular*. The building was restored in 1799 and is open to tourists, an elegant remembrance of Spanish history.

Unzaga sent a report of this action to Carlos III, who approved of his assistance. Carlos III gave orders to supply more arms, ammunition, clothing, blankets and medicines from Latin America. Carlos emphasized that all the operations were to be done under complete secrecy to maintain the Spanish position of neutrality.

On January 1, 1777, Unzaga retired and Bernardo de Gálvez was appointed as the new Governor of Louisiana. Gálvez married Doña Marie Felicitas de Saint-Maxent, a Louisiana-born woman whose father, Gilberto Antonio de Saint-Maxent, had immigrated from northeastern France and married a wealthy widow named Elizabeth de La Roche. Gilberto enriched himself in the fur trade and eventually amassed a fortune that included four plantations. The couple had six daughters and four sons. The sisters were the celebrities of Nueva Orleáns society, similar to the Schuyler sisters in the American colonies. Without the assistance of dating apps or algorithms, the sisters lined up an impressive list of husbands who were distinguished Spanish military officers and French political elites. The oldest sister, Isabel, married Unzaga in 1775. A cosmopolitan, erudite woman, Isabel and her husband hosted Prince William, George III's son, when he visited Havana in 1783 while the peace negotiations were underway.[5] In a wedding that was the social event of the season, their sister Maria Victoria married a career naval officer who fought in Gálvez' campaigns across the Gulf of Mexico and at the Siege of Pensacola.[6] Antoinette Marie Joseph married a Spanish Count and governor of several territories in the Americas. Marie Anne Josephine married an Army brigadier general from Spain who served under Unzaga[7] and the youngest sister, Marie Héloïse Mercedes tied the knot with a French Baron in 1804.[8]

Gálvez was elated that his efforts in learning French were truly well spent. Marie Felicitas was a beautiful, intelligent nineteen-year-old widow with a two-year-old daughter, and according to popular accounts, their marriage was for love.[9] Her portrait shows a woman with very large dark eyes and a petite mouth, her hair fashionably dressed with ribbons and feathers.* Gálvez was seriously ill at the end of 1777, and fearful that he could die, married Marie Felicitas in a quiet ceremony at his home. She helped to nurse him back to health — fortunately for the American Revolution.

---

*Assassin's Creed fans, please note that Marie Felicitas did not look like her diabolical avatar featured in Assassin's Creed Wiki Fandom.

Felicitas and Bernardo became the power couple of Louisiana society. The marriage greatly benefitted Gálvez and his policy goal of harmonizing Spanish rule over the former French province. Felicitas was a true partner for him. During his extensive military campaigns against the British across the Gulf of Mexico in 1780 to 1781, Felicitas managed the Spanish Louisiana administration.[10] In 1782, Gálvez was stationed in Cap-Haïtien with Spanish and French troops preparing for a final assault against Jamaica. Felicitas braved an unpredictable sea voyage to join him. She was several months into her third pregnancy and gave birth to their son Miguel at the encampment.[11]

Spies and Supplies in Nueva Orleáns

Shortly after appointing Gálvez as Governor in February 1777, the court in Madrid sent him two royal orders. The first noted that goods were en route to Nueva Orleáns warehouses that were decidedly not in the standard merchant shopping cart, including medicinal quinine, bolts of woolen and twill fabric for military uniforms, a hundred barrels of gunpowder, and 300 muskets with steel bayonets. The second letter confirmed that these unusual goods belonged to Carlos III. Since, as the dispatch instructed, it would be "inconvenient" to send these goods in the king's name, they were to be entrusted to ship to General Lee's agent. Gálvez and the Spanish officials were to avoid all connections with these transactions, so that the King and Spanish officials could never be implicated if the supplies and the Americans were captured. After some deliberations, the Spanish selected Miguel Eduardo, who had also served as official interpreter in Havana. Unfortunately, the British suspicions of Eduardo were far too high after his arrest while traveling to Philadelphia in 1776, and the British increased their monitoring and diplomatic objections.

The British diplomatic consul in Nueva Orleáns and their spies soon circulated reports suggesting that the shipment invoices revealed the goods actually belonged to the King of Spain — casting doubt on Eduardo's transactions. To resolve the dilemma and confound the British, Gálvez launched an almost comic drama of deception. Starting with the cloth for military uniforms, Gálvez announced that the cloth had been chewed by moths, presumably an unpatriotic species, and was no longer suitable for the king's army of fussy fashionistas.

The cloth was then purchased by a trusted merchant, who whisked it away for clandestine shipment to the rebels. To ship the barrels of gunpowder out of the warehouse, Gálvez asked the same reliable merchant to switch one of the barrels in the warehouse with a powder of the same weight. The merchant then knocked in the top of this decoy barrel in full view of the warehouse staff to prove that it was not explosives, which must have been a tense moment. Once this stratagem was demonstrated, the actual barrels of gunpowder were shipped out of the depot with a voucher signed by the superintendent of the warehouse. Gálvez engineered similar excuses for the rejections and disappearances of crates of quinine, muskets, and bayonets that later mysteriously reappeared in the supplies shipped up the Mississippi to the US Army.

Gálvez corresponded with his uncle, José de Gálvez, about the need for secrecy in these endeavors. He suggested that later consignments be smuggled into the port of Nueva Orleáns without an official registry or bills of lading, which would not implicate the King of Spain in these transactions. Carlos III agreed by Royal Order in 1777, authorizing Gálvez to proceed, "as it might seem most proper and convenient in this so interesting and delicate matter."[12]

In the spring of 1777, the Continental Army again requested aid from the Spanish in Nueva Orleáns. This time the request was from Colonel George Morgan stationed at Fort Pitt (now Pittsburgh), asking for assistance to attack the British outposts at Mobile, Alabama and Pensacola, Florida. While the court in Madrid was not ready to openly support a Patriot attack with boots on the ground, Gálvez clearly would have welcomed the chance. He wrote back to Morgan that, "Although it would please me greatly I cannot enter into it. You may rest assured that I will extend my permission and whatever assistance I can, but it must appear that I am ignorant of it all."[13] This sentiment on paper was accompanied by a flotilla well-stocked with arms, ammunition and provisions.[14] But hyperactive British spies were watching, and Gálvez soon received an angry official protest from Peter Chester, the British Governor in West Florida.

The Patriots continued to request aid, and Patrick Henry, the newly elected governor of Virginia, also wrote to Gálvez for assistance. In a letter to Gálvez in October 1777, the Virginian extolled the benefits to the Spanish of trading with the Continentals and of Spain retaking Florida from the British. Henry wrote that, "Indeed, if you were once more in possession of the two Floridas, you might enjoy a great part of the Trade of our Northern States." He suggested that the

Americans establish a port at the mouth of the Ohio to trade with the Spanish on the Mississippi. Henry sent an additional message to Gálvez in January 1778, asking for a huge cash loan.[15]

Gálvez came to the assistance of the contentious and difficult James Willing, younger brother of Thomas Willing, Robert Morris' partner in Philadelphia.[16] Willing was acquainted with Pollock during his earlier career as a merchant in Natchez, Mississippi. Returning as a captain in the Continental Army in 1778, Willing launched a series of raids against British and American Loyalist civilians. The rebels destroyed and confiscated much of their property along the British side of the Mississippi and West Florida. Panicked refugees began arriving in Nueva Orleáns. Gálvez issued a proclamation to confirm both Spanish neutrality and hospitality to those fleeing the conflict.

Pollock sent assistance to Willing, and with the quiet permission of Gálvez, Willing arrived in Nueva Orleáns. Among the property confiscated was a British sloop mounted with sixteen guns, which was refitted and re-christened as the *Morris* to sail as an American ship. All this activity was carefully watched by British spies. Word reached British General William Howe, still in the American battlefields further north. Howe grumbled that Gálvez's conduct regarding the *Morris* was "very extraordinary." A British officer on board a sloop of war soon called at Nueva Orleáns to protest Gálvez's actions and to demand the return of the British property seized, including the *Morris*.

A debate raged between the Patriots, led by Pollock and Willing, against the British and American Loyalists as to which seizures were legal as privateering, and which were illegal as piracy. According to the British, the Americans were pirates, and according to the Americans, they were privateers. Governor Chester sent two warships to forcefully press the case for the British side, and eventually some of the ships and property were returned to the British. Chester was furious over the Spanish assistance to the Patriots. He ended his demand letter with, "I cannot conclude this letter without once more Remonstrating against your Subjects transporting military Stores and Clothing up the River Mississippi destined for the Colonies in Rebellion, under Spanish Colours and Passports."[17] Despite the angry protests from the British and their ever-watchful spies, Gálvez and Team Carlos in Havana persisted in aiding the US Army. The supply-laden barges and boats continued their silent passage up the Mississippi to American ports.

The Battles for the Mississippi

In an era before interstates and freeways, the mighty Mississippi River was once a leading transportation route, stretching 2,300 miles down the middle of the country from its origin in a cold glacial lake in Minnesota to the warm salty waters of the Gulf of Mexico. Controlling the Mississippi was crucial for the British, who held the Northwest territories and Canada. When news of the Spanish declaration of war reached Lord George Germain, the British secretary of the colonies, he wrote to the British governor general of Canada with a sweeping battle plan. Germain's grand scheme was to invade the American Midwest from the north and capture all the Spanish fortresses on the Mississippi River. Once these forts were conquered and the British moved closer to the Gulf Coast, Germain planned to coordinate with General John Campbell, who held the British Fort at Pensacola, Florida, in the territory that Britain had seized from the Spanish in 1763. Germain envisioned that Campbell would fight the Spanish along the Gulf Coast and their two forces would meet in Natchez, Mississippi.

Critical to these British plans for conquest were their alliances with Native American nations, which they'd carefully tended as the dust settled from the French and Indian War. George III's Proclamation of 1763 prohibited colonists from settling west of the Appalachian region and ruled that Native Americans were to be treated as subjects of the King, including in any disputes with the then-British colonists. The colonists, including Washington, had planned to seize more Native American land west of Appalachia and were angry with the Proclamation. While the Proclamation seemed surprisingly benevolent compared to the treatment that native peoples usually received from the British, their motives were highly strategic. Lord Hillsborough, who served as Secretary of State for the Colonies from 1768 to 1772, told his colleagues that the Proclamation had two primary goals: to keep the American settlements near the coast and dependent on Britain, and to leave the Native Americans undisturbed so His Majesty could continue to reap the benefits of the fur trade.[18] Regardless of their sketchy motivations, this strategy was highly effective: in battles along the Mississippi, many Native American nations joined forces with the Redcoats to attack both the Patriots and Spanish soldiers.

An International Alliance and A Friendship

Fernando de Leyba was a career military man from a family of knights who served in the Spanish military for decades. Leyba enlisted as a youngster and was promoted to sub-lieutenant in the Aragon regiment when he was sixteen. He was deployed to Cuba and was captured during the British invasion of 1762. He was shipped home as a prisoner of war and was reassigned to duty in the Mississippi region. In Bernardo de Gálvez's orders to Leyba, he stressed "the greatest secrecy," instructing Leyba to "learn all the news occurring in the English part (of Illinois), concerning the war of this power with the colonists, the situation of both parties and their plans so as not to allow himself to be surprised in case of any unforeseen design." Gálvez also requested that Leyba report any correspondence with the American rebel leaders to him.[19]

Leyba was soon managing the covert weapons shipments to the Americans that Gálvez and Oliver Pollock had underway. In March 1778, he took two swivel guns from the King's Storehouse in Nueva Orleáns and evaded British spies to deliver the materials to the Americans.[20] Leyba arrived in St. Louis with his wife and infant daughter in June 1778, living in a two-story stone house originally built for a fur trading company. Leyba packed up and shipped a boatload of cloth for uniforms for American troops.[21] Once Leyba was settled in his new command post, he contacted George Rogers Clark, the American military leader in the Mississippi region, to congratulate Clark on his victory in Kaskaskia, Illinois. (Kaskaskia was both the name of the town and of the Native American nation whose homeland was in the region.)

Clark, a native Virginian, was appointed by Governor Patrick Henry to lead an expedition into Kentucky in early 1778, then part of the Virginia colony. The American colonists defied the British Proclamation of 1763 and built illegal settlements which the Kaskaskia nation attacked. Clark was fighting to take the Native American territory between Appalachia and the eastern banks of the Mississippi, breaking British law and relying on Gálvez and Pollock to supply his men with weapons and provisions. At the start of his campaign, he used some of the remaining powder at Fort Pitt that Unzaga supplied to Linn the previous year. Clark and his troops captured Kaskaskia in July 1778 and Vincennes, Indiana, during a wintry campaign in February 1779. The credit lines that Pollock established to purchase supplies for Clark were supposedly backed by the state of Virginia. However, Pollock in turn had to rely on his own personal credit and on Gálvez, who "loaned" Spanish government funds to Pollock. These funds were usually delivered under cover of night by Juan Morales, Gálvez' private secretary.[22]

Leyba and Clark were at very different points in their lives, with different cultures and experiences. At the time that the two men met, Leyba was 44 years old with a wife and two children. Clark was 25 years old and single. Leyba had over 25 years of experience in the Spanish military and was a by-the-book officer with a distinguished military family background. The independent-minded Clark was in the militia – an informal DIY group at best – and had served for only four years. Leyba was educated with training and studies in mathematics and engineering, while Clark had little formal education and was trained as a land surveyor. One personality trait that they shared was sociability; both men were extroverts. Leyba enjoyed card playing and wine, and Clark was a social dancer. Despite all their differences, a true friendship and bromance developed that continued until Leyba's death in 1780.[23]

Leyba wrote to Clark in July 1778, noting that as soon as his military preparations were in order, "I shall come in person to congratulate you on your happy arrival at the Kaskaskias."[24] Leyba later referred to Clark in a letter in May 1779 as "Mon cher ami", my dear friend.[25] Leyba gave Clark the 18th-century equivalent of a five-star review in his correspondence with Gálvez, often referring to Clark as Don Jorge Roger Clark. Clark wrote glowingly of Leyba in his report to the Governor of Virginia in September 1778, "This gentleman [Leyba] interests himself much in favor of the States, more so than I could have expected. He has offered me all the force that he could raise, in case of an attack by Indians from Detroit, as there is now no danger from any other quarter."[26]

When Clark visited Leyba's home in the late summer of 1778, Leyba hosted him in a grand style.[27] From the inventory of Leyba's possessions listed in his will, he clearly enjoyed a party. He owned large numbers of chairs, stools, dinnerware, cookware, a Spanish guitar known as a bandurria, over 400 bottles of wine, and kegs of aguardiente, traditional liquor from Spain that contains up to 60% alcohol — which must have been a rock star party. Leyba wrote to Gálvez of the visit, "... where I entertained thirty guests on his [Clark's] first visit which lasted two days, giving dances on both evenings and supper to all the ladies and dancers, and lodging in my home."[28] Clark fondly mentioned Leyba's wife and two daughters in his correspondence, referring to them as "Madame Lebau and my two favourites the little Misses."

This friendship also started the rumors of a romance between George Rogers Clark and Theresa de Leyba, a woman who reportedly was a relative of Leyba's, either a sister or a niece. The first mention of the story in US sources was published much later, in 1848. According to the tale, Clark was deeply in love with Theresa when he met her in San Luis and heartbroken that he was unable to marry her, due to his financial insolvency from funding American troops and supplies. Manuscripts based on later interviews with Clark's family include the quote that Clark was "bankrupt in everything but love for her."[29] The letter from Clark's niece also said that her uncle sadly reminisced about this mysterious woman when he was intoxicated. The niece wrote that Clark felt if he had been well-treated by the government – a reference to the US government not honoring the debts that Clark incurred for military expenditures – "I would have had an elegant aunt whom I [his niece] would have loved very much."[30] Theresa lived in Nueva Orleáns for several years after Fernando de Leyba's death. A play was written about their romance in 1929 with a fascinating and historically inaccurate cast, that staged Theresa in a convent in Nueva Orleáns and Clark wandering despairingly outside the convent walls.[31] According to one account, Theresa returned to Spain and really did enter a convent in Mérida. Unfortunately, this sad tale of love on the Western Front has not (yet) been verified, despite the earnest research of reliable scholars relentlessly digging through archives in Spain and the US.

The Attacks on Fort Carlos and San Luis

In February 1780, Leyba received news of the declaration of war between Spain and Britain, and rumors and reports began to swirl that the British planned to attack Spanish forts along the Mississippi. Leyba began to prepare for the invasion, which was a challenging task given his limited resources in San Luis. Leyba initially requested reinforcements of 200 additional troops, but the Spanish military declined the request and advised him that he had to defend San Luis without reinforcements. Spain was engaged in a wide theater of war with the

British and had to prioritize defense of its empire in the Caribbean and Central America; the loss of Havana in 1762 remained a bitter memory. Spain also hoped to reconquer its former possessions in Florida and Jamaica, and retake Gibraltar and Menorca in Europe — quite a project plan!

Leyba began to reinforce San Luis in April. He planned to reorganize and ship available cannons from other forts in the region to San Luis, construct defensive stone towers for the artillery, and build retrenchments around their defensive position. San Luis was founded in 1764 by Gilbert Antoine de St. Maxent, Bernardo de Gálvez's father-in-law and two French fur traders, who named the town for the French King. In the late 1770s, it was a small settlement with a total population of 1,300 settlers, 485 of whom were enslaved people.[32] Leyba planned to construct several defensive stone towers but was able to finance and complete only one. While the exact dimensions of the tower are not documented, construction was planned with standard Spanish military defenses, meaning the tower would have been about 30 to 40 feet high and 30 feet in diameter, with window openings spaced in a semi-circle. The defenders moved five cannons to the top and fired from this vantage point. San Luis residents, including enslaved people, dug entrenchments. These barricades were more formally constructed than simple trenches, with defensive earthen mounds and logs to hold the piled dirt. Building the entrenchments required extensive coordination, and a former French officer who continued in Spanish service directed the labor of digging and moving earth with picks, shovels, and hoes.[33] Without bulldozers or excavators, all this work was accomplished by hand in about five weeks. Without reinforcements from Nueva Orleáns or Havana, Leyba sent messengers to the nearby towns asking for volunteers to join the fight. By early May, the Spanish and San Luis settlers had prepared as thoroughly as they could.

The Native American and British forces began their attack on May 26, 1780. Most of the soldiers were Native Americans who were motivated by their fierce opposition to the Spanish and French settlers in their homelands. Leyba later wrote that the Native American soldiers advanced "with an unbelievable boldness and fury, making terrible cries and a terrible firing."[34] The church bell rang out the alarm, and the Spanish and San Luis troops quickly rushed into their planned battle formations. The troops began firing cannons, scrambling in the small circular top of the tower to organize the rammers, buckets, cannonballs, and fuses[35] needed to maintain steady rounds of cannon fire. Leyba was ill and had to be assisted into the tower to direct the defenses. The troops in the entrenchments fired muskets and rifles. The battle raged for two hours. The Native American soldiers finally broke off their offense, unwilling to sustain more casualties. As they withdrew from the battlefield, they destroyed crops and livestock.

Across the river from San Luis, a smaller force of predominantly Native Americans attacked the settlement at Cahokia. The defenders in Cahokia were from Clark's Illinois Regiment of Virginia, local militia, and Kaskaskia soldiers who had allied with the Americans. The Americans had some field cannons and were relatively well supplied with gunpowder and muskets. The battles ended with victories for the Spanish and Americans, but at a high cost for the small population.[36] Leyba, who never recovered from his illness and the emotional stress of his wife's recent death, died a few weeks later. After his death, he was honored by Carlos III with a posthumous promotion to the rank of colonel.

Skirmishes and conflicts continued in the region until the final peace negotiations in 1783, without a clear victory or seizure of territory for the British, much to Germain's disappointment. The British did not secure the western banks of the Mississippi and implement their grand plan to link with the British troops fighting along the Gulf Coast and Florida. This failure was important for the success of the Spanish and the Americans in the next series of battles, as the British continued their campaign to divide the northern and southern colonies. The southern colonies were in turmoil with civil conflict between the American Patriots and the Americans Loyalists who were willing to stay neutral or fight for the British. Rebellions and resistance from enslaved African Americans added to the tumult and uncertainty. With the western front secured, the Spanish now turned to their next campaign: reconquering the territory along the Gulf Coast from Alabama to Florida.

Chapter 9

The Civil War and the Desperate Pursuit of Happiness

British ships at a distance had the wish of every enslaved man and woman on board. Some of the enslaved people swam or sailed out with the tide, claiming freedom as their desperate hands grasped the ships' rails in jubilation. For others, these ships sailed forever on the same horizon, never out of sight, never landing until the watchers turned their eyes away in resignation, their dreams mocked to death by slavery.* The dreams of those enslaved and their desperate pursuit of life, liberty, and happiness was the unfulfilled hope of the American Revolution. To the British, these dreams and the fear that these aspirations created among their American oppressors were tactics in the British strategy to divide the colonies between North and South and win the war. To destabilize the southern colonies and recruit the additional troops and logistics forces that they needed, the British promised freedom to enslaved men and women owned by American Patriots who joined the King's Army.

The British gained the Spanish territories on the Gulf of Mexico from Alabama to Florida in 1763. If their military operations in the South were successful, they reasoned that they could completely encircle and control the southern colonies both politically and geographically. For three harrowing years, the British were close to succeeding, as they leveraged the work and support of enslaved people. As they soon learned, the Spanish had their own campaigns underway to recapture their former empire. In the South, the Revolutionary War was fought on multiple battlefronts. American Patriots fought directly with American Loyalists and Loyalists joined British troops fighting against the Continental Army and state militias.

---

* Inspired by Zora Neale Hurston and the opening lines of her classic, *Their Eyes Were Watching God.*

African Americans fought for their freedom, predominately siding with the British. Despite terrible risks and cruel punishments, thousands of African Americans escaped from bondage to join the British cause. They supported the British through skilled labor, including carpenters, blacksmiths, construction workers, river pilots, ferrymen, coopers (who created barrels and casks, essential before FedEx packaging) and hostlers (who managed horses and oxen).[1]

The wealthiest states in America were (obviously) slave-based economies in the South, comprising Virginia, Maryland, North and South Carolina, and Georgia. Many slaveholders viewed the enslaved as a severe risk, particularly during wartime. Let's do the math — and please bear with me, there's a point to the numbers. The Americans and British greatly expanded the number of enslaved people in the years before the American Revolution. Over 364,800 people were trafficked into the American colonies in the 1760s, the highest ten-year total in the history of the British slave trade.[2] Virginia was the California of 18th century America, the most populous and wealthiest of the colonies. Of the three million Americans in the Revolutionary period, about 25% lived in Virginia.[3] Of those Virginians, 40% were enslaved human beings, almost 200,000 people, comprising nearly half of all enslaved people in the thirteen colonies.[4] "The wealth of the country consists in slaves, so that all one eats rises out of driving and whipping these poor wretches," said an appalled British officer who was stationed in Virginia. "You cannot conceive how it strikes the mind upon the first arrival to have all these black faces with grim looks around you."[5]

The remaining four southern colonies also had high populations of enslaved people, averaging about 40% to 50% of the total population. In South Carolina, African Americans outnumbered the colonists. Only Virginia and South Carolina, whose wealth corresponded directly with the number of slaves, were profitable colonies for the British; Massachusetts, with the fewest number of slaves, was the least profitable.[6] Jamaica, with a slave population of about 90%, was more profitable than all the thirteen colonies combined.[7] The British astutely promised freedom to enslaved people who were considered the property of Patriots but did not offer the same guarantee to those owned by Loyalists.

The first shot at unraveling the southern colonies started in Virginia, with a proclamation in November 1775 by Lord Dunmore, the British Governor of the colony. Dunmore declared that "...*Negroes*, or others (appertaining to rebels) [were] *free*, that are able and willing to bear arms, they *joining his Majesty's troops.*"[8] Dunmore was convinced that enslaved people would be eager "to revenge themselves by which means a conquest of this country would inevitably be effected in a short time."[9]

Dunmore's proclamation hurtled a thunderbolt into the volatile political and economic landscape. Even without text messages and TikTok, news of Dunmore's offer spread with astonishing speed among African American communities, and enslaved people, some as far away as New York, began to join the British cause. The risks and perils of escape attempts were horrifying and heartbreaking. Captured enslaved men were brutally tortured. Often they were hung, and their bodies burnt. Their severed, rotting, heads were placed on posts at crossroads as a warning to others.[10] Punishments included selling the enslaved to the faraway sugar plantations of the Caribbean or to the lead mines of Appalachia, where the working conditions were brutal and very often deadly. The Virginia Committee of Safety threatened enslaved families by warning that the "fury" of the slave owners would be unleashed "against their defenceless fathers and mothers, their wives, their women and children."[11] The enslaved men who did escape were forced to make the distressing choice between their personal freedom and never seeing their family and friends again.

Despite these perils, hundreds of enslaved people responded to Dunmore's proclamation. And not only men of military age — women, children and older men also answered the call.[12] Dunmore formed the "Lord Dunmore's Ethiopian Brigade," which mustered between two to three hundred African American volunteers. The term "Ethiopian" was a rare homage by the British to Africans, some of whom were aware of the history of the East African Christian Kingdom.[13] One of the local papers reported that Dunmore issued uniform shirts to the men that boldly read, "Liberty for Slaves" in huge letters. The Ethiopian Brigade marched into combat in early December 1775, the first recorded event of newly freed African American soldiers fighting against the Patriot militias on the offensive. This action was the initial skirmish in the Battle of Great Bridge fought on December 9, 1775. The Virginia militia was reinforced by the arrival of the North Carolina militia. The casualty rate among the British troops was disastrous,[14] forcing a retreat. Dunmore attempted to negotiate an exchange of African American prisoners, but the Patriot militias refused to exchange these prisoners and instead re-enslaved them.[15]

While Dunmore's first battles with the Ethiopian Brigade were a loss, he won the media war. The Patriots were terrified of the prospect of a rebellion among enslaved people. Washington and his leadership were apoplectic. The Americans intercepted Dunmore's letters to the British command in Boston in which Dunmore wrote, "We keep them in continual hot water…the Negros are flocking in from all quarters." Washington worriedly wrote to Richard Henry Lee in late December of Dunmore's "diabolical Schemes." Washington was convinced that if Dunmore was not "crushed before Spring, he will become the most formidable Enemy America has — his strength will Increase as a Snow ball by Rolling; and faster, if some expedient cannot be hit upon to convince the Slaves and Servants of the Impotency of His designs."[16] But African Americans were not convinced of the "impotency" of Dunmore's plans, and the British expanded their recruitment. Reflecting the fears in the South, the media brutally trolled Dunmore calling him "black as an Ethiop" and a "murderer."[17] Miguel Eduardo, the Spanish agent captured en route to Philadelphia and still in British custody through this period, wrote that, "It is against this official that the Americans show their greatest rancor."[18]

Fears of a slave uprising gripped southern plantations. Bloody slave rebellions had been staged in Jamaica, Surinam, and St. Vincent. Newspapers reported on an uprising in Surinam, where a force of Africans and Native Americans overwhelmed the Dutch Army, burning plantations and towns and killing their enslavers. British troops stationed in America were redeployed to Jamaica and St. Vincent to fight the rebellions there, and revolutions started in Antigua, Montserrat, St. Kitts and Barbados. On the political and legal fronts, the anti-slavery movement was well underway in the northern states, and African Americans challenged the legality of slavery in courthouses across the south.[19]

The British persisted in their policy of freeing the enslaved in return for enlistment and support, to the fury of the Americans. During his visit with Dunmore, the commander of the British Army, Sir Henry Clinton, personally met with soldiers of the Ethiopian Brigade, which was the first time that a British general spoke with African Americans in uniform. Clinton must have been impressed: when he camped in North Carolina later that spring, seventy enslaved men escaped to his camp, and Clinton formed a dedicated regiment of free African Americans named the "Black Pioneers." From his New York office, Clinton released the Philipsburg Proclamation in June 1779,[20] extending the offer of freedom to include enslaved women as well as men. In a stunning display of humanity, Clinton instructed his junior officers that the soldiers in the Black Pioneers were to be treated with "tenderness."[21] The regiment was later stationed in New York, the British stronghold for most of the War. African Americans enlisted at the highest percentage of their demographic. An estimated 5,000 to 6,000 African Americans fought for the Patriots – from Crispus Attucks, the first man to die in the revolution at the Boston Massacre in 1770, to the 1st Rhode Island regiment that stormed the British redoubt at the Siege of Yorktown in 1781. But the overwhelming majority of African Americans – over 20,000 enslaved men and women – fought in the British Army.[22] The southern colonies exacerbated the trend by their reluctance and sometimes outright refusal to allow African Americans to voluntarily enlist in the US Army, though slave owners were very willing tomandate their enslaved to serve in their places.[23]

The Ethiopian Brigade suffered a terrible smallpox epidemic. Dunmore was distressed over the losses, writing that, "a fever crept in amongst them [Ethiopian Regiment] and carried off a great many very fine fellows."[24] Those who survived were placed with Clinton's Black Pioneers and transferred north to New York on British ships. There, they lived in settlements of freed African Americans called "Canvas Towns" and "Negro Barracks," determined to build a new life. These formerly enslaved people must have experienced a profound culture shock. While circumstances in times of war were dire, especially during the harsh winter of 1779 and 1780, their new life was a stunning contrast to their enslavement. They were actually paid for their work! Clinton stipulated that the Black Pioneers be allowed to choose their occupations.[25] While this point sounds trivial now, it was a surprisingly thoughtful consideration by 18th century standards. The freed people could worship at the Anglican Church, baptize their children, and legally marry, which was prohibited under slavery. Entertainment was now open to them: they drank and partied at taverns with their own music, cheered at boxing matches and horse races, and attended the theater. Othello, a Shakespearian play about an African man in Italy in the 16th century, was a favorite during this period, and still is today. Freed women dressed up for "Ethiopian Balls," which British officers attended as well. These integrated social events were bitterly ridiculed by the Patriots.[26]

Freedom Riders and Freedom Writers

Among the soldiers in the Ethiopian Brigade who sailed north to New York with Clinton's fleet was Titus Cornelius, the famous freedom fighter known as "Colonel Tye." He was the feared nightmare of every American slaveowner; think of Denzel Washington's *The Equalizer* on horseback with a musket and pistol. Tye left the British Army to lead his own troops, known as the "Black Brigade." The title "Colonel" was given to him out of respect, not as a formal military role. The Brigade numbered as high as 800 men, both black and white.[27] His men attacked US Army troops, militias and supply trains across New Jersey and New York.[28] Riding swiftly through the countryside, the men destroyed supplies, mustered cattle and horses, burned houses and farms, and took prisoners back to New York. One of Tye's first recorded raids in the summer of 1779 was at the plantation where he had been enslaved. He and his men commandeered eighty cattle and twenty horses and captured two prisoners, which must have been quite a personal triumph. Frightened Americans petitioned New Jersey Governor William Livingston to crush Tye and his men, but the Governor and his troops were unable to defeat them. Tye was killed in his fight for freedom in September 1780, but his brigade did not stop fighting with his death. He was succeeded by Colonel Stephen Blucke, a free Black man from Barbados, and an officer in the Black Pioneers.[29]

The African Americans' fierce resistance and dedication to freedom evoked widespread fear in the South,[30] as southern Americans feared that a "Third Column" allied with the British could defeat them. James Madison, later the fourth US President, reported in 1774 that a slave plot was discovered to welcome and assist British troops. He warned in 1775 that the British were instigating a revolt among enslaved people, a frightening scenario in which "we will fall ... by the hand of the one that knows that secret" of Virginia's vulnerability.[31]

Boston King was astonished by his welcome, "They [the British] received me readily, and I began to feel the happiness of liberty, of which I knew nothing before."[32] King escaped slavery in South Carolina in 1780 when the British invaded Charleston. He served as a soldier and as a courier traveling through enemy lines — a perilous assignment that risked re-enslavement, imprisonment or worse. In August 1781, many enslaved people formed partisan bands that raided Virginia farms and plantations, and the American troops were dismayed by the "most alarming times" during the shoreside raids by African Americans.[33] In the spring and summer of that year, Cornwallis led the British Army up the James River to attack and occupy Richmond, Virginia. Over 4,500 African Americans joined him, including enslaved people from plantations owned by Washington and Jefferson.[34]

While African American leaders and orators of the 19th century are most often recognized in history, numerous African Americans fought with their quills and their voices throughout the colonies during the 18th century. African Americans challenged their own enslavement in a revolution that championed freedom. Most of the written petitions for freedom that are preserved originated in the North, of course, where the African Americans had more support. Four Black community leaders in Boston – Peter Bestes, Sambo Freeman, Felix Holbrook, and Chester Joie – hand-delivered one such petition to each representative in the Massachusetts legislature in the early 1770s. "We expect great things from men who have made such a noble stand against the designs of their *fellow-men* to enslave them," they proclaimed. They argued that "*as men*, we have a natural right" to laws that enabled their freedom, including the right that the Spanish provided to their enslaved people, that of coartación, which allowed enslaved people to work for their freedom.[35]

Benjamin Banneker, a scientist, mathematician, and surveyor, directly confronted American leaders, including Thomas Jefferson, for their oppression of African Americans while proclaiming their own freedom from tyranny. He called out Jefferson, "how pitiable it is to reflect that altho you were convinced of the rights and privileges ... of mankind ...that you should at the same time counteract ... in detaining by fraud and violence so numerous a part of my brethren under groaning captivity and cruel oppression."[36] Lemuel Haynes, a poet, preacher, and US Army soldier, wrote in his 1776 essay, "Liberty Further Extended," that "a Negro may Justly Challenge, and has an undeniable right to his Liberty...the practice of Slave-keeping which much abounds in this Land is illicit." Despite the more supportive environment in the North, his essay was not published until late in the 20th century, and only one fragmentary copy survived.[37] Fortunately, this document and others did survive, and now, we can say their names. While the moral paradox of Patriot slaveholders fighting for their liberty was apparently lost on the Patriots, this incongruity was annoyingly obvious to British thought leaders. Samuel Johnson, the renowned British writer and critic, rolled his eyes in exasperation and observed, "how is it that we hear the loudest yelps for liberty among the drivers of negroes?"

Phillis Wheatley, the unofficial Poet Laureate of the American Revolution, was kidnapped from her home in Africa at age seven and sold to the Wheatley family in Boston. The family tutored her, and after she quickly learned English, she progressed to Latin and Greek. Her first poem was published when she was eleven years old. Wheatley wrote poems, letters and posts to and about the powerful men in the revolution, from George III to George Washington, and chronicled the events of the war. Wheatley penned a poem to George III when he repealed the British Stamp Act, a taxation scheme that angered the Americans.[38] Wheatley sent a poem to Washington when he was appointed Commander-in-Chief in 1775, with a letter "Wishing your Excellency all possible success in the great cause you are so generously engaged in."[39] Washington wrote to Wheatley, thanking her "most sincerely for your polite notice of me" and complimenting "the style and manner exhibit a striking proof of your great poetical Talents."[40] Washington concluded his letter with an invitation for Wheatley to visit his military head-quarters. In an action that will still warm the hearts of wishful writers across the centuries, Washington assisted Wheatley to find a publisher for her work.

The Bloodiest Hour

The British military operation opened their 1778 campaign in the South with an attack on Savannah, Georgia. In the 1770s, Savannah was a frontier outpost with a peacetime population of 750 people. During the war, refugees fled to the town, swelling its population. The once-profitable trade in indigo and commodities drastically declined during the war. Winds blew across the sandy soil during the summer season, filling the houses with dust.[41] The streets were unpaved and there were few buildings; the cobblestone avenues and beautiful antebellum mansions that now enchant visitors were built later in the 19th century. Georgians were ambivalent about the war and were the only colonies who did not send delegates to the First Continental Congress in 1774. The Georgians faced armed resistance from Native Americans and depended on British military assistance.[42]

So, why invade a backwater outpost like Savannah, you ask? Great question! At first look, the small town appears an unlikely target, but Team George III had a plan. From his war rooms in London, George III carefully analyzed the military campaigns throughout the revolution, and he and the British military leadership believed that Savannah was the launch point to conquer the South. Lord George Germain, the Secretary of State for the Colonies from 1775 to 1782, advised General Clinton to split South Carolina in two, separating the back country from the seacoast.[43] In George III's view, once the rogue South Carolinians came to their senses and supported their lawful King, the British would march through North Carolina to capture the real prize: Virginia.[44]

In the words of a prominent historian on the Savannah battle and later siege, "As usual, it was blacks who made the difference."[45] In late November 1778, a British expeditionary force of 3,500 sailed from New York to attack Georgia.[46] The British soldiers and smaller warships arrived on Christmas Eve, guided by Samson, an African American river boat pilot who safely navigated the British ships from the Atlantic coast up the Savannah River. In the 18th century, without sophisticated radar, this knowledge of coastal waterways was critical. Samson continued to support the British and Loyalists over the next few months of battles, piloting expeditions in Georgia and the Carolinas. Samson was so effective that he became a marked man, in constant danger from the US Army that sought his arrest or death. Once the British landed, Quamino Dolly, an enslaved man of AARP age, led British soldiers on the only solid earth passageway through the rivers and swamps. This route enabled the British to attack the Americans from the rear, rather than a frontal assault.[47] The British quickly captured Savannah in late December 1778 and continued their relentless march through Georgia.

In January, reinforced by their Native American allies based in San Augustin, the British captured Fort Morris and took 200 US Army soldiers as prisoners. Hundreds of Carolina Loyalists joined the British in February. The fighting continued, and Augusta, Georgia was captured by the British, then recaptured by the US Army. By the end of March, Congress was so desperate for reinforcements that they urged the South Carolinians to raise a force of 3,000 African Americans. The slave-owners would be paid $1000 per enslaved man as compensation. The enslaved men were promised emancipation and, if they managed to survive gunfire, cannons, starvation, and disease to the war's end, a bonus of $50.*

---

* Insert Eyes-Rolling emoji here — $50 to the enslaved soldier and $1000 to the owner?

The proposal was championed by John Laurens, a US Army officer and the son of one of the largest slaveholders in the colonies, Henry Laurens.[48] An ardent supporter of emancipation, he wrote to his father asking him to free his enslaved human beings "instead of leaving me a Fortune."[49] This was a courageous act by any century's standards, which few of his contemporaries emulated. His close friend, Alexander Hamilton, supported his plan. The proposal was debated in the South Carolina House of Representatives. Despite the enemy at the gates, the representatives voted down the proposal by an overwhelming count of 72 to 12.[50]

The Patriot leadership knew that they had to disrupt the British southern campaign, and in the summer of 1779, they plotted to recapture Savannah. The grueling month-long siege began in September 1779. The US Army relied heavily on the French for this campaign. Washington and General Benjamin Lincoln, a former town constable turned soldier from Massachusetts, could not muster the number of troops that were needed. The Continental and militia troops numbered about 3,000 and included many immigrants. The French landed with 5,000 troops, including 750 men[51] from Haiti, Martinique, and Guadeloupe, more than double the American forces.[52] The Afro-Caribbean troops were free men of color and enslaved men seeking freedom in exchange for their service. These troops initially formed their own regiment of Chasseurs Volontaires (volunteer light infantrymen) and they fought together with the French and US soldiers as the battle raged on. The French dressed in their summer white uniforms, while the Afro-Caribbeans wore coats of blue wool, with yellow piping on lapels, yellow collars, green cuffs, and shoulder epaulets that must have been miserable in the summer heat. Among the Chasseurs Volontaires were men who later led the Haitian revolution in 1791, including Andre Rigaud, Louis-Jacques Beauvais, Jean-Louis Villatte, and Henri Christophe. Christophe was probably 12 at that time; birth dates of the enslaved are difficult to trace, and this age is the closest estimate. According to one report, he was injured in the fighting with a gunshot wound. He survived to become the first President of Haiti.[53] A memorial to the Chasseurs Volontaires was erected in 2007 in Savannah and includes statues of the Haitian soldiers and the young boy Christophe.

The British were secure within their redoubts built with African American labor and reinforced with southern Loyalist militia troops. The French, Patriot and Afro-Caribbean troops launched their final and fatal charge in the dawn light of October 9. They withstood a deadly barrage of cannon fire and musket and grapeshot, which was a package of small balls of ammunition stuffed in a canvas bag, resembling a cluster of grapes. Upon firing, the bag disintegrated, releasing the lead balls as multiple projectiles that spread into a deadly, devastating impact. One hour after the charge began, the bugle sounded for retreat.[54] The Chasseurs Volontaires desperately tried to defend their fellow soldiers as they ran for cover.[55] The British and Loyalists shot at the retreating men who headed towards the swamp. The scene after the battle was horrifying. An aide to British General Prevost later wrote that, "such a sight I've never seen before." Hundreds of American and French soldiers were killed, wounded and captured. Many of the dead were mangled by grapeshot and some were impaled on the abatis, the sharpened stakes that defended the fortress. The British buried the dead American and French troops who were killed near the fortress. The famed Polish nobleman, cavalry officer, and immigrant, Casimir Pulaski, was found dead and tangled in the abatis, as were many of his cavalry men and their horses. A shortage of linen bandages heightened the trauma for the wounded.[56] Casualties were high; the Americans suffered 150 casualties of the 1,500 engaged, and the French lost 650 of their 3500.[57] The hour of that charge is believed to be the "bloodiest hour" of the American Revolutionary War. When the news reached London, cannons were fired in celebration, as the British appeared to be steadily marching towards their goal of dividing the colonies and conquering the South.

"France and Spain must save us"

In late December 1779, after the French Navy departed, Clinton began to send ships and troops from New York City south to Charleston. The combined sailors and soldiers numbered over 13,000 men on over 100 troopships and warships. The winter was so bitterly cold that, for the first and to date the only time on record, all the saltwater estuaries along the entire northeast were frozen solid. The British, Hessian and Loyalist troops struggled to maneuver their ships through the stormy cold seas. When US General Lincoln learned that Clinton's Army was heading south from New York, he sent a message to Washington and to Congress that he needed reinforcements. His resources included 3,600 regulars and militia, French volunteers, and a Spanish volunteer, Jordi (Jorge) Ferragut Mesquida.

Ferragut immigrated to the US as a merchant sailor in 1776 and joined the South Carolina Navy, changing his name to George Farragut* to sound more American. The US Army reinforcements began arriving in March 1780. The reinforcements numbered about 1,500, far fewer than the worried general hoped for.[58]

On April 1, the British and Hessian soldiers began the work to prepare for the siege, digging the trenches and constructing the breastworks, which were shoulder high temporary fortified walls to protect the soldiers firing from behind them. No, the British and Hessians did not do all of the digging and building. When word of Clinton's Philipsburg Proclamation reached the enslaved people, thousands rushed to claim their freedom. As they had done in the Siege of Savannah, they dug ditches, chopped down trees to make lethal points for abatis, and packed the soil and wood that constructed the fortifications. The initial siegeworks for Charleston were completed only 800 yards from the US Army troops.

The British pushed relentlessly forward, capturing more territory, yard by yard, cannon barrage by cannon barrage as the days and weeks passed. The Americans fired back, volley after volley. The British pushed to a second line of trenchworks, then a third. As the danger of a British victory crept, South Carolina Governor John Rutledge, the man who had tried to persuade the Spanish into a joint military action against the British earlier that year, and the Privy Council attempted to negotiate with the British. They offered to betray the revolution and proposed that South Carolina would remain neutral for the rest of the war, in return for the preservation of slavery. John Laurens was horrified.[59] British General Prevost turned down the offer and the siege continued. Finally on May 12, 1780, the US Army and French surrendered. The British captured 5,500 prisoners, half from the scarce forces of US Army.

In the aftermath of the Patriot losses at Savannah and Charleston, more African Americans escaped slavery. A quarter of the enslaved population of South Carolina, about 25,000 people, and a third of Georgia's, fled to the promise of freedom that the British offered.

------

*The Farragut Metro stations in Washington DC are named for his son, Admiral David Farragut. Admiral Farragut fought for the Union in the Civil War and is remembered for his battle cry, "Damn the torpedoes, full speed ahead."

Most of these people encountered cruel disappointment. The British were overwhelmed by the number of people in urgent need of food and shelter. Many were ill and required medical attention. While Clinton acted with humanity, their treatment from the British generals Howe and Cornwallis was indifferent.[60]

The defeat at Charleston was the worst military disaster in the Revolutionary War.[61] The collapse of the US forces at Charleston was quickly followed by the Battle of Camden in August 1780, described by 20th century US Army historians as "the most crushing defeat suffered by United States on a major field of battle during the Revolution."[62] The loss was humiliating for the US military leadership and soldiers. The US soldiers were led by General Horatio Gates, the hero of Saratoga, and were twice the number of British troops. With bayonets gleaming in the summer sun, the experienced Redcoats charged towards the militias, who broke ranks and ran. The US Army briefly rallied, and the Delaware militia held the line, but it was too late. An estimated 2,000 Americans were killed, wounded or captured, including General de Kalb. Only 700 of the 4,000 in Gates' forces rallied after the battle.

The country was shaken by these defeats. Patriot leaders watched despairingly as Team George III's plan and the British southern strategy surged towards success. Hamilton wrote grimly to John Laurens after the loss of Charleston, "If we are saved France and Spain must save us."[63] As Hamilton and the US military leaders soon learned, Spain's plans to challenge the British in the South were already underway. With a powerful military campaign that swept from Central America through the Gulf Coast to the final triumph in Pensacola, Florida, the Spanish thwarted the British plans to divide and conquer America.

Chapter 10

Spain and Latin America on the Southern Front

In the sweltering heat of the Louisiana bayou in the autumn of 1779, one of the most diverse forces ever assembled in North America marched to challenge the British Army in the southern theater of the American Revolutionary War. The men followed a young rising star of the Spanish military, Bernardo de Gálvez. The troops numbered over 600, and included veteran Spanish soldiers, Mexicans, Louisiana militiamen and local citizens, free African Americans, and American Patriot volunteers. Gálvez was joined by his aide-de-camp, the Irish American Oliver Pollock. Gálvez' campaign swept along the American Gulf Coast, battling from Nueva Orleáns to Baton Rouge, through Alabama, culminating in the lengthy, complex siege of Pensacola. His father, Matías Gálvez, defeated the British in the jungles of Honduras, Nicaragua and Guatemala. To the relief of the Continental Army and militias, who were suffering serious losses in the southern colonies, the Spanish forced the British to divert their military resources away from the Americans.[1]

"… to shed the last drop of my blood for Louisiana"

War against Britain was finally and openly declared with the awkwardly titled "The Treaty Offensive and Defensive Alliance Against England," signed at Aranjuez Palace and formally announced on June 21, 1779.[2] Under the treaty, Spain agreed to provide military support for France in its military campaigns in the American colonies. The French agreed to support Spain in its quest to repossess Gibraltar and the island of Menorca off the Spanish Coast, and East and West Florida. To the benefit of the struggling Americans, the treaty also stated that neither Spain nor France would "lay down its arms until the independence [of the United States] is recognized by the Kingdom of Great Britain."[3] The British were aghast, and George III stated that this was "the most serious crisis that this nation ever knew." The Americans were cheered and encouraged. Washington noted, "I promise myself the most happy events from the known spirit of your [Spain] nation. United with the Arms of France, we have everything to hope over the Arms of our common enemy, the English."[4] Jefferson wrote that Spain's declaration "has given us all the certainty of a happy issue to the present contest."[5]

Realizing that a declaration of war meant an attack on his adopted home, Gálvez increased his military preparations. Gálvez' confirmation of his full appointment as Governor arrived with the news of Spain's entrance to the war. A skilled speaker, he assembled the inhabitants of Nueva Orleáns to announce his appointment as Governor and called on the citizens to support him in the pending conflict with the British. In a dramatic oration, his voice rang out, "...although I am disposed to shed the last drop of my blood for Louisiana and for my king ...I do not know whether you will help me in resisting the ambitious designs of the English. What do you say? Shall I take the oath of governor? Shall I swear to defend Louisiana?"[6] The crowd applauded thunderously and carried Gálvez on their shoulders to the cabildo, the Spanish colonial municipal building.

The game plan for the Spanish was to seize the well-fortified British bases along the northern Gulf Coast, sweeping from Nueva Orleáns to Baton Rouge through Alabama to reach the heavily armed fortress at Pensacola, Florida. The first stage of the long, complex campaign was waged from June 1779 to mid-October 1780.

While arranging for food provisions in July 1779, Gálvez inaugurated a quintessential American tradition: the long-range Texas cattle drive. Spanish cattle ranching was a vast industry in the 1770s and 1780s. Spanish ranches and settlements extended across Texas, from El Paso in the west to Nacogdoches in the east.[7] From 1692 to 1793, Spanish clergy and missionaries built 26 missions stretching from east to west Tejas, as the Spanish called the territory. Gálvez dispatched an emissary to the Tejas Governor to request authorization for the first official cattle drive. The next month, cattlemen herded 2,000 Longhorns to supply Gálvez' troops. Over the three years of the war, more than 9,000 cattle were rounded up on the ranches between Bexar and La Bahia and driven overland into Louisiana to distribute to Spanish forces in Nacogdoches, Natchitoches, and Opelousas.[8] The cattle ranching industry was continued by Texan and African American cattlemen, and cattle drives across the state continued into the 1890s.

Gálvez's first target for this campaign was the British Fort Bute on the Manchac Bayou, about 115 miles up the Mississippi River from Nueva Orleáns. As the troops marched in challenging conditions through dense forests and mosquito-infested swamps to Manchac, Gálvez preceded them and continued to muster volunteers. He succeeded in recruiting another 600 men among the German and Acadian immigrants, and 160 native Americans. Throughout the long march in the intense humidity and heat of the bayou, Gálvez created a sense of esprit de corps among the men despite their differences. A Babel of languages hummed in the humid air: German, Acadian French, Choctaw, Atakapa, Creole, and the Spanish of the Mexicans, Canary Islanders, Cubans, and peninsular Spaniards, with the Irish lilt of the bilingual Pollock. If any 18th century man could lead this diverse force, that man was Bernardo de Gálvez. His attitudes towards African Americans and Native Americans were progressive by 18th century standards, and in some cases, recent 21st century standards. As he later wrote in reflections on his military service, "What does the king care if his soldier is black or white, if the nobility of his heart denies the color of his face?"[9]

Gálvez and his troops reached Fort Bute on September 6. Most of the British garrison had retreated to Baton Rouge upon learning of Gálvez' advance, and the fort was taken after a brief skirmish. Saint-Maxent, who previously surveyed the structure of the fort, was the first to charge into the compound.[10] The success encouraged the inexperienced volunteers and bonded the troops, a psychological gain that Gálvez needed. After resting his men, Gálvez marched farther north on the Mississippi River, to the British stronghold near Baton Rouge, which was surrounded by an eighteen-foot moat. As Gálvez noted in his report back to the Captain General in Havana, he was very concerned about his inexperienced troops and the fact that many of his men had families. Fearing that the human toll of a direct assault would be far too costly, he led with an artillery bombardment. Sending a diversionary detachment to a small grove of trees as twilight fell, these men chopped trees, dug earthworks, and fired at the fort while the British unsuccessfully bombarded them with cannons throughout the night. With the remaining men working in the darkness, Gálvez surreptitiously installed his cannons in a garden on the opposite side of the fort. In the morning, the British realized their mistake and opened fire on Gálvez' troops. Gálvez' troops launched an artillery barrage from their secure vantage point and wrecked the fort. By midday, the British officers proposed a truce, the terms of which included the surrender of their fort in Natchez, Mississippi.[11]

The troops continued their march along the Gulf coast in September. To reinforce Gálvez' men, 650 soldiers from the Infantry Regiment of Spain arrived from Havana with provisions and supplies.[12] The next two victories were achieved with the diplomatic assistance of Oliver Pollock. Pollock had written George Rogers Clark, the American military leader in the Mississippi region, stating his belief that the Natchez inhabitants would join the American Patriots and the Spanish when they had a chance. Pollock sent a letter to the inhabitants, informing them of Spain's declaration of war and urging the inhabitants to give up the Fort in Natchez.

The militia and civilians gathered at the fort were in a quandary. The terms of the surrender given by the British officer at Baton Rouge were countermanded by messages from the commanding officer at Pensacola, General John Campbell. Campbell had a force of over 1,000 men, including Loyalist troops from Pennsylvania and Maryland. Campbell urged the inhabitants to join him against the Spanish. The diplomacy and personalities of Pollock and Gálvez prevailed, and Fort Natchez was surrendered. The Spanish campaign had succeeded in its initial sweep of the south. As Gálvez later wrote, "It had so fortunate a result that with the loss of only one man and of two wounded, we have taken all the English settlements which they had on this river ..."[13]

Gálvez' success stunned the British. General Campbell initially refused to believe the reports, suspecting that these news updates were a ploy to lure the British out of the strong fortifications of Pensacola. The British in San Augustín also panicked at the threat of a Spanish attack, and importantly for the US Army, requested more troops from General Clinton. The fort commander wrote in December 1779, "Should we receive a similar visit from the Havanna, I shall do what ought to be done; but I have not the gift to perform miracles."[14]

The news of Gálvez' feats reached Carlos III in Madrid, who commended Gálvez for "the happy success of the expedition carried out with such spirit and speed ... and the great valor and courage shown by their scanty forces."[15] Carlos III promoted Gálvez to Brigadier General. The welcome news also reached a weary General Washington in a report sent by Juan de Miralles, who advised Washington that the Spanish would soon move against Mobile and Pensacola from their bases in Cuba and urged the General to move more forces to Georgia.[16]

Miralles continued to monitor British troop movements to discern whether these reinforcements were destined for the Carolinas and Georgia, or directly to Florida. These reports of the Spanish victories were greeted with relief in Washington's headquarters as the British continued to succeed in their attacks in the South and on Charleston. Washington and his officers understood the value of stretching the enemy's forces along numerous fronts of battle, redirecting British firepower and soldiers from attacking the US Army. By the end of October, Congress approved General Nathaniel Greene as commander and ordered Lieutenant Colonel Henry Lee's and Baron Von Steuben's forces south. Desperate to reinforce US troops, Congress ordered all units drawn from Delaware and states southward to the South.[17]

The Stormy Gulf of Mexico

With the start of the New Year in 1780, the Spanish prepared for the final phase of their southern campaign against the heavy fortifications and infrastructure at Mobile and Pensacola. This phase required significant military troops, supplies, and naval reinforcements from Cuba, Spain and other regions to face large forces of British Regulars and American Loyalist troops.

Gálvez initiated his march against Fort Charlotte in Mobile on January 10, 1780. Many of the men in this campaign were from the Cuban garrison, joining the artillery, fixed infantry, and militia of Louisiana. A small contingent of 26 American Patriots joined forces, bringing the total to over 1,400.[18] Transport to Mobile Bay in the stormy Gulf was plagued by shipwrecks and storms. During the landing of February 10 through 12, Saint-Maxent directed the disembarkation of soldiers from ships stranded on sandbars. The loss of supplies due to shipwrecks was massive, and the story later circulated that the ever-confident Gálvez even thought of abandoning his mission. He persevered, utilizing the artillery from one of the ships to establish a battery at the entrance of Mobile Bay. In an encouraging and almost proverbial demonstration of making lemonade from lemons, the men began to construct ladders to scale the walls of the fort from the wreckage of their ships. As the troops embarked on the remaining ships to continue up the Bay, a small vessel arrived with the welcome news that reinforcements were underway from Havana. By February 20th, the billowing sails of five warships were sighted.[19] These troops were from a veteran Spanish infantry, the Regiment of Navarre, and the combined forces assembled for the assault on Mobile.

In the following days the adversaries exchanged a series of gifts and double-edged pleasantries that were characteristic of the often-gentlemanly manners of 18th century warfare. Under the influence of the Enlightenment, war was viewed as a business conducted by professionals, in contrast to the scorched earth combat that emerged in the 19th century.[20] A Spanish officer acquainted with Captain Elias Durnford, the British commander, was sent to negotiate. Gifts were exchanged, with Durnford sending wine, chicken, fresh bread and mutton, and Gálvez reciprocating with Spanish and Bordeaux wines, tea biscuits, corn cakes and – most persuasively – Cuban cigars.[21] The culinary exchange ended with Durnford's final statement that given his position, honor required him to resist with whatever tactics he deemed necessary.

While Durnford waited for rescue troops from Campbell in Pensacola, Gálvez and his men continued the arduous work of building a battery to bombard the fort. They situated several of the eighteen-pound cannons and completed the earthworks and trenches to prepare for a siege. On March 11, scouts reported two nearby British camps with an estimated force of 600 men, the relief mission from Campbell.

The next day, the Spanish batteries of heavy cannons began firing. The intense barrage filled the skies with smoke and cannon balls blasts shook the air. Gálvez' men smashed the parapets (the low protective walls along the edge of a roof) and embrasures (openings in the walls that enable cannon fire). The British tenaciously returned fire. By late in the afternoon, the British realized that their defense would not hold and hoisted a white flag into the sunset of the Alabama sky. The British requested a cessation of hostilities to negotiate the surrender, finalized on March 14, 1780. News of the victory at Mobile was cheered in the US, which was struggling through difficult times. Gálvez' letter announcing the victory was read on the floor of Congress.[22]

Gálvez had wanted to move quickly against Pensacola, but the authorities in Havana postponed the campaign in a decision reached by the junta de guerra in early May 1780. The British continued to reinforce Pensacola, and to the relief of the US Army, diverted some of their forces from Savannah.[23] Gálvez sailed to Havana on August 2 to lobby the junta for prompt movement of forces against Pensacola. The junta agreed to provide him with 4,000 men, including reinforcements from Mexico and as many troops as could be spared from Puerto Rico and Santo Domingo.[24] To support the Pensacola campaign, the Spanish Army of Operations had departed from Cádiz, Spain on April 28, 1780. This Army comprised six regiments of over 7,600 men and 100 artillerymen. Alejandro O'Reilly, then Captain General in Cádiz, prepared the embarkation of the troops. These reinforcements endured two terrible blows that thwarted their speedy deployment. The first was the British blockade that forced them to remain in port, and the second was a terrible devastation by disease that swept the fleet. By the time that Gálvez was ready to launch his campaign, only one-third of these men were healthy enough for duty.[25]

In mid-October 1780, Gálvez finalized preparations for the invasion of Pensacola. This coincided with the dangerous hurricane season and Gálvez' date of departure was strongly opposed by naval commander José Solano y Bote, who calculated that one of the Gulf's terrible storms was approaching. Solano was an experienced combat veteran who conducted industrial espionage in British shipyards, explored the wilderness of the Orinoco River with a team of geographers, and fought in 1762 against the British. Solano rose to a high rank in the Spanish Navy and was known for his competence, creativity, and efficiency.[26]

Unfortunately, Gálvez prevailed. The powerful fleet of eleven warships and fifty-one transport ships set sail on October 16, 1780. Two days later, the fury of a Gulf hurricane devastated the fleet, scattering the ships throughout the Caribbean, the Campeche coastline, and the Mississippi River. The remainder of the squadron straggled back to Havana on November 17. The damage to the fleet was an appalling setback for the Spanish, and they had to reset their campaign for the conquest of Pensacola.

The Longest Siege of the War in America

Chastened but undaunted, Gálvez organized a final campaign that earned him the accolade, *Yo Solo* – I alone – approved by Carlos III for the Gálvez family crest.[27] This victory dealt the British a stunning defeat in the spring of 1781, disrupting the British hold on the southern colonies and weakening the dominion of the British Navy on the Atlantic coast and in the Caribbean.

At Pensacola, Gálvez faced a series of difficult challenges. The first was entering and securing control of Pensacola Bay, followed by establishing a base on mainland Florida. From there, the Spanish disembarked artillery, weapons, ammunition, food, and gunpowder. They then combined forces from Nueva Orleáns, Mobile, and later reinforcements from Havana. The soldiers hauled the weapons and provisions across marshy swampland, a difficult manual operation without the benefit of oxen teams or tractor trailers. The landing base was at a point close enough to the British fortifications to begin the siege but far enough not to be destroyed by enemy fire. The British fortifications comprised Fort George and the smaller nearby Fort Crescent.

On February 28, 1781, Gálvez and a squadron of thirty-six ships under the command of Captain José Calvo de Irazabal sailed a second time for Pensacola. This fleet was later joined by the *Galveztown*, Gálvez's private brig, a captured British vessel that was a gift from his American allies.[28] On March 4, they reached Santa Rosa, a 40-mile-long barrier island that provided a harrowingly narrow passage for the large fleet. A shore battery was stationed at Barrancas Colorados, opposite the western shore of the island, compounding the danger to invading ships.[29] Gálvez' plan was to land the Army on Santa Rosa, and wait for the reinforcements from Louisiana and Alabama. The Army disembarked on March 9, safely shielded from the cannons of the shore battery and patrolling British frigates. British commander Campbell, fearing the worst, managed to slip a brig out to Jamaica in a desperate bid to recruit more soldiers as reinforcements.

An acrimonious dispute started between Gálvez and Calvo de Irazabal over how to maneuver the Spanish naval fleet into Pensacola Bay. how mthe Santa Rosa barrier island. The convoy had attempted to enter the bay on March 11, with Calvo leading in his warship, the huge sixty-four cannon *San Ramón*. To Calvo and his officers' alarm, the ship touched bottom on the sandbar. When Gálvez ordered a second attempt, Calvo, concerned for both shallow water and British artillery, countermanded him. Calvo refused to take the fleet through the narrow passage into the Bay and moved the warships out to deeper water. Gálvez objected, urging them forward. Acrimonious messages were hurled back and forth between the two men. On March 14, Calvo wrote Gálvez asking, "...why then do you intend the conquest without a plan?"[30] Gálvez responded that if Calvo had courage and honor, he would sail his ships into the Pensacola Bay following the *Galveztown*'s lead. Calvo refused to move his ship and sent

Gálvez another nastygram, calling Gálvez "a spoiled upstart and traitor to king and country." Calvo threatened that if Gálvez continued his disrespect, he would hang Gálvez from the towering beams of the *San Ramón*.[31]

For six days, anchored at sea in their respective ships, the two men remained at a standoff. Gálvez feared that the campaign would be lost. The turbulent weather of the Gulf could once again scatter the ships, and reports had reached him that the British were sending reinforcements from Jamaica. On board *Galveztown*, Gálvez decided on a dramatic and daring course of action. After sending one of his men to sound the entrance of the Bay, he risked his ship and his personal safety with a charge through the entrance. Amid a fierce barrage of screeching cannon balls and artillery from the British and the cheers of the Spanish soldiers on the opposite side, the *Galveztown* was able to sail over the sandbar, leading the way for the Spanish warships.[32]

The Spanish fought the Siege of Pensacola as a classic and rigorous siege operation, based on the designs and protocols developed by the French military during the 17th century. The first siege line was constructed parallel to the enemy's position close enough to allow the soldiers to fire cannons at the enemy, but not so close as to endanger their own troops while coverage was built. Combat engineers directed the digging of immense trenches, deploying wheeled structures to guard against enemy fire. Once this first line was constructed, the engineers built the approach trenches or zigzags that defended the troops against incoming fire while they engineered the second trench closer to the target. This process continued until the soldiers were close enough to the enemy fort walls to plant mines in the walls or barrage the fort with cannon and artillery fire to force collapse and surrender.[33] The siege operations were essentially an "artillery duel conducted at increasingly shorter ranges."[34] Think of an American football game, in which the team possessing the ball pushes down the field 10 yards by 10 yards, to advance the team and move further to position for a goal kick or a touchdown, or in this case, blow up an enemy fortress.

Early in the morning of Friday, April 27, the Spanish heard the British cutting down the trees between their fortifications and the parallel trenches constructed by the Spanish. The British fired cannons and howitzers from their advantaged position on the fort parapets. Both sides continued to build redoubts and trenches under heavy fire. By dawn on Sunday, the full-scale attack on the extensive Pensacola fortifications began. The Spanish troops were positioned in a long 800-meter trench about 500 meters from the British fortifications and fired smaller cannons against the British fort.[35] For American readers, 800 meters is 875 yards or about seven football fields including end zones; 500 meters is about four football fields. For soccer fans, 800 meters is about eight soccer fields based the FIFA recommended length of 105 meters. (Please note that the meter was not officially established until 1790, so this is an approximation to provide a comparison of the extent of the siege.)

On March 24, the Spanish Army and militias moved to the center of operations, with troops moving from Santa Rosa to join the forces arriving from Mobile. During the first weeks of April, Fort George and the surrounding redoubts were reconnoitered and encampments established. Extensive preparations for the siege began. The men dug trenches, bunkers, and redoubts and built a covered road to shield the troops from the constant fire of British cannons, grapeshot, grenades, and howitzers. Over 1,500 men worked in 12-hour shifts. On April 12, Gálvez was slightly wounded by a musket shot, reportedly from Native Americans allied with the British. The command was formally given to Colonel José de Ezpeleta, Gálvez' personal friend and comrade-in-arms.[36]

On April 19, a massive fleet was sighted heading towards the Bay. Ominous rumors rippled through the ranks that British reinforcements had arrived in Pensacola. To his relief, Gálvez learned that these ships were from Havana. The fleet had departed ten days earlier, successfully skirmishing with British ships en route to Pensacola.[37] Reports of a British squadron sighted near Cape San Antonio had reached Havana. Concerned that this fleet could support Pensacola, Cagigal and Solano rushed reinforcements to Gálvez.[38] The fleet of 36 ships carried 1,700 crewmen and 1,600 soldiers, 640 of whom were from the Havana garrison and the remainder from the Spanish Army of Operations. The Spanish force then totaled 8,000 men.[39] Among the diverse troops were soldiers from Puerto Rico, Honduras, and Guatemala,[40] and Jeronimo Giron y Moctezuma, a ninth-generation descendant of the Mexica (Aztec) leader who fought against Cortes in 1520.[41] Haitian soldiers from the Chasseurs Volontaires were deployed from Charleston.[42] Solano and Gálvez cooperated closely together, and Solano remained to assist Gálvez after their troops disembarked on April 22.

Francisco de Miranda was on board this fleet and took daily notes on the events. Miranda was born in Venezuela in 1750 and became a leader in the revolutions in Latin America in the early 1800s. As Miranda and the reinforcements from

Havana disembarked, he noted that, "All the army welcomed us with infinite joy, for not only were they fatigued with the endless and not well-combined Marches that they had made in the 42 days since they had landed ... they considered all their work useless and were in despair of the enterprise."[43]

The Gulf continued to send its tempestuous storms, and on May 5 and 6, a hurricane again struck the Spanish ships. Miranda wrote, "A heavy rain and strong wind which came at 1 o'clock in the morning flooded our camp, tore down our tents, and gave us a terrible night. There was not a single bed that was not made into soup because all the tents were rotten. This lasted until 5 in the morning, when each one spread his rags out in the sun. The trenches were flooded likewise, and you can imagine the work that the troops had standing in water up to their waists." The Spanish Navy was forced to withdraw, fearing that the fierce sea would crash the wooden ships on the shore. The Spanish Army was on its own to continue the siege. The troops were miserable in the flooded, muddy trenches, and Gálvez encouraged them with an extra ration of brandy.

On May 8, a massive blast ruptured the grueling two-month siege. With a direct hit, Spanish artillery blasted the ammunition storage depot in Fort Crescent. Black smoke billowed into the sky as barrels of gunpowder exploded. Miranda "saw a great column of smoke rising towards the clouds, and later we found out that the explosion had been inside the circular fort ... which battery was all in flames." Ezpeleta, commanding the light infantry, led the charge into the destroyed fort. Gálvez and two companies of grenadiers marched into the city and were "very well received by the people in the vicinity."[44] The fall of Fort Crescent positioned the Spanish for their assault on Fort George. Heavy fire continued against Ezpeleta's position until three o'clock on May 10, when a white flag was hoisted from Fort George. The Spanish captured 1,113 British prisoners and seized more than 200 barrels of gunpowder, 2,000 muskets, and a substantial number of howitzers, mortars, and swivel guns.[45]

Into The Heart of Darkness

While Bernardo de Gálvez campaigned through the Gulf of Mexico and the Florida panhandle, the Spanish launched another major warfront in Central America. The conflict ranged across the globe from the jungles of Honduras,

Nicaragua, and Guatemala to the mountains and granite outcrops of the Maratha and Mysore kingdoms in India. The fighting deflected the British military and naval resources from attacking American soldiers. The battles and skirmishes in the extreme wilds of the jungles were ferocious, deadly and relentless. In the words of one historian, the physical and psychological toll on the soldiers was brutal, in a vastly different physical world from the forests and fields of Europe.

Carlos III wrote in a report to Navarro that after winning back Mobile and Pensacola, "the second most important objective" was Central America. The British had long annoyed the Spanish with logging operations on the coasts of Honduras and Nicaragua, concessions that the Spanish had to make in the peace deal in 1763.[46] The Spanish considered this territory as part of their empire, which the British usually ignored. Both European powers ignored the Maya, a sophisticated civilization that had thrived for thousands of years in the region. The strategic location of Central America was the deciding factor and if you look at a map, you'll understand why.[47] The San Juan River flows 119 miles from the Caribbean to the eastern end of Lake Nicaragua, along the border of Costa Rica. The western end of Lake Nicaragua is about eleven miles from the Pacific Ocean. You can visualize a shortcut through the American continents connecting the Atlantic and Pacific oceans. This path between the seas had been a goal of the Europeans since Columbus sailed in 1492. Long before the United States "helped" to "acquire" the then province of Panama from Colombia in 1903,* the Spanish and other powers were formulating ideas to leverage these natural lakes and waterways. Team Carlos understood that with a strong military and commercial presence in Central America, the British could launch offensives to seize the precious silver and gold mines of Mexico and Latin America. At a meeting in Paris in early 1778, Aranda, Floridablanca, and Vergennes discussed Spain's goal of expelling the British from Central America.[48] José de Gálvez wrote to the Governors in the Yucatan, Mexico City, Panama, Trinidad, Cartagena and Bogotá, instructing them to prepare defenses of their territory and for an offense against the British in Central America.[49] Precise orders and instructions arrived from Madrid beginning in February 1780, and continued almost weekly while the battles raged.

---

* Please note that this disturbance is not to be confused with the US plans announced in 2025 to take the Panama Canal from the Panamanians (again).

The first stage involved shipping military supplies and silver pesos from Oaxaca, Mexico. More supplies, equipment and funds were shipped from Colombia, Ecuador and Peru. Team Carlos in Central America was led by Matías Gálvez, the Captain General of Guatemala 1778, and three more veteran military commanders who arrived in 1781 and 1782, enabling powerful and effective military leadership in a difficult landscape.[50] Troops were recruited throughout Spain. Two regiments comprised of soldiers from Guatemala and Mexico, the Fijo de Guatemala and the Castilla de Campeche, were deployed to join the campaign. Militias, a multiracial force of citizen-soldiers from Honduras and Guatemala, also fought in the Central American campaigns.[51]

The fighting began in September 1779, when the Spanish attacked the British Fort Omoa, a seaport in the Gulf of Honduras. The Spanish force was initially overwhelmed by the British, who sent in reinforcements from Roatan, an island in the Bay of Honduras. The fighting was brutal, with hand-to-hand combat in the hostile jungle terrain. The difficult physical and psychological conditions can be compared to the 20th century experience in US soldiers in Vietnam[52] — except that neither the Spanish or the British were equipped with rain ponchos, two-way radios to communicate through the dense vegetation, or C-rations for a half-decent meal. The men suffered "jungle rot" from wet clothing and shoes, which led to tissue death and gangrene. Amputations were performed in unsanitary conditions without anesthesia. The men were plagued with the incessant buzzing and sting of mosquitoes, bites from disease-carrying kissing bugs, and strikes from venomous snakes. Leeches persistently dropped from the trees and hid in the jungle streams, crawling up pant legs and gorging themselves on the men's blood. Given limited visibility and jungle, the men strained to hear, see or smell a clue to their enemy's presence.[53] As with many who endured combat injuries and PTSD in 20th century Vietnam, the man who entered this jungle warfare in the 18th century left a different, often traumatized, man.

After fierce fighting and the arrival of reinforcements, the Spanish retook Fort Omoa in November of 1781, with Matías de Gálvez leading the charge. The British commanded their troops from nearby Jamaica, and in January 1780 the British attacked a Spanish fort on the San Juan River. Despite reinforcements, this Spanish fort fell. The British troops marched on to Fort San Carlos on Lake Nicaragua. The British bombarded the fort for 20 days with heavy artillery and cannons but were unable to defeat the Spanish, who continued their momentum and targeted two remaining British strongholds. Between December 1781 and March 1782, the Spanish sent more troops, eventually capturing Roáton, and mopping up the remaining British fortifications. The soon-to-be famous Lord Horatio Nelson, later regarded as one of Britain's leading naval commanders, was a young twenty-two-year-old in the San Juan River campaign. Pessimistically and presciently, he wrote, "How it will turn out, God knows!"[54] Nelson was correct, the battles were a huge loss for the British. Over 2,500 men lost their lives and the British concluded their ambition to divide the Spanish Empire through Central America.[55]

Onwards to ... Virginia

The Spanish victories in Pensacola, the Gulf of Mexico, and Central America impacted the outcome of the American Revolution, disrupting the British campaigns and clearing the way for American and French forces fighting toward the climactic land battle at Yorktown six months later. With Spanish and French fleets now commanding the seas, the balance of power shifted. The French were able to concentrate their naval strength and bring it to bear against the British during the war's pivotal final days, in the Battle of the Chesapeake and the Siege of Yorktown.[56]

Chapter 11

"Now or never"

"We are at the end of our tether,"* General Washington wrote discouragingly in April 1781 to John Laurens, his aide-de-camp, as he sent the young man off on another fund-raising mission in Europe, "... now or never our deliverance must come." The Army could not transport provisions because the wagon drivers refused to accept paper Continental dollars, hospitals were without medicines, soldiers were again "approaching fast to nakedness & that we have nothing to cloathe them with." Washington ordered troops to march to support the Southern Army, but "how either can march without money or credit, is more than I can tell."[1]

The rebellion was in its sixth long year since the Declaration of Independence. The terrible strains of the conflict and blockade continued to erode the agrarian-based economy and a population ravaged by a nightmarish smallpox epidemic.[2] The army suffered through a winter camp at Morristown in 1780 that was colder and crueler than Valley Forge. Three serious mutinies erupted, which the British gleefully publicized throughout Europe.[3] The Continental currency continued to hyper-inflate, and finally collapsed in May 1781. General Henry Clinton's work at establishing an effective espionage network was a grave threat to the Americans. A French commander worried that only one highly placed American traitor could determine the fate of the rebellion,[4] and Clinton succeeded in finding that one. George III was optimistic in September 1780, writing that, "America is distressed to the greatest degree. The finances of France, as well as Spain are in no good situation. This war, like the last, will prove one of credit."[5]

---

* A tether is a short rope that secures a horse and allows it to graze or rest. Washington was an excellent horseman, and his horses were well cared for.

George III certainly had a point. The strains of the continual spending were stressing the public funds of nations as wealthy as Spain and its rich Latin American empire. The French were losing confidence in the US Army and political leadership, and were unwilling and unable to commit the financial, naval and military resources to support the war if it continued. According to documents captured by the British and noted by Clinton in his personal narrative, the planned Yorktown campaign was the last time the French court would commit troops or ships to the American Cause.[6] As the US Army mutinied, the currency collapsed, and the Americans wearied of years of war, time was running out.

Today's menu? Roasted Shoe Leather

"The oldest people now living in this Country do not remember so hard a Winter ... the severity of the frost exceeded anything of the kind that had ever been experienced in this climate before,"[7] Washington wrote to Lafayette in 1780. The winter of 1780 at Morristown was colder, darker and more desperate than Valley Forge. Problems with supplies continued to plague the army. When General Greene took the southern command in December 1780, only a third of the 2,500 men were adequately clothed and equipped.[8] The icy roads worsened the supply shortages, making it nearly impossible to deliver the limited provisions to the suffering soldiers. For the first and only time in recorded history, the saltwater estuaries froze solid along the entire eastern seaboard, preventing transport of goods by boats.[9]

Joseph Plumb Martin was among the troops and he wrote of the shortages and sleeping in the snow, "Sometimes we could procure an armful of buckwheat straw to lie upon, which was deemed a luxury..."[10] When Martin and his fellow soldiers arrived in December 1779, the snow was already more than a foot deep as the men dug into the cold earth to construct their winter huts. They quickly realized that once again, they did not have enough food. Hunger cynically stalked the brave and the fearless, mocking their courage. Martin gnawed off black birch bark as his only meal in four days, watching other soldiers roast and eat their old shoes. He sadly noted that one American officer "killed and ate a favorite little dog." Many of us in the 21st century, surrounded by fast food chains, food delivery services, and mega grocery stores, can barely imagine this relentless hunger that the soldiers endured day after day after day.

"What was to be done?" questioned Martin, there among the angry troops. "Here was the army starved and naked ... [expected] to do notable things while fainting from sheer starvation." Martin speaks to us from those perilous days, his words echoing across the centuries, "Reader, suffer what we did and you will say so too."[11] The serious mutinies among these loyal, dedicated men began near the end of the war,[12] after the soldiers experienced years of hunger, a lack of clothing and supplies, and the frustrating knowledge that despite all their steadfastness, they did not receive their promised pay. Two Connecticut regiments walked out in protest, threatening to return home. This upheaval was diffused, but it was a troubling presage to the serious mutinies that erupted across the Continental Army.[13]

On the bitterly cold New Year's Eve of December 31, 1780 in the Morristown winter camp, the soldiers of the Pennsylvania Line celebrated with a rare ration of rum, ordered by Washington. The real celebration for many of the enlisted men – from their perspective – was that they had served their three-year enlistments and could now return home. Enough of relentless hunger, of shabby clothing, and of no pay in worthless Continental dollars. Their sacrifice was over. Their officers had a different point of view: the soldiers had enlisted for the duration of the war, not for a three-year term. The disheartened men were pushed beyond their limits and launched the first mutiny of the Pennsylvania Line. Muskets blazed from a handful of men and then more soldiers with weapons and knapsacks rushed out of their huts and on to the parade ground. The officers frantically tried to reason with men. The mutinying soldiers seized ammunition, horses, wagons and other provisions, firing shots over the heads of their comrades who tried to intervene.[14] After several weeks of negotiations, the soldiers reached a settlement. The men who were scheduled to end their enlistments were allowed to leave.

News of the Pennsylvania Line mutiny reached the soldiers camped in New Jersey a few weeks later. These soldiers had the same grievances as the Pennsylvania men. Washington and the military leadership were devastated by the mutinies, fearing, as Washington wrote, "this dangerous spirit ... would speedily infect the whole army." The punishment for the New Jersey mutineers was severe: twelve of the leaders were executed by firing squad. Mutinies also erupted in the southern region of the war. In October 1780, General Nathanael Greene was appointed to lead the dwindling army that was now in South Carolina. Greene was distraught to learn that the supplies were desperately low, and once again, the troops were half-starved, ragged and unpaid. Shortly after his arrival, soldiers from the Maryland unit tried to desert with their weapons but were warned that they would be discovered before they were able to travel a safe distance. The men returned to camp, and an altercation broke out when the officers reprimanded them. One man angrily shouted and swore back at the officers. He was accused of "encouraging mutiny and desertion"[15] and sentenced to death by firing squad. The shots rang out that early evening and his body crumpled to the bloodied ground. The US Army was strained to the breaking point.

The Money Men

The man at the center of the firestorm of the collapsing economy, bankrupting currency, overdrawn accounts and desperate, constant requests for money was Robert Morris, an immigrant from England. Morris immigrated from Liverpool, England in 1747 to the bustling port city of Oxford, Maryland, at age thirteen, to join his father, a British merchant and international agent for a large firm of tobacco traders. Morris became involved early in rebel politics by resisting the Stamp Act and signing the non-importation agreement to boycott British goods in 1765.[16] He served in the Continental Congress, signed the Declaration of Independence, and after the Revolution was elected to the first United States Senate. He was appointed to the committees to manage imports of arms, cartridges and gunpowder and to establish a colonial navy.[17] He rose to be one of the wealthiest men in Philadelphia, and he unconditionally pledged his personal and business finances to sustain the Continental Army. He drew on his own credit to pay soldiers and spies, purchase supplies and provisions, and sent his merchant fleet throughout the Caribbean and Europe to trade for needed supplies and equipment.[18] As a representative of Pennsylvania, Morris also administered the substantial funds granted to Congress by his adopted state.[19] Loyal to Washington, he supported the General during the divisive attempts by his rivals to unseat Washington as Commander-in-Chief. He weathered fierce charges of corruption and war profiteering, the vicious barrage of gossip and rumor that swirled around his intertwined political and personal transactions that were often unavoidably close. Morris became known as the chief financier of the Revolution, loyal to the Cause through each dark and desperate day that turned inexorably into months and then years. He rose to such prominence that his signature was trusted more than the Continental currency itself, and his personally signed notes of "Long Bobs" and "Short Bobs" sustained the moribund colonial economy. Morris understood the importance of Spain and Latin America in financing the rebellion. Morris established close business relationships with Gardoqui, Miralles, and Rendón, and corresponded with Team Carlos to ask for emergency loans and to expand the lucrative trade with Havana — one of the few opportunities for Americans to earn silver currency.

Morris sometimes partnered with Haym Salomon, who immigrated from Poland in 1775, initially settling in New York. Salomon was from the Sephardic Jewish community that immigrated to Eastern Europe after being expelled from Spain in 1492. Eventually, he joined the vibrant Sephardic Jewish community in New York, the descendants of those who arrived in 1654, in an epic journey worthy of a Netflix series. The community fled the Spanish Inquisition in 1492 to Brazil, then had to flee again when the Portuguese recaptured Brazil in 1654. When sailing from Brazil to the Netherlands, one of the ships in their convoy was captured by Spanish pirates who threatened to sell the passengers into slavery. The Spanish pirate ship was then captured by a French merchant ship, whose heartless captain dropped them off in New York without their baggage or money.[20] Salomon married Rachel Franks, a descendant of the original 23 Jewish immigrants who had survived and prospered.

Salomon was imprisoned by the British government in New York for his pro-Revolutionary views but escaped to Philadelphia in 1778 and joined Morris to assist with the country's calamitous finances.[21] He negotiated the war subsidies and loans from France and the Netherlands, which he endorsed and sold in bills to merchants in America. The treasurer of the French Army in America appointed Salomon as their paymaster, a huge undertaking that he provided free of charge. He also managed a loan to the Spanish agent in Philadelphia, Francisco Rendón, when his funds were cut off by the British b lockade.[22] He lent money to American political leaders, including three future US Presidents, Jefferson, Madison, and Monroe.[23] As Madison wrote, "When any member was in need, all that was necessary was to call upon Salomon."[24]

Both men were financially strapped during the summer months before the Battle of Yorktown, as they scrambled to gather the cash that Washington and the US Army desperately needed. Salomon was able to provide the Continental Army with $20,000 through bills of exchange, not in silver. Morris wrote to Navarro in July 1781, advising him that the paper money had collapsed and requesting an urgent loan for Yorktown.[25] The men watched despairingly as the Yorktown campaign drew closer and the Army struggled with supplies. The supply commissaries tried to conscript horses and wagons to move food and provisions, and the impoverished citizens did not want to cooperate unless they were paid in hard currency. Some hid their wagons and teams to prevent them from being "commandeered" or seized.[26] Morris visited the Yorktown camp in August. Washington pleaded with him to find the money to pay the troops, "I must entreat you, if possible, to procure one month's pay in specie..."[27] With no other options, Morris advanced a large sum of his personal funds for the Yorktown campaign, writing later that, "While I was in advance, not only my credit, but every shilling of my own money, and all of which I could obtain from my friends."[28]

The same summer that the men frenetically worked to fund the campaign, the hyper-inflated Continental currency finally collapsed in May 1781. The Council in Philadelphia began to publish the month-to-month rates of currency to silver and gold coins, and exhausted consumers then multiplied the official rate by three. The paper currency-to-silver ratio was officially 175 to one, but the people calculated the rate at 525 to one, for actual prices in the markets. A procession was held in Philadelphia to spiritedly mark its collapse, with people marching with dollars in their hats as paper plumes. An unhappy dog trotted alongside, tarred and pasted with the worthless paper.[29] As Mercy Otis Warren despaired, "The immense heaps of paper trashed, denominated money ... that fluctuates from day to day."[30] The American economy was in shambles. Agriculture was the dominant sector and production decreased by about 50% during the years of the war. Reports of food shortages among the civilian population started in the early years of the War, and the situation worsened by 1781.

Crowdfunding the Revolutionary War

As George III had happily noted, the finances of the Spanish government were also strained by the war. In addition to supporting the Revolutionary War, the Spanish military funded a costly siege and blockade of Gibraltar from 1779 to 1783 and planned a grand assault for 1782. The French and Spanish had also spent resources in a pricey and failed campaign to invade Britain in 1779.[31] In response to the financial crisis, on a warm August day in 1781, Carlos III and his ministers issued a Real Orden to kick off a massive crowdfunding campaign across the Spanish empire, from the towns of Alta California, through the American Southwest, and into Latin America. This war tax was a one-time "donativo" that required Spanish citizens to pay two pesos and Native Americans to pay one peso for the war effort. When word reached California, Junípero Serra, a Catholic priest who founded eight of California's 21 Spanish missions, was concerned that the Native Americans at his missions were not financially able to pay the requested peso. (The reason that the Native Americans did not have the wealth to pay a tax was that the Spanish confiscated their land.) Serra covered their share from funds collected by the mission. Serra referred to the English as "perfidious heretics" and included George Washington and the Patriots in his prayers. In 1778 Serra wrote, "We prayed fervently last evening for the success of the colonists under one George Washington, because we believe their cause is just and that the Great Redeemer is on their side."[32]

Spanish and Latino soldiers sent their donations from Santa Fe, the oldest State Capitol in the US where the Palace of the Governors still watches over the peaceful, grassy plaza. The small town of Tucson, Arizona contributed their silver, as did the Spanish citizens of Tejas. Martín de Mayorga, the Viceroy of New Spain, organized the collection across Mexico, El Salvador, Guatemala, Honduras and Costa Rica. Many donativos were sent from Mexico, including the present-day states of Guadalajara, Veracruz, Yucatan, Puebla, and Oaxaca, and the cities of San Luis Potosí and Mexico City.[33] The records of the donors and their sums were handwritten in elegant calligraphy with artistic drawings and occasionally decorated with bright red ink made from cochineal bugs.

The donors were from the military, ranches, churches, guilds (labor unions) including miners and silver makers, and gun powder producers and card factories.[34] Their ethnic backgrounds were varied and reflected Latin America's diverse and effusive culture after centuries of intermarriage, with groups listed as Españoles, Indios, Mestizos, Mullatos, Lobos and Coyotes. The crowdfunding campaign was a success underscoring the importance of fund-raising and shipments of silver from Latin America to continue Spain's global wars.

Ambush on the high seas

The good news that reached the Americans during this period were the reports of battles in distant oceans and lands. In 1780 and 1781, the highly experienced Spanish Admiral, Luis de Córdova y Córdova, captured major British convoys en route to the American colonies and the Caribbean, preventing the crucial supplies from reaching the British. Across the ocean, the rulers of the Mysore Kingdom, Hyder Ali and his son Tipu Sultan, rallied their armies of tens of thousands to fight major battles against the British military and East India Company. Americans eagerly followed the campaigns of these two Muslim leaders, toasting them at parties and meetups and composing rap songs to celebrate their victories.

Córdova enlisted in the Spanish Navy at age eleven when he joined his father's ship. During the Revolutionary War, he was over 70 years old with decades of experience in Latin America and Europe. In August 1780, Carlos III and Floridablanca learned from their intelligence sources that a huge British military and merchant convoy was en route to America from the south coast of England, and Carlos approved plans for an ambush. Córdova commanded the attack from the Spanish base in Cádiz.[35] The chase began in the early morning hours of August 9. By manipulating the stern lamp of his command ship, the *Santísima Trinidad*, Córdova tricked the British merchant convoy into following his ship instead of their warship. In the dawn light, the merchant captains realized that they had been duped but were unable to escape. This victory was the single largest loss of British merchant ships during the war.[36]

A list of the captured merchant ships with their cargos and destinations rivals an Amazon distribution center on Prime Day: ships rigging and masts, clothing, meats, wines, beer, horses, mules, flour, iron works, and military supplies and ammunition (which are not available on Amazon) that were destined for New York, Jamaica, India, and the Caribbean islands.[37] The financial impact was so severe that insurance rates for British shipping jumped by 25%, further straining the British economy.[38] Over 1,800 officers and men from the East India Company were captured.

On His Majesty's Secret Service

Fighting in uncharted wilderness without GPS or spy satellites to even locate the US Army in the vast wooded terrain seriously hindered Clinton and the British. By 1779, Clinton determined that he needed a comprehensive overhaul of his espionage and reconnaissance operations. In May of that year, he appointed Captain John André, his twenty-nine-year-old aide-de-camp, as his lead intelligence officer. André was popular in the American Loyalist society, and a frequent partier in the British-occupied cities of Philadelphia and New York. The multi-talented military officer was also an artist, poet, actor, singer and writer. A man who knew how to enjoy life, he organized the mega-party known as the "Mischianza" in Philadelphia in 1778, in honor of the British General Sir William Howe. The Mischianza, from the Italian word for medley or mixture, featured a boat regatta along the Delaware River, three musical bands, a tournament of jousting knights, and a sumptuous banquet. The ballroom glittered with mirrors that reflected the lights of an extravagant number of glowing candles. The party guests danced until four in the morning, toasting what they were certain would soon be a British victory.[39]

Upon his appointment as intelligence officer, André began organizing data and recording almost daily reports into a hardbound "intelligence" book. A born spymaster, he brought his personal charm and likeability to his role, convincing his social contacts in Pennsylvania and New York to assist him. With his own spies, André was soon able to stipulate the types of information that he needed, including locations and strengths of US units and supply depots, identities of commanders, troops movements, and activities near British lines.[40] André focused attention on the many American deserters, requiring that they be sent to headquarters for interrogation. British spies closely monitored and reported on the French naval and army troops movements. André recruited among the American Loyalist community and further expanded his operations.

Spies on both sides used ciphers for their covert communications, the 18th century equivalent of data encryption. Without a Signal app or other digital options, these messages were written on paper and could be read if captured by the enemy. The modern day US National Security Agency (NSA) describes André's technique as Substitution Cipher, in which the letters and numbers of a message are changed according to a cipher key held by one person, and can only be deciphered by another person who has that same cipher key. For example, using a substitution cipher, the word CRYPTOGRAPHY could be scrambled to DOHQMRZOFQYH, with a cipher key that designated C=D, R=O, Y=H, each letter consistently substituted throughout.[41] Washington and his troops also implemented cipher codes in their messages, as well as correspondence between civilians and political leaders. André upgraded the use of ciphers among British spies.

From your US high school history book, you may remember André's final and most daring espionage mission and Major General Benedict Arnold's betrayal as they tried to capture Washington and West Point fortress in New York. By taking West Point, strategically located on the Hudson River, the British planned to further their strategy to divide the colonies. A complicated man, Arnold was a rising star in the Continental Army and successfully fought in key battles in New York, New England, and Canada, during which he was seriously injured. He believed that the American alliance with France, a Catholic monarchy, was a mistake. The British offered a bribe of £20,000 to betray the Revolution. Peggy Shippen Arnold, his wife and a close friend of André was complicit in the conspiracy, communicating with British intelligence on Arnold's behalf.[42]

By the summer of 1780, Arnold had maneuvered his appointment as commander of West Point. André arrived on the British ship *Vulture* and met with Arnold on the riverbanks on September 20 and the two men conferred for several days. The *Vulture* was spotted by the Patriots, who fired on the ship while it was trapped in the low tides of the Hudson River. The ship withdrew, and André was stranded in enemy territory. Arnold advised him to travel back to British lines by land, and to change out of his uniform into civilian clothes. As he hurried to safety, André was stopped at a checkpoint. One of the American soldiers wore a Hessian coat, and André, mistaking him for an ally, gave himself away. He had forgotten the dire clothing shortages plaguing the Continental Army and militias. As recounted in Chapter 5, American soldiers had stripped warm coats from captured Hessians out of sheer necessity — a small act of desperation that now, four years later, helped expose one of the most dangerous spies of the war. André was caught and prosecuted as a spy. Despite Clinton's best efforts to rescue his officer, André was hanged on October 2, 1780. As an eyewitness later wrote, André tied on his own handkerchief as the customary blindfold, and slipped the noose over his neck, asking that, "I pray you to bear me witness that I meet my fate like a brave man."

Washington was devastated by Arnold's treachery. He had traveled to West Point with his aides to meet with Arnold on the morning that André was captured and was puzzled by Arnold's sudden and unexplained departure. When Hamilton and Lafayette returned to brief Washington on the papers captured from John André, Washington was close to tears. "Arnold has betrayed us," the shocked General exclaimed, "Whom can we trust now?"[43] Hamilton and another aide raced off in hot pursuit of Arnold, but they were too late — he'd already boarded a waiting British ship and escaped to the safety of New York. Consider the frightening thoughts and restless nightmares that Washington must have endured with this betrayal and his razor-thin near capture. His arrest would mean reprisals against his beloved family, the possible collapse of the Revolution, and imprisonment and death by hanging — or worse. Sentences for treason in the 18th century were cruel and savage. Drawing and quartering, literally tearing a live man to pieces, was enforced as a penalty for treason. The spy network marched on after André's death. Clinton appointed Captain George Beckwith to the unit. Beckwith expanded André's spy network, and coordinated analyses with the Hessian commander of the garrison in occupied New York. Beckwith became more active in political reconnaissance, enrolling agents in Philadelphia to infiltrate Congress.[44] The British continued to monitor the Americans' French allies and Washington's mutinous army with increasing success.

In 1781, Clinton's espionage team captured a trove of letters from the Americans and French, written after a conference at Wethersfield, Connecticut. Jean-Baptiste Donatien de Vimeur, Comte de Rochambeau and the leader of the French Army in America arrived with 7,000 French troops in July 1780. Rochambeau and their officers met to prepare for the approaching campaign with De Grasse's naval and military reinforcements. For the British and Clinton, "the most interesting piece of intelligence" from the captured mail was "an intimation from the court of France that this was the last campaign in which the Americans were to expect assistance of either troops or ships from that nation, as she began to be apprehensive that her own exigencies would put it out of her power to continue her support if the war should be protracted much longer." In other words, the French planned to give up the fight for the American cause after the Yorktown Campaign. Clinton was certain that, "because it was now manifest that, if we could only persevere in escaping affront, time alone would soon bring about every success we could wish."[45] The unfolding Siege at Yorktown was the "now or never" for the fate of the American Revolution.

Chapter 12

La Habana, The Key to the New World

By August 1781 Havana had glowed as the "Key to the New World" for over 250 years since its founding early in the 16th century. The pride of the Spanish monarchs, the envy of the British, and the target of the pirates in the Caribbean, Havana was central to the Spanish management and protection of their New World Empire. Most importantly for the scene that was about to unfold that helped to finally win the American Revolution, Havana was the center of vast wealth and resources. The government in Havana was funded through the centuries by the wealth of the silver and gold mines in the Viceroyalty of Peru and Mexico, with the Mexican mines leading construction financing in the late 18th century.

The rise of Mexican silver is reflected in the revenue numbers of the situado, the tax subsidy, that was shipped from Mexico to the Treasury in Havana. Taxes more than tripled from the 1750s to 1769, with an annual average of approximately 1.48 million pesos. During the last years of the American Revolutionary War, this tax reached its all-time high of 10.6 million pesos[1] or about $22.1 billion today. The Treasury also prospered from taxation of the lucrative trade and commerce, as thousands of ships docked annually in the harbor. One British merchant observed that silver flowed so freely in Havana that he likened it to the lands of the biblical King Solomon.[2]

The walled city was built to the specific architectural standards of early cities in Spanish America, with carved gates that enclosed whitewashed houses with red tiled roofs, stately mansions with heavy wooden doors and large courtyards, three main plazas, and a Franciscan monastery, Dominican university and Jesuit college. Tall, elegant royal palms swayed in the sea breeze. Flocks of multi-hued birds, including native Cuban parakeets, orioles, woodpeckers, quail doves and zunzuncitos, the world's smallest hummingbirds, flew among the trees and endemic colorful flowers and vines. The new construction and militarization of the city after Havana was lost to the British in 1762 were completed. By the late 18th century, Havana was regarded as the most fortified city in the world.[3]

The city's population underwent a dramatic transformation as well. The number of Habaneros increased steadily after 1762, as a wave of Spaniards moved to Cuba, driven by the island's extensive military expansion.[4] The 1778 census counted over 40,000 people, and another 40,000 in the suburbs, known as Havana Campo.[5] The cobblestones clattered with the stomp of soldiers, the hoofbeats of horses, and the wheels of wagons. In preparation for the war with the British, Carlos III and his military leadership sent twelve battalions of troops from Spain. Team Carlos expanded and upskilled the local militias, which had supported the regular troops at Pensacola in 1779.[6] By day, many of the enlisted militia men were bakers, butchers, artisans, carpenters, and barbers but when the island was threatened they turned into citizen-soldiers.[7] The wealthy merchants and plantation owners comprised many of the militia officer corps. During the late 18th century, relations between the Spanish and Afro-Cubans were relatively peaceful — or, as peaceful as relations could be between enslavers and enslaved. Key reasons for this stability were the demographics and the militarization of the island. Free Afro-Cubans were a minority, about 15% of the population. Most of this free population lived in Havana, where many men served in the militia.[8] The enslaved people, while numerous, were a minority in the overall population and they worked in urban occupations or on small farms. The brutal conditions of the large, high-production sugar plantations were not fully operational until later in the 19th century.

The 18th Century Dynamic Duo

There are many famous Dynamic Duos in books and movies, but you've probably never heard of the two men who decisively impacted the fate of the Revolutionary War in its last days: Saavedra and De Grasse, or more precisely, Francisco Saavedra de Sangronis and François Joseph Paul, Comte de Grasse. These two men joined forces as the American military was close to collapsing. Together, they managed to raise funds for the Battle of Yorktown and negotiated the military and naval resource allocation strategy to defeat the British Navy at the critical Battle of the Chesapeake, shortly before Yorktown.

Many historical accounts never mention our esteemed hero, Saavedra, misreporting him as a mere "customs officer" who had to be persuaded to assist De Grasse in his mission. His name was misspelled in some reports as Salavedra.[9] In reality, Saavedra was a former soldier and special agent appointed by Carlos III to assist the French and Americans. His title was an official of the Secretary of State and General Bureau of the Spanish Indies.[10] Saavedra's superpower was getting things done well, quickly, and discreetly — a quality that could explain why his valuable contribution has been underappreciated. He was born in Sevilla, a great center of the Enlightenment movement, and was a fan of bullfights and operas. An educated, insightful man, in 1780 he presciently wrote, "What is not being thought about at present, what ought to occupy the whole attention of politics, is the great upheaval that in time the North American revolution is going to produce in the human race."[11]

Saavedra was a close friend of Bernardo de Gálvez and the two men were classmates at the famed military academy at Avila. They bonded during a road trip through Spain in 1775. As Saavedra wrote, "We traveled by horse, and I had a very entertaining journey, because he related several episodes from this life, which were a real novelty. Anyway, we forged a very close friendship which in a certain way was to become the foundation of my destiny."[12] The two men fought in the Spanish war with Morocco, where both were wounded. They were later assigned to duty in Havana. Saavedra was at the siege of Pensacola as the personal representative of the powerful minister of the Indies, José de Gálvez, Bernardo's uncle.[13] There, Saavedra served as an understated, driving force behind the scenes, ensuring that food and other critical supplies were speedily shipped in from Cuba.[14] By May 1781, Saavedra was back in Havana, ready for his next mission to support De Grasse and the French fleet heading for Yorktown.

De Grasse was from Bar-sur-Loup, a small French town north of Grasse, the elegant center for the perfume industry and his family's namesake. The Admiral was a strong-willed military man with decades of experience, including fighting in India against the British during the Seven Years' War. He sailed from France to the Caribbean in March 1781, determined to keep his promise "to do the impossible." Among De Grasse's "impossible" tasks was to raise enough cash to fund both the French and American armies.

De Grasse received an urgent dispatch from his Army counterpart, Rochambeau. "Papa" Rochambeau as he was known, was 55 years old when he arrived in America in 1780. A seasoned veteran and commander, he was a strong partner for Washington and the beleaguered US military. In July 1781, Rochambeau and his 7,000 French Army troops marched from their landing point in Rhode Island to Virginia to rendezvous with the US Army. Rochambeau had a dim view of the financial support that the US military was receiving. In September he confided to a colonel in his command as to the dire financial situation in America, "The cupidity of the [financial] dealers is extreme. Their naked troops do not take a crown from the pocket of the most patriotic business man except at an unheard of interest."[15] Rochambeau wrote to De Grasse of their desperate need for reinforcements of military supplies, financing, and manpower: "I should not conceal from you, M. l'Amiral, that these people are at the very end of their resources or that Washington will not have ... half the number of troops he counted upon having."[16] Rochambeau was running out of money. The expected shipments of cash had not reached him and he worried that any hard currency would be captured by the British blockade.

On July 16, De Grasse arrived on the island of Saint-Domingue, now known as Haiti. José de Gálvez sent instructions to Saavedra, then in the Spanish city of Santo Domingo, requesting him to confer with De Grasse about "the operations that must be executed." Saavedra and De Grasse met for the first time on July 17, 1781. Saavedra joined De Grasse at dawn the next day on board the *Ville de Paris*. The Spanish and French had an impressive list of ambitions for damaging the British, including aid for the US and conquering Jamaica. The Bourbon Kings, Carlos and Louis, were determined to capture Jamaica, or recapture it, since the Spanish had occupied Jamaica from 1509 until the English invasion in 1655. Jamaica provided enormous wealth to Britain through sugar production, an inexpensive and indispensable source of food energy. While the two men strategized, De Grasse worked to fulfill his promise to Rochambeau to raise the 1.2 million livres, equivalent to about 270,000 pesos, and sail to the Chesapeake Bay as soon as possible. This assignment proved to be very challenging, even for a man as competent as De Grasse. He met with merchants and planters of the Cap Français (now Cap-Haitien in Haiti) offering his own plantations in Haiti as collateral. Saavedra wrote that in late July, De Grasse printed notices and posted them throughout Cap-Français, offering bills redeemable at the Treasury of Paris at a profitable rate of interest in return for hard currency. Having experienced unacceptable delays in the past when lending to their court, the French citizens declined, even at interest rates offered at 25%.[17] De Grasse wrote to Team Carlos on August 3, asking for a loan of 500,000 silver pesos.[18] The Spanish and French routinely exchanged currency in the Caribbean, for expenses such as covering salaries for French troops and hospitalized Spanish soldiers in Cap Français.

Team Carlos planned for cash reserves as early as March 1781. Cagigal, José de Gálvez, Urriza, and Bernardo de Gálvez exchanged a flurry of missives during the summer of 1781. On June 19, 1781, Urriza, the Intendente of Havana, wrote to José de Gálvez that "following the Real Orden of March 17, [they] had prepared beforehand for the delivery of one million pesos to the French commanders."[19] Urriza advised that this same day they had received a sealed letter from the Viceroy of New Spain that the silver coins from the mines in Zacatecas and Chihuahuas were ready for shipment, confirmed in a report from Cagigal to José de Gálvez.[20] Transport vessels and warships were stationed to speedily sail from Vera Cruz with all or part of the needed money. As spring turned to summer, however, these sailing ships were stalled by the unpredictable winds in the Caribbean. After much discussion among Team Carlos,[21] they transferred 100,000 pesos from the taxes designated for Puerto Rico and Santo Domingo to the French Treasury in Cap-Français in July.[22] This money was still far below the amount needed. The Spanish Treasury remained alarmingly low on funds as August approached.[23]

In the Room Where It Happened

De Grasse again conferred with Saavedra, who reassured him that he was confident that silver was available in Havana. Saavedra departed for Havana on August 5 onboard the *Aigrette,* and hurriedly met with "the generals, then the intendant and the treasurer,"[24] expecting to readily arrange the funds. Saavedra soon learned that the transport ships carrying the silver had not arrived from Vera Cruz. Saavedra, Cagigal and Urriza hastily conferred as to how to solve the cash shortage.[25] The wealthy families had responded earlier in July to an appeal for funds from the Crown. As Saavedra noted, "The course of action that seemed preferable was to appeal once again to the local residents, emphasizing the urgency so that each person would voluntarily give what they could." Could the citizens of Havana respond a second time? If they were willing, and as loyal subjects, Saavedra anticipated that they would be, but were there enough silver pesos in the city to fund two armies to battle against the British Empire?

Saavedra kicked off the crowdfunding campaign, and "Word was immediately spread among the neighbors."[26] On August 16, he posted paper notices throughout the city that "anyone who wished to contribute towards aiding the French fleet with his money should send it immediately to the treasury."[27] Saavedra, Cagigal and Urriza waited expectantly at the Treasury rooms, close to the Plaza de Armas. Saavedra's request went viral. The citizens of Havana gathered barrels, chests and sacks of gleaming coins, piled them into waiting carriages and wagons and sent them through the streets to the Treasury. Within six hours, twenty-seven men and one woman raised the huge sum of 500,000 Spanish pesos, about $1 billion today, weighing over six tons.[28] Two French officers coordinated loading the funds on a French ship, which raced to join their fleet as De Grasse waited in the harbor.

Who were these men and women, their stories almost lost in history, who stepped forward to aid America in her moment of great need? An elite group of twenty-some families dominated Havana in the mid-18th century. Among older, Cuba-born families, fortunes were made in the sugar and tobacco plantations, merchant trade, and cattle ranching. Spanish civil servants appointed to Cuba advanced themselves by becoming landowners, leveraging the sugar industry, and marrying into the older family dynasties.[29] The Spanish Crown increased the titles of nobility that were doled out among the wealthy and influential, including those who lent money to the Crown. Titles of Marqués and Conde – Marquis and Count – often popped up in the roster of celebrity families. The lenders and donors for the emergency collection were prominent merchants, militia men, and plantation owners, anybody and everybody with money and influence. In the 18th century Spanish Empire, "Vecinos," as these elites were called, referred to property-owners with privileged social status. Today, "vecinos" translates simply as neighbors without the requirements of money or celebrity.* The Beverly Hills equivalent was Plaza Nueva, where the fabulous Cárdenas sisters and Alejandro O'Reilly lived in their elegant homes.[30]

---

*For a 21st century update of the term, see the Mexican telenovela series, *Vecinos,* about neighbors in a rented apartment building in Mexico City in 2005.

When the news of the successful fundraising reached Spain, the leadership understood the impact of their funding of Yorktown on the outcome of the American Revolutionary War. In the words of General José Solano y Bote, the King noted "with great pleasure the gains in the North, the effects of the aid with the triumphs are well known."[31] Carlos III quickly recognized the contributors in a Real Orden on September 5, 1781. The King acknowledged that the "Vecinos" had crowdfunded the silver pesos for the glory of His Majesty and their allies "en bravissimo tiempo."[32]

In his letter to José de Gálvez of February 1782, Cagigal notes that the King specifically mentioned the Marques de Cárdenas de Montehermosa and the Marques de Real Socorro in his acknowledgement.[33] The Cárdenas family was prominent in social and business circles and family names appear frequently in the militia rosters. The Volunteer Cavalry Regiment and the Volunteer Infantry Regiment list the Cárdenas among the prestige appointments.[34] The nine largest sugar plantations were owned by Ignacio de Cárdenas, the brother of the Marques de Cárdenas de Montehermoso. Nicolas Cárdenas, another brother, served as captain of cavalry.[35] The one woman on the list of donors is Doña Bárbara Santa Cruz,[36] the Marquesa de Cárdenas. Doña Bárbara was born in Havana in 1720, and married Augustin de Cárdenas y Castellon in 1746. Augustin was the first Marques de Cárdenas de Montehermoso and received his title in 1765. Augustin was also a Sublieutenant in the First Battalion of the Volunteer Infantry.[37] Doña Bárbara was widowed at that time; her husband had predeceased her in 1771.[38] Her son, Don Gabriel Maria de Cárdenas y Santa Cruz, testified to the family's assistance in December 1781 at a hearing at the Cabildo and City Council.[39]

The Marqués del Real Socorro, Antonio José Beitia y Castro, was born in Havana in 1751 and was the son of a Basque immigrant. His rich dad was a successful businessman and real estate mogul who was awarded the title of Marques de Real Socorro in 1770, qualified as "Hacendado Prestamista de La Corona", Landowner Lender to the Crown.[40] Antonio, the second Marques, inherited one of the fastest-growing estates in Cuba, and was a Lieutenant Colonel in the militia.[41] The Marques managed the expenses of the regiments for Vera Cruz and Campeche and corresponded with Cagigal and José de Gálvez during the urgent crowdsourcing, and he offered his cash on hand.[41]

The mention of a woman among the fundraisers may have inspired the meta myth of the diamond ladies, which continues to resurface online after 250 years.

According to these legends, either the French women in Cap Français offered De Grasse their diamonds or Francisco de Miranda persuaded the women of Havana to donate their diamonds. The Miranda story originated from one source: Miranda himself. At the time that he made this claim in the 1790s, Miranda had fought in the French Revolution and was in prison during the Reign of Terror. His loyalty to the French Revolution was challenged, as was the loyalty of many innocent people and he was imprisoned. Miranda and his lawyer argued at his trial that he supported the French during the American Revolution by organizing the collection of silver in Havana. This is certainly a story that a person might embellish while hearing the guillotine's blade rising and falling near their prison cell.[43]

As his admiring friend, Thomas Paine, described Miranda, "the whole of his life has been a life of adventure."[44] Miranda did lead an extraordinary life. The native Venezuelan fought in Pensacola during the American Revolution, in the French Revolution, in Morocco with the Spanish Army, and led the revolutions in Latin America against the Spanish in the early 19th century. In the age of long, difficult, and dangerous sea voyages, he globetrotted throughout the world. His ports of call included Russia, Greece, Turkey, Belgium, the Netherlands, Spain, and Denmark. A gregarious, intelligent and charming man, he was well-liked by many in his travels. He became a confidante of Catherine the Great in Russia.[45] During his two-year travel in the US after the war, he met and partied with many famous Americans, including Washington, Thomas Jefferson, Phillis Wheatley, Samuel Adams, Alexander Hamilton and Thomas Jefferson.[46] The story of Miranda leading the fundraising in Havana was one of the few adventures that Miranda did not live.

THE Naval Battle of the American Revolution

As Saavedra wrote in July, De Grasse's plan was "to [take] possession of the Chesapeake Bay ... in order to cut off the retreat and prevent the reinforcement of the army of Lord Cornwallis who was in that area." At the same time, Saavedra noted, "Washington, Rochambeau, and Lafayette, who had already agreed to the plan, would encircle him [Cornwallis] on all sides with their respective troops and totally destroy him or oblige him to surrender." The British had other plans. They had no intention of losing the British Army at Yorktown, and a fleet of warships was on the way to rescue and evacuate their troops.

De Grasse commanded French sailors and marines on French ships for the most decisive naval battle of the American Revolution. He sailed from France with an armada of warships and a convoy of French merchant vessels. He also ferried infantry reinforcements for Rochambeau. His command-ship, the *Ville de Paris*, was reportedly the largest warship on the 18th century seas. A gift of the "people of Paris" to the Americans, the *Ville de Paris* was an imposing vessel of 110 guns on three-gun decks. With his armada stationed in the Caribbean, De Grasse planned to take only twenty-four warships and leave five or six of the ships to protect French commerce. He suggested to Saavedra that four to six Spanish warships could join his fleet as they headed to the Chesapeake. Saavedra replied that "because Spain had not yet formally recognized the independence of the Anglo-Americans, there could perhaps be some political objection to taking a step that appeared to suppose this recognition."[47] To ensure that De Grasse had the number of warships that he needed, Saavedra requested additional Spanish warships to protect the French merchant ships in Santo Domingo. With this support, De Grasse was able to sail with all his warships to fight the British rescue fleet heading to Yorktown, at the entrance of the Chesapeake Bay.

The two men then worked out the military and naval resource allocation plan for the following nine months, known as the De Grasse-Saavedra Convention, while onboard the *Ville de Paris*. The first goal stated in this agreement was "To powerfully aid the Anglo-Americans by defeating the English fleet and dislodging them from the southern provinces." The next two goals were to drive the British out of the western Caribbean Sea and "to conquer Jamaica, the center of their wealth and power in that part of the world."[48] De Grasse planned to support the French and US Armies in Virginia during the late summer, and return to the Caribbean in November 1781.[49] Fully briefed of the gravity of the situation, and anxious to sail north, De Grasse updated the Spanish leadership in Cuba and Bernardo de Gálvez. Gálvez had the authority to request the French ships and troops for his military maneuvers. He released these ships and the French corps at Saint-Domingue that were designated for Spanish military aid.[50] On July 20, Saavedra, a Type-A planner, returned to the *Ville de Paris*. De Grasse insisted that Saavedra stay onboard for lunch, where De Grasse optimistically hosted "a grand banquet for ladies and officers." Saavedra returned to his office and spent the night manually writing six copies of the plan. De Grasse dispatched a frigate to speedily sail north to update Rochambeau that he was on his way with firepower and reinforcements. After receiving the funds, De Grasse began the voyage to the north. British spy ships prowled the waters of the western Caribbean. De Grasse feared that the British had discovered his mission. Realizing that he was critically pressed for time to reach Yorktown, the Admiral decided to take the war fleet with its precious cargo through the old Bahamian Channel, "the famous dreaded channel, where no French fleet had ever passed."[51]

The arrival of De Grasse at Chesapeake Bay on September 5, 1781, was harrowingly close for 18th century military maneuvers. On September 1, British Admiral Thomas Graves sailed from New York with a fleet of nineteen ships and sighted the Chesapeake Bay in the dawn light of September 5. De Grasse's men were also on the lookout in that early morning — for the French ships of Admiral Barras scheduled to join them. The French soon realized that the oncoming ships plowing across the seas were British and not their French reinforcements. The sailors hastily sprinkled the ships' decks with sand to soak the blood soon to splatter on the wooden decks in the morning battle. De Grasse entered this battle with his entire fleet, as arranged by Saavedra and Bernardo de Gálvez, and had at least five more warships than Graves. The battle raged through the day and into the night. Wood shattered, canvas sails ripped, cannon balls screamed through the air, and the cries of wounded and dying men rolled across the churning waves. Finally, both sides halted to appraise the damage, care for their wounded and briefly mourn their dead. Repairing their ships on September 6th, the fight resumed the next day. The fiercely dueling navies drifted south from the Chesapeake towards North Carolina.

By the 9th, De Grasse decided to pause the fighting and sail back towards the Chesapeake. To their relief, there to greet them in the waters of the Bay were the reinforcements of Barras. The French navy was now in full command of the entrance of the Chesapeake, enabling the siege and land battle of Yorktown to unfold. The most important naval battle of the American Revolutionary War had been fought and won by the French. A council of war was held by the British Navy. Admirals Graves and Hood concluded that given "the position of the enemy, the present condition of the British fleet ... and the impracticability of giving any effectual succour [aid] to General Earl Cornwallis ... it was resolved that British squadron ... should proceed with all dispatch to New York." The British ships withdrew, leaving Cornwallis and his army to defend themselves against the combined American and French forces. News of the defeat of the British Navy at the Chesapeake Bay reached a shocked George III in London. He confided to the Earl of Sandwich, "I nearly think the empire ruined ... this cruel event is too recent for me to be as yet able to say more."[52]

"Demonstrative gestures of the greatest joy"

Back in Virginia on that warm August day, Rochambeau may have squinted in the summer sunshine. Was he really seeing this? There in the distance the normally reserved George Washington was "waving his hat at me with demonstrative gestures of the greatest joy. When I rode up to him, he explained that he had just received a dispatch ... informing him that De Grasse had arrived."[53] De Grasse wrote to Rochambeau on August 30 from the *Ville de Paris*, anchored in the Chesapeake Bay. He noted his "great pleasure" in arriving at the Bay, and that he had departed on August 3rd from Santo Domingo. He explained that the fleet stopped in Havana for the silver and added that he was ferrying the 3,200 reinforcements that Rochambeau had requested.[54]

The French quickly disembarked with the barrels and chests of silver pesos. Washington, still without any cash for payroll or supplies, had pre-arranged with Robert Morris to borrow half of Rochambeau's silver coins. Morris continued to scrounge for coins to send to Yorktown. The currency and supplies raised in Paris by John Laurens reached Boston on August 25 but could not be shipped overland to Yorktown in time to prepare for the siege. The French Court believed that this latest request for funds from the Americans was excessive, and Laurens had difficulty raising the amounts that were required.[55] The American officers quickly distributed the coins from Havana directly to the soldiers, many of whom had never been paid in silver and had received only worthless Continental dollars — if they had been paid at all. Rochambeau was relieved as well. Both shipments faced the same obstacle: no viable route for overland transport to Yorktown. As Rochambeau wrote to Aranda on October 24, 1781, "the residents of Havana remitted in 24 hours to Monsieur De Grasse, 1,200,000 [livres] that were of the greatest necessity to me, my [funds] having arrived in Boston when overland transport has not yet enabled" the currency to reach him.[56]

De Grasse strode off the Ville de Paris to the waiting crowd of American and French officers. In true French fashion, he embraced Washington – who was finally meeting someone taller than himself – and kissed him on both cheeks, greeting him as *mon petit cher General*, which translates as "my dear little General."[57] (French people do these things.) Washington's staff shook with suppressed laughter — nooo one referred to the austere Washington as "cher" or "petit." The remainder of the coins were managed by the harried French Commissary, Claude Blanchard. Blanchard wrote that later that night, the floor of the room housing the silver collapsed under the weight of the coins, breaking apart with a tremendous noise and sending both the coins and his assistant tumbling into the basement below.[58] (The assistant wasn't hurt.)

News of the emergency collection in Havana reached British General Clinton, who understood that this fresh infusion of funds reanimated the exhausted American rebels. Clinton wrote in his memoirs, "as the hard money procured from the Havana (amounting in a very short time, as was reported to me, to half a million dollars) had encouraged the farmers back to market with their produce and was beginning to give a life and figure to all their measures, I had proposed to the Admiral a plan for shutting up that port [Philadelphia] and attempting such a blow against the place itself as might disperse the Congress, ruin public credit, and totally overset their schemes and preparations for the campaign."[59] While the British Navy had raced to rescue Cornwallis at Yorktown, Clinton believed that the British would soon achieve "such a blow" to end the Revolution.

From Philadelphia, Rendón monitored the events and dispatched reports to Team Carlos in Havana. Horses raced to Philadelphia to bring news of the latest troop movements and naval battles, which were difficult to ascertain with limited communication and observation technologies. Rendón's correspondence preserves a surprisingly timely account of the unfolding battle at Yorktown as confusion and uncertainty rolled through the countryside. The US Army and Congress updated him frequently as they confirmed their news reports. Rendón wrote to Cagigal on September 15, 1781, that the "English in New York are in great commotion" and that "the Americans embarked at Head of Elk on September 7 to go down into Chesapeake Bay and the French were to follow them."[60] A Congressman from Virginia messaged him that De Grasse and Barras won the naval battle at the Chesapeake and blockaded Cornwallis at Yorktown. Rendón hurried to send the news to Cagigal as a ship to Havana was departing.[61]

With the supplies and payroll in place, the French and American armies began the challenging Siege of Yorktown on September 28, 1781. The armies totaled 18,000 men: 8,000 US Army and militias, and the 10,000 French soldiers, including De Grasse's 3,200 marines. The Yorktown Siege was fought in classic European style, similar to the Siege of Pensacola six months earlier. Highly experienced French engineers managed the artillery engineering and trench placement. The best and brightest of US Army leadership was on the field, including Hamilton, Von Steuben, Benjamin Lincoln, Knox, and Lafayette. The 1st Rhode Island Regiment of enslaved African Americans, who were promised their freedom for their service, fought under the command of Hamilton. Rendón reported that Lafayette's troops were reinforced by Virginia militia men: "when they saw those fellow citizens surrounded by dangers, came running in coveys, every man armed with his carbine, to enlist under the banner of Lafayette."[62]

On October 7, Rendón sent Bernardo de Gálvez a remarkably detailed account of the unfolding siege, "so as to paint the most complete picture." Writing of Washington's deceptive tactics to lure Clinton into thinking that the US Army would attack New York, Rendón noted that Washington, "deceived the enemy by the number of all kinds of preparations". Once the ruse was in place, "the combined [US and French] army marched rapidly to the northern end of the Chesapeake Bay." According to Washington and Rochambeau's plan, as Rendón noted, "Certainly the way in which Lord Cornwallis was so completely surprised cannot be exaggerated ... he found himself completely surrounded by land and by sea."[63]

The fighting and artillery barrages continued relentlessly through the first two weeks of October. The sounds of shovels and picks clanged as the troops dug trenches and pushed artillery closer and closer to the British stronghold. Two important redoubts were captured, with a French officer and Hamilton leading the parallel assaults. In a desperate move on October 16, Cornwallis attempted to evacuate his men across the York River. Sudden gusts of violent wind and rain slashed through the boats and the river roiled with waves. The men frantically tried to steer the boats, but Cornwallis had to abandon the evacuation. As the morning sunlight crept over the battlefield on October 17, a drummer and a British officer waving a white flag of truce approached the French and American lines. In a stunning turn of events, Cornwallis surrendered at Yorktown, the last major battle of the Revolutionary War.

Feliz Navidad, Próspero año y Felicidad

From his home office in Philadelphia, Rendón excitedly wrote to Cagigal that a special courier arrived at 2:00 AM on October 22 with a letter from De Grasse to Congress, "reporting the agreeable news that on the 17th Lord Cornwallis with his whole army had been taken prisoner."[64] With the surrender concluded, the tension that had gripped Philadelphia for months finally lifted, and the celebrations began. George and Martha Washington returned to the city in November 1781. Philadelphia was grappling with a housing shortage. In addition to the standard influx of people for Congress and the military, Rendón reported that two hundred families evacuated to the city from South Carolina.[65] Rendón offered the Washingtons his home for the holiday and was pleased that they accepted his offer over the other distinguished invitations that the couple received.

The Washingtons moved in for Christmas and Rendón wrote that, "General Washington did me the honor of living in my home all the time that he spent in the city"[66] during that winter. Rendón hosted a dinner party for the Washingtons, inviting Knox and Howe and their wives, members of Congress, Robert Morris, and several more guests.[67] Rendón's pantry was stocked for the holidays with chocolate, guava jellies, wines, fresh tropical fruit, and Cuban cigars. Let's imagine the stressed-out General Washington and Rendón's guests enjoying a warm fire with dessert chocolate and smoking aromatic cigars. Perhaps some men and women silently dared to think that Yorktown might be their last major battle?

Chapter 13

The Rocky Road to Peace

The Battle of Yorktown was the last major battle of the Revolutionary War — but the Americans of 1781 did not know this. George III viewed the defeat as "very unfortunate" and vowed to continue fighting.[1] Clinton knew that he could deploy over 40,000 troops for another campaign: 15,000 from his stronghold in New York, another 9,000 in South Carolina and Georgia, and thousands more in the Caribbean that he could move north to America.[2] Clinton was certain of his intelligence that Yorktown was the last campaign in which the nearly bankrupt French would assist the Americans. Washington and his leadership had only small numbers of soldiers, silver pesos, and supplies. Why did the British curtail their military campaigns when so many factors were in their favor?

The short answer is that the Spanish, French, Dutch and Indians kept the British very busy during the two-year period between Yorktown in 1781 and the peace treaty signed in September 1783. Once again, Britain was compelled to prioritize other theaters of war across distant continents. Manpower and firepower were drawn away from the American Revolution, a conflict that had grown increasingly unpopular in England. In the war's closing years, Britain commanded nearly 100,000 men across its empire, but only three in ten of these men were deployed in America.[3] The formidable British Empire found itself dangerously overstretched. King George remained firmly committed to his imperial ambitions to establish an empire on which the sun never set,* and the British continued to battle the Spanish, French, Indians, and Dutch.

---

* By the 19th century, the British had colonized or stolen – depending on your point of view – so much land around the globe that that there was always daylight in at least one of "their" territories.

The Spanish persisted in the brutal jungle warfare that ended with their victory in Honduras in 1782.[4] The combined Spanish and French navies challenged the British at Gibraltar. In the Caribbean, the Spanish invaded the British Bahamas and supported the French in their massive joint campaign to retake Jamaica. The French and British navies fought the Battle of Cuddalore in 1783, known as the last Battle of the American Revolutionary War. No, that's not a typo, Cuddalore, India, is recognized as the final battle between the French and the British. Hyder Ali was succeeded in 1782 by his son, Tipu Sultan, the "Tiger of India," who continued the fierce fight for Indian independence until his death on the battlefield in 1799. The British had declared war against the Dutch in 1780, and fighting continued through 1784. The British blockaded Dutch ports and fought to take Dutch colonial possessions in the Caribbean and West Africa.

"Nothing could be more hurtful"

Meanwhile, in America, the British intensified their naval blockade. In May 1782 Rendón wrote to Havana that the British military "is not inclined to continue the war against the United States by the same methods used heretofore."[5] Instead, the British "new plan" that arrived with General Carleton escalated the blockade of American ports with two heavily armed warships and fourteen armed privateer frigates. The ships were "scattered around all the ports of the continent, so that no ships ...can safely enter into or out of them," he wrote.[6] The blockade was the most severe of the entire war and continued through 1783.[7] The prices of imported goods increased to even more astronomical levels. Without earning silver from Havana and international ports, merchants and laborers were unable to pay taxes. Prominent businessmen wrote despairingly about "the amazing number of repeated losses that we have sustained"[8] and that mail to Europe was severed as, "Our ports have been totally shut up." Rendón was "certain that nothing could be more hurtful to these states than that method of waging war against them."[9]

The Spanish and Cubans intervened to assist the blockaded Americans. Rendón wrote to José de Gálvez that "many merchants have elected to carry on their trade by exporting flour by way of the Ohio and Mississippi Rivers and selling it in Nueva Orleáns." The American merchants requested that Rendón communicate the desperation of their situation to Team Carlos. "They have asked me to write letters to the Governor of Nueva Orleáns to explain the objective of their expedition," Rendón wrote to Havana.[10] With Spanish approval, Americans throughout the colonies, including Maryland and Virginia on the Atlantic coast, increased their shipments on the Ohio and Mississippi Rivers and trans-shipped the goods through Nueva Orleáns to Havana. There, they were paid in desperately needed silver and gold.[11] Rendón continued his support of the trade in wheat flour and other commodities. The number of American ships in the flour trade increased from 31 in 1780 to over 200 in 1782. Oliver Pollock moved from Nueva Orleáns to Havana in 1782, working officially as an envoy from Congress to support and administer this commerce.[12] After the British seizure of the Dutch port of St. Eustatius in early 1781, Havana became Philadelphia's main trading partner. The Dutch sold tons of weapons to the Americans through the port of St. Eustatius throughout the war, much to the annoyance of the British. In defiance of the heightened blockade, the Spanish and Cubans continued to outmaneuver the British blockade and ship after ship docked at the wharfs in Philadelphia.[13]

The Man Who would Not be King

Despite all the assistance from the Spanish and French, America's financial situation remained dire. A proposed plan to give US Army veterans a pension floundered, and it was clear that Congress could not raise the cash for a pension or back pay owed to the men for their active-duty service. The veterans were also frustrated with Congress's failures to deliver basic needs of clothing and shoes. In January 1783, even the stoic, serious Washington slipped into sharp sarcasm, "The Army, as usual, are without pay; and a great part of the Soldiery without Shirts." He continued, "Congress must have concluded that the army had made a habit of encountering distresses and difficulties and living without money, that it would be impolitic and injurious to introduce other customs into it."

The soldiers and officer corps decided that it was time to act. As one young officer in the Newburgh encampment wrote in May 1782, the solution was apparent: dissolve the Continental Congress and crown George Washington as the King of the United States. Petitions circulated among the soldiers that made veiled threats if Congress did not honor their pensions. High-ranking generals and officers raised the prospect of a military takeover of the government. Washington categorically refused the plan. "Banish these thoughts from your Mind," he admonished. The dissident officers planned a meeting for March 11, which Washington countermanded, stating that only he could order a meeting of all officers. He scheduled a session for March 16, 1783 and his tone that day was conciliatory and powerfully effective. As he walked slowly towards the podium to address the 500 angry men, he reached into his pocket for his prepared speech and took out his spectacles. No one had seen the General wearing spectacles before. He adjusted the glasses and gazed out at the men. "Gentlemen," he said, "you will permit me to put on my spectacles, for I have not only grown gray, but almost blind in the service of my country." The raging room was silent. Fierce dissidents were calmed, and some men openly wept. The shouts for a military coup were stilled — and the fledgling republic was saved.[14]

Congress was not as fortunate a few months later. In June 1783, soldiers lost patience when plans to finance their salaries and pensions with import duties collapsed due to lack of funds. Congress was out of cash and out of silver pesos. The soldiers of the Philadelphia Line, who mutinied in 1781, sent another petition to Congress in threatening language, demanding their money. For two days, eighty armed soldiers marched from Lancaster to Philadelphia to confront Congress. They seized several arsenals of weapons and rumors spread that the men might raid the local bank. By then, the rebellious soldiers numbered over 400. As the politicians locked themselves in the State House, soldiers surrounded the building, shouting and waving their muskets and bayonets in the air. Twenty-eight-year-old Alexander Hamilton was sent to defuse the situation. Unable to secure help from the Pennsylvania state militia, Hamilton informed the frightened Congressmen that they should flee Philadelphia. Unsurprisingly, Congress agreed, and the politicians hastily escaped to Princeton, New Jersey.[15]

The Book of Negroes

Judith Jackson was desperate and anguished. Where was her daughter? How could she rescue her? She ran through the chaotic refugee settlement in New York City, frantically asking for help. Jackson's war years were marked by tumult and danger, and she thought that finally, she and her daughter were safe. In 1775, when Dunmore issued his freedom proclamation, the enslaved Jackson fled to the British carrying her two-year-old daughter. She worked for the British Army as a laundress, traveling with them from Virginia to the battlefields in South Carolina. Jackson returned to New York with the British Army and expected to sail to Canada in the autumn of 1783.[16]

Clinton remained in New York after the defeat at Yorktown, where African Americans were protected. Carleton arrived in May 1782, and Clinton departed shortly afterwards. Carleton, who didn't think that American independence was a foregone conclusion,[17] entered a tumultuous situation with almost impossible demands to negotiate. American Loyalists clamored to restart the military campaigns against the Patriots and demanded the return of the property that had been confiscated by the rebels, a condition that the Patriots flatly refused. Many African Americans, including Jackson, had devoted years of service to the British Army, staking their lives on a promised freedom that now glimmered before them. Both the Loyalists and the African Americans wanted to evacuate from the colonies as quickly as possible. More troubling, the freedom-loving Patriots demanded the return of their formerly enslaved people, terrifying African Americans. As Boston King reported, "The dreadful rumour filled us with inexpressible anguish and terror, especially when we saw our old masters coming from Virginia, North Carolina and other parts and seizing upon slaves in the streets of New York, or even dragging them out of their beds."

Carleton and Washington met in May 1783, to negotiate the terms of the settlement. Carleton coolly informed Washington that British ships were already departing with African Americans. Carleton persisted in his aristocratic British manner stating that regardless of the terms of the draft treaty, "no Interpretation could be put on the Articles inconsistent with prior Engagements binding the National Honour which must be kept with all colours."[18] Washington kept his composure while an uproar broke out in the room, and the Patriots accused the British of breaking their agreements. Carleton held his ground. As part of his work to manage the evacuation, he organized "The Book of Negroes," which listed the names of 2,831 men, women and children granted freedom for helping the British cause.

One of the "old masters" arriving from Virginia was a slave trader with a bill of sale that claimed Jackson and her daughter. Jackson was shocked, and petitioned

Carleton directly in September 1783. She detailed her service to the British, and that the Virginia enslaver "wanted to steal me back to Virginia" and "took all my Cloaths which his Majesty gave me ... and stole my Child from me and Sent it to Virginia." Although the enslaver was a Loyalist and not a Patriot, Carleton sided with Jackson. He honored her place in The Book of Negroes. Two versions of what happened next are recorded in historical accounts: one is that the slaver trader did kidnap Jackson's daughter.[19] The second version, taken directly from The Book of Negroes, is that the British rescued Jackson and her daughter and they departed for Nova Scotia onboard a British ship* – aptly named *Danger* – and sailed into as much of a happy ending as the harsh 18th century could offer African American women.[20]

"The pile of rocks called Gibraltar"

The Spanish were still determined to win back Gibraltar from the British, which they lost in 1704, and mounted a campaign at a staggering cost. Gibraltar, a small rocky peninsula on the southernmost tip of Spain, was a strategic location that dominated sea routes between the Mediterranean and the Atlantic. With 2.6 square miles of land, Floridablanca grumbled that the "pile of rocks called Gibraltar" was an unworthy cause for one of the greatest single campaigns of the war.[21] The Spanish also wanted to retake the smaller island of Menorca, located about 50 miles from the Spanish mainland. While the island is now a beloved tourist destination, it was then hotly contested, with the Dutch, British, Spanish and French grabbing ownership from each other in waves of invasions and peace treaties. In another outcome of the Seven Years' War, the British controlled Menorca and turned it into a strategic naval post and a base for privateer raids. In 1781, Floridablanca and Vergennes finalized the agreement for a joint attack on Menorca, launching a massive fleet with 58 ships carrying 8,000 troops.[22]

---

*As I'm sure you guessed, dear Reader, I envision the happy ending. Please check the online database The Book of Negroes: African Americans in Exile After the American Revolution. For a beautiful dramatization of The Book of Negroes, please view this series on streaming services.

Although 2,000 British and Hessian soldiers were stationed in the island's fortress of San Felipe, the British did not know the attack was coming, and with their resources stretched from Central America to India, could not send reinforcements in time. The Spanish and French fleets encircled the island, choking the flow of food and provisions on which the British garrison depended. In early January 1782, the Spanish and French troops landed and fought their way to San Felipe,[23] bombarding the fortress for five months as British casualties climbed. The British garrison, starved, weakened and wounded, finally collapsed in early February, waving a white flag over the damaged stone walls. The Spanish and French redeployed their troops and navies and turned to their next target, Gibraltar.

The Spanish started their siege of Gibraltar in 1779 and launched the final assault in 1782. Their goal was to prevent the British from resupplying their 5,000 troops and support personnel in Gibraltar and force a surrender. In this assault, the Spanish and French navies surrounded Gibraltar with 35,000 troops and warships. The bombardment began, and the combined navies fired 40,000 artillery rounds at the British fortifications — approximately one round for every second of the fight.[24] The British had to respond and resupply their troops. In September, British Admiral Howe, who was transferred from duty in America, sailed from England with 34 ships of the line and an additional 31 transport ships carrying food, military supplies and other needed provisions to the British garrison of 5,000 soldiers. A violent storm scattered the Spanish and French ships, and Howe was able to deliver provisions to their garrison. After the British unloaded the relief provisions, Howe departed, and Spanish Admiral Córdova began a chase on the seas. With copper sheathing, the British had the advantage and outdistanced the Spanish ships. As the distance between the fleets lengthened, the Spanish had to admit defeat. The longest siege the British endured during the war finally ended.[25] While the Spanish failed to retake Gibraltar, they succeeded in redirecting the British to battlefront far from America.[26]

It's Better in The Bahamas

Apparently, Spain and Britain agreed that "It's better in The Bahamas," and both countries wanted real estate on the thousands of islands, keys, and inlets scattered like jewels in the Atlantic Ocean north of Cuba. Both countries, as usual, blithely dismissed the native Lucayan people who already claimed the islands as their home. The Bahamas were in the disinterested hands of the Spanish after Columbus landed in 1492, briefly captured by the Patriots in 1775, and were back in the hands of the British.

As Carlos III and his ministers prepared for their assault on San Augustin, Florida, they determined that capturing the Bahamas should be the first step in their campaign.[27] Cagigal organized the warships and transport ships for the 300-mile journey from Havana. With much of the Spanish Navy already deployed for battle in Jamaica and internal political differences as to the allocation of naval resources, Cagigal searched for resources to escort his fleet to the Bahamas.[28] Alexander Gillon arrived in Havana early January 1782 with the *South Carolina* and six smaller warships. Cagigal met with him to discuss leasing his warship as an armed escort for the Spanish Army's transport ships. The two men made an informal agreement under which the Spanish would rent the American vessels until eight days after the surrender, in addition to a specified bonus for the actual conquest.[29] Cagigal boarded the *South Carolina* in late April, leading a fleet of eight American warships and 57 Spanish and American transport ships. Miranda, Cagigial's aide-de-camp, was among the crew. Miranda was fluent in English and was the designated translator between Gillon and Cagigal. The men began the adventure of the only joint military expedition of Americans, Spanish, and Cubans during the war. From the Spanish point of view, their decision to include Gillon in the expedition almost lost the campaign.[30]

The target was Nassau, where the British fleet and fortifications were located. The success of the campaign depended on surprising the British so they couldn't send for reinforcements from South Carolina, which was still under British occupation. Weather conditions during the first days of the campaign slowed the fleet, and the expedition entered the New Providence Channel on May 2. On May 6, the fleet reached Nassau, and Cagigal sent Miranda to negotiate with the British. At this very strategic hour, Gillon decided to completely disrupt the campaign by demanding immediate payment of 70,000 pesos from the Spanish for expenditures that he had incurred in preparing the ship plus a 300,000-peso insurance policy for the *South Carolina*. Gillon threatened that if Cagigal did not pay up immediately he would not move his ships, blocking the Nassau port for the rest of the squadron, and effectively sabotage the mission that he had agreed to.

While the altercations began between Gillon and Cagigal, the ever-adventurous Miranda sailed to the British garrison. Miranda told the commanding lieutenant that the British had twelve hours to surrender, or the Spanish would start firing. The lieutenant managed to send a small fast ship to South Carolina to request reinforcements. Hours passed. With many of his men ill and no reinforcements on the way, the lieutenant agreed to a surrender.[31] The first, only, and last joint military expedition between the Spanish and Americans concluded, although disputes over the terms of the agreement and payments lasted for years. Rendón reported from Philadelphia that news of the victory, "had caused widespread rejoicing among the people here, because they know the importance of that conquest." British privateers were based in the Bahamas and were within striking distance of American merchant ships traveling to Havana and other global ports, posing a "grave danger" to the Americans. Rendón added that the British were "now blockading the Delaware River with three or four war frigates and several privateers."[32]

"The Standing Toast of My Table"

On the other side of the globe, the British were challenged by an alliance of two powerful kingdoms, the Mysore and the Maratha. These military alliances between the kingdoms were, at best, complicated, with shifting alliances and political strategies, often following the adage of the enemy of my enemy is my friend. The Maratha initially sided with the British while the Mysore fought against the British in a lengthy series of wars to determine who would rule India. The French East India Company, also determined to establish their commercial presence in India, allied with the Mysore against the British East India Company in 1778. By the late 1770s both Indian kingdoms had united to fight against the British.[33]

Hyder Ali, also creatively spelled as Hyder Ally by the Americans, was one of the first Indian leaders to fully comprehend the impact of British ambitions to his homeland.[34] Ali was an astute politician as well as a brilliant military leader, and claimed descent from the Prophet Mohammed.[35] As a Muslim ruler with

Hindu subjects, he wisely continued the diversity and inclusion* policies of the Mughal rulers in India. He based his government on respect for Hindu deities and the leading Brahman caste, with elaborate coins that placed the figures of Siva, Parvati and Vishnu near his signature. Ali and his son continued the established system of grants and gifts to Hindu institutions.[36] In their portraits, both men are elegantly attired in elaborate turbans and hold intricately carved swords and bejeweled daggers.

The Second Mysore War raged from 1780 through 1784, with fortuitous timing for the Americans. In contrast to the perennially undersupplied Continental Army that the British fought on the American battlefields, the Mysore were a powerful and well-supplied military force. Ali started his campaign in July 1780, thundering into the Carnatic on India's southeastern coast with an army of over 100,000 men. Many soldiers were cavalry troops on horseback, with elephants in the rear guard. In the words of one contemporary Mughal historian, Ali's army "covered the plains like waves of an angry sea, with a trail of artillery that had no end."[37] The abundant artillery and cannons included Tipu's feared rockets, which he had innovatively fitted with iron tubes to increase their range and accuracy.[38] The Mysore rulers' immediate goal was to isolate the British in their stronghold at Madras (now Chennai). Ali and Tipu defeated the British East India Company in September at the Battle of Pollilur, which was the worst defeat in India in the 18th century that the British suffered. The artillery cannonade from the skilled Indian troops was devastating. As a British soldier wrote, "Our fate was for above an hour to be exposed to the hottest cannonade that ever was known in India" and that the soldiers were "mowed down by the scores."[39]

The US leadership understood the importance of these two Muslim leaders in drawing British forces from the American battlefields. Hyder Ali and Tipu Sultan were discussed in letters by American leaders and in media reports. These Indian leaders were well aware of the American Revolution, and Tipu Sultan reportedly endorsed the Declaration of Independence.[40] The Americans across the ocean eagerly awaited news of the Mysore rulers' victories, cheering on the men that they viewed as allies and a force that diverted the British military power from them.

---

*These rulers were committed to diversity and inclusion (D&I). Equity? Not so much, given that they were 18th century Sultans. But two out of three was excellent for their times.

Throughout the years of the Revolutionary War, the demands for East India Company troops to fight in India decreased the number of Company troops that could be sent to the US.[41] "Hyder Ally is the standing toast of my table," wrote Benjamin Rush, a signer of the Declaration of Independence and Surgeon General of the Continental Army. "The enemies of Britain anywhere and everywhere should be the friends of every American."[42] Local news outlets and social media reported on Ali's progress against the British. *The Maryland Gazette* wrote that "our friend Hyder Ali, was driving the British out of Bengal into the Indian Ocean.'"[43] The Pennsylvania state government purchased a merchant vessel, transformed it into a warship armed with sixteen cannons, and renamed it the *Hyder-Ally*. To recruit sailors and marines for the new warship, the Americans composed a rap song in Ali's honor with the lines, "From an Eastern Prince she takes her name/ Who, smit with freedom's sacred flame/ Usurping Britons brought to shame/ His country's wrongs avenging."[44]

In 1781, the British, French, and Mysore battled for Cuddalore, a port city in southeast India on the Bay of Bengal. Hyder Ali worked to align his cavalry and land troops with the French.[45] After the death of Hyder Ali, the British attempted to retake Cuddalore. The French, still allied with the Mysore, fought the British in June 1783. The French Navy prevailed, and the British were forced to withdraw their supply fleets. The news of the Peace Treaty in Paris reached the two warring sides in late June. Cuddalore was the last fight between the British and the French in the Revolutionary War.

The Mysore pressed on with their campaign against the British, winning victory after victory until the British surrendered their garrison at Mangalore in 1784. Tipu Sultan maintained his alliance with the French, sending delegations to their court. Jefferson noted in 1788, "The Ambassador from Tippoo-Saïb arrived ... where a magnificent reception was prepared for [him]."[46] The Mysore challenged the British again in 1790 and continued the fight through 1799. With peace treaties signed with the Spanish, French, Dutch, and Americans, the British military and the East India Company hurled their combined forces against the Mysore in a determined campaign to finally conquer India. In May 1799, the "Tiger of India" roared on the battlefield for the last time at Seringapatam, where Tipu Sultan was killed.[47] Reportedly, a leading British General celebrated his death, saying, "Now, India is ours." That was the British point of view, of course;

India's point of view was far more complex and another story unfolded in the next centuries.

The Unpeaceful Peace Negotiations

The peace negotiations in Paris were anything but peaceful, marked by treacherous betrayals, backstabbing side deals, and broken agreements. The British worked to undermine Spain and France by signing a separate peace treaty with the Americans, convincing them to betray the two countries without whose aid they would have lost the Revolutionary War. The key British diplomat in Paris was William Petty Fitzmaurice, the Earl of Shelburne, who rose to the office of Prime Minister in 1782. Shelburne negotiated directly with Benjamin Franklin, against the wishes of the French.

Both men agreed that a separate peace would force Spain and France into more reasonable terms for the British. Obviously, Franklin did not let the French know about this side deal with the British — despite the difficult state of their own finances, France continued to provide economic support to the Americans.[48] John Jay pushed the treachery even further. Without Franklin's approval, he sent word to Shelburne that the Americans were willing to abandon the French alliance.[49] Jay also proposed a back-stabbing deal to the British to undermine the Spanish. As Adams wrote in his journal, Jay urged British diplomats to send their troops from New York to Florida to attack the Spanish.[49]

Jay's goal was to persuade the British to retake Florida from Spain.[51] Since Franklin and Jay could not guarantee safe passage for the British troops from New York to Florida, the British declined. When Britain did sign the peace agreement with Spain, all of Florida was assigned to Spain, with no discussion on Florida's northern boundaries. This side arrangement contradicted Britain's direct agreement with the US and, in a painful payback for his meddling, Jay was later assigned the difficult negotiations between Spain and the US over the Florida borders.[52]

Shelburne worked to seed the disputes over the navigation rights of the Mississippi and Florida boundaries, which would later prove problematic for relations between the US and Spain.[53] The Spanish viewed the lower Mississippi River as part of their empire, and were not willing to relinquish control or offer free rights of navigation to the Americans. From the Spanish point of view, the Mississippi and the port of Nueva Orleáns were part of their empire in North America that had existed since the 1500s. Spain controlled both banks of the lower Mississippi River and established Fort Saint Joseph in the north on the shores of Lake Michigan.[54] The Spanish were no more willing to give free navigation rights to the Americans than the Americans were willing to give free navigation rights to the Ohio River that flowed eastward from Illinois to Pennsylvania.

Rendón and the Spanish were aware of some of the treachery, as Arthur Lee continued to exasperate Spanish diplomats. "Mr. Arthur Lee, the present head of that party and a member of Congress, an extremely turbulent and dangerous man, was the first to become suspicious of the French in the negotiations of 1777 and 1778," Rendón wrote to Team Carlos in Havana. "Those same men now want to tie themselves very tightly to Great Britain. It is Arthur Lee who has always opposed all the wise measures which Congress has considered adopting."[55]

In Madrid, William Carmichael continued to monitor the peace negotiations, and he received a confidential copy in French of the preliminary treaty drafted between the US and the British in November 1782. The treaty was not favorable to Spain and Carmichael understood the frustration of the Spanish court.[56] Lafayette joined Carmichael for a week in Spain, to use his star power to push along a better deal between America and Spain and lobbied for the formal recognition of the independence of the US.[57]

The bickering and backstabbing ended on September 3, 1783, when Britain signed the Treaties of Versailles with Spain and France, and the Peace of Paris treaty with the US. Spain had reason to celebrate; Carlos III had recaptured Menorca and Florida and pushed the British out of most of Central America.[58] Fireworks lit the night sky in Madrid's Parque del Buen Retiro. But Spain failed to recapture Gibraltar, which is still under British control.

The negotiations over the navigation rights on the Mississippi River between Spain and the US continued after the peace treaties were signed. Carlos III assigned his best man for the job, Diego de Gardoqui. In May 1782, Gardoqui arrived in New York City, then the capital of the US. Gardoqui viewed life in the Big Apple as a big snoozer. He wrote to a fellow diplomat that, "As you know, this country produces only food, and everything else comes to us from Europe. As for the rest, there is still no news, just the toasts and teas … but with an infinite difference in the entertainments and other matters in that country, so that my life is reduced to getting along with people as best I can, and to my books and papers."[59] His home was near Jay's, who was then the Secretary for Foreign Affairs. The ever-diplomatic Gardoqui managed to create a viable working relationship with Jay during the strained negotiations over the Mississippi River. As Gardoqui wrote in a private letter to Floridablanca in August 1785, "Minister Jay and his house have made a good impression on me. I have just been with him in high good humour; He told me that he must scold me a great deal, to which I replied that I would do no less, but that for every argument, he must take a meal with me at this the King's house, to which we have both agreed."[60] The negotiations continued past Gardoqui's diplomatic assignment, finally concluding with the Treaty of San Lorenzo in 1795 that resolved territorial disputes and navigation rights.

Everybody Loves A Parade!

Gardoqui knew how to throw a party, and for George Washington's Inauguration as President on April 30, 1789, he planned a rock star celebration. Craftsmen, carpenters, and artists worked on his large, elegant house in Hanover Square, near today's Battery Park.[61] The workers installed lanterns, flowerpots, and arches with foliage. They created two magnificent gardens adorned with statues painted in an imitation of marble that represented the virtues of Spain. On the canopy constructed over the gardens, artists placed thirteen stars, representing the US colonies. The sunlight shone through the overhead canopy, glowing on the statue of Fame and the coat of arms of two Spanish provinces. The crowning touch at the doors were Spanish and American flags, enlaced with the motto, "Natural Union."[62] Politicians, businessmen, celebrities and influencers flocked to the party and refreshments, which, given Gardoqui's elegant tastes, probably included chocolate, tropical fruits, wines, and Cuban cigars.

At sunrise on April 30, a military salute was fired from Fort St. George, and crowds gathered at Washington's home at Franklin House. Church bells rang throughout the city for thirty minutes. At noon, crowds moved to Federal Hall, newly reconstructed as the seat of the US government, now a national monument. The parade began when a military escort of 500 men arrived at Franklin House at 12:30 PM to escort Washington to the Hall.[63] Washington rode in a stagecoach drawn by four horses with his large entourage that included

Congressmen and military leaders. During the last steps of the parade, Gardoqui and the Comte de Moustier, the French representative, walked directly behind George Washington.[64] The dignitaries briefly met in the Senate chamber, where Gardoqui and Moustier were seated in the very first set of rows directly next to the senators and cabinet officials. At 2 PM, Washington was escorted to the outer balcony in front of the Senate chamber, overlooking Broad Street, and the first President of the United States was sworn into office. The crowds of citizens burst into thunderous applause. Shouts of "Long Live George Washington, the President of the United States!" reverberated through the city streets. Later that evening, the sky was lit with fireworks, and the dramatic lantern displays that Gardoqui had carefully prepared. The newly built *Galveztown* joined the celebrations. The original ship that had played a pivotal role in Pensacola was retired, and Bernardo de Gálvez ordered a new ship built in New York shortly before his death in Mexico City.[65] Gardoqui wrote that, "the [ship captain] saluted [Washington] with fifteen cannon-shots, five vivas for the king, and other honors — the first shot being so powerful in its detonation that it surprised the immense pageant by land and sea, meriting not only the general applause and hand-clapping of all."[66]

Gardoqui was seated near Washington for the Inauguration Ceremony. He must have reminisced about the long, long road that he and his country had traveled for the American Revolution, beginning in 1775 with smuggling weapons to the desperate Patriots in Massachusetts. He remembered the days and nights spent managing the collections of military hardware, uniforms, and blankets throughout the war. The continuous worry as to whether the critical supplies would reach America or be stopped and seized in the relentless blockade by the British Navy. The weeks spent waiting for news of victory or defeat in the many battles between the Spanish and the British, in Florida, Alabama, Missouri, Honduras, Menorca, Gibraltar and the Bahamas. The long journey was fraught with difficulties and challenges, but Gardoqui had persevered for fourteen years. Now, here at the first Presidential Inauguration, Gardoqui celebrated the victory of the American Revolutionary War and the new nation of the United States of America that the Spanish and Latin Americans had helped to create.

Bonus Feature: Money, Money, Money
Currency Units in the American Revolutionary War era
8 silver reales or pieces of eight or bits = 1 silver peso
1 Continental paper dollar when issued in 1775 = 1 silver peso
5 to 5.5 French livres tornesas or tournois = 1 silver peso
1 British pound sterling = 3.354 dollars
1 US silver dollar minted in 1794 = 1 silver peso

Source:

Bethell, Leslie, Ed., The Cambridge History of Latin America, Volume 1. Cambridge: Cambridge University Press, 1984

Spanish Peso to US Dollar Values based on Economy Cost Comparator

In his book, *Brothers at Arms: American Independence and the Men of France and Spain who Saved It,* Professor Larrie Ferreiro uses the rates of one silver Spanish peso in 1775 to US $2,083 in 2010 as the Economy Cost Comparator. I've used this ratio as the basis to approximate the value of the Spanish pesos during the Revolutionary War in today's dollars.

Professor Ferreiro provides a detailed and compelling analysis on the use of the Economy Cost Comparator based on the national gross domestic product (GDP) deflator instead of the Consumer Price Index (CPI). His calculations use 1775 as the basis year. All modern prices are keyed to the year 2010 and converted to US dollars using purchasing power parity rates.

Source: *Brothers at Arms: American Independence and the Men of France and Spain who Saved It,* Ferreiro, Larrie D., New York: Albert Knopf, 2016, pp. 339-340.

Continental Currency and Depreciation

Prices and Inflation During the American Revolution, Pennsylvania, 1770–1790, by Anne Bezanson, et. al., is the foundational economic history analyzing price volatility in Pennsylvania during the revolutionary era. If you are interested in understanding the impact of hyperinflation on prices of daily commodities, this work provides a detailed study, and documents the complete collapse of the currency in 1781 shortly before the Battle of Yorktown. Originally published by the University of Pennsylvania Press in 1951, the book is available on the Internet Archive and Google Books. The book was re-released in the Penn Press Anniversary Collection in 2016.

Afterword

Sunlight glowed through the arched windows of the gleaming dome crowning the Main Reading Room of the Library of Congress, where I sat at a wooden desk waiting for a volume of the *Diplomatic Correspondence of the American Revolution,* a rare book from 1830. I was researching a letter in the Congressional Committee of Secret Correspondence – yes, our Congress was keeping secrets from its start. This set of twelve volumes was published in Boston in 1829 and 1830, and contained documents written during the Revolutionary War, including correspondence with the Spanish leadership. This letter was written by Benjamin Franklin from Paris in March 1777, noting that the Spanish had covertly shipped 3,000 barrels of desperately needed gunpowder to the Americans; the cargo was waiting in New Orleans. I'd begun my research in the early 2000s and had located only two complete sets of this correspondence. One set was priced at a very expensive $1,500, and the other was here at the Library of Congress.

These letters were a stop along the lengthy paper trail – literal and figurative – that I had started when I first learned that the 1781 Battle of Yorktown was funded by silver currency from Havana. While reading *The First Salute: A View of the American Revolution*, author Barbara Tuchman mentioned this event. There were two versions of the story. One held that the funding was part of a series of standard transactions between the Spanish and French governments. The second, more romantic version, posited that the treasury in Havana was empty and the hard currency essential to fund the campaign was raised directly by the people of Havana. As a Latina with an interest in history, I was surprised that I'd never heard of this event. I began my twenty-year quest to track down and write about the true story.

Tuchman's book led me to *When the French were Here*, by Stephen Bonsal, about the essential role of the French in the Revolutionary War. Bonsal was a

Pulitzer Prize-winning journalist as well as a diplomat, a veteran, and an advisor to President Woodrow Wilson. Fortunately, Bonsal had donated his papers to – where else – the Library of Congress. I went there with his book in hand, and the talented staff guided me to a box of yellowing, typewritten papers that contained Bonsal's research. In the box was a handwritten letter from his son, Philip, a career diplomat who had served in Spain and Cuba. "Dear Daddy," the letter from December 1946 began, "You will remember that a good many months ago you wrote me about the assistance said to have been rendered by the ladies of Havana to [French] Admiral de Grasse's fleet in 1781." Philip had requested research assistance at the Archivo de Indias in Sevilla, which houses more than 80 million pages of documents related to the administration of Spain's colonies in the Americas and the Philippines. Philip enclosed a report from the Archivo about the last-minute fundraising by the people of Havana to save the American Revolution. The record showed that the second version of the story was true! I copied the 1946 report and mailed it back to the Archivo, asking for copies of the documents referenced in their original report. A few weeks later, a thick envelope arrived from Seville with copies of the handwritten documents in Spanish.

I also discovered key documents related to Spain's involvement in the American Revolution were in the *Diplomatic Correspondence*. When my requested volume with Franklin's letter arrived at my desk at the Library of Congress that day, it was an original publication from 1830. Early 19th century books were constructed by printing the content on a large sheet of paper, which was folded twice to produce four sheets that were then cut at the edges to produce eight pages – think of opening a large napkin and refolding it twice. The center fold was stitched into the book binding. I'd handled books from that era before and kept a sharp kitchen knife at my desk at home to slice through the edges of the uncut pages. When I tried to open the book to Franklin's letter, I was shocked to see that the page was uncut. Not having a kitchen knife at the Library of Congress, the librarian kindly cut open the pages for me. After almost two centuries of unseen silence, Franklin's words on Spain and Latin America's assistance to our new republic were brought to light.

Gratitude and Acknowledgements

I am grateful to the professionals who've provided their excellent guidance and expertise. The Library of Congress Manuscript Division and the Hispanic Reading Room were pivotal in assisting me to start this research, and I appreciate the recent support from Henry Widener on the Library staff. The staff at the Archivo General de Indias in Sevilla, Spain, have answered my research requests and forwarded documents since 2000. Special thanks to Antonio Sanchez de Mora, Magdalena Canellas Anoz, Isabel Simó Rodriquez, and Maria Antonia Colomar Albajar. Manuel Olmedo Checa at La Real Academia de Bellas Artes de San Telmo de Málaga, Joaquín Mª Domínguez, SJ, and Antonio Laserna Gaitán at the University of Granada kindly answered my queries and provided documents. Tanya L. Marshall directed me to the Yale University Beinecke Collection. Professor Larrie D. Ferreiro provided guidance on the intractable topic of currency valuation from the 18th century to today's dollars. Stephen L. Kling, Jr., shared his knowledge and ensured that I knew about the valuable American Revolutionary War in the West conference. I've received research assistance from the Beinecke Rare Book and Manuscript Library at Yale University, the Daughters of the American Revolution (DAR) Library, the Cuban Research Institute at Florida International University, and the South Carolinian Library. The editors at the Weider History Group, which published two articles that I authored, coached me on how to make history narratives compelling, with appreciation to Bill Horne, Jim Paschall, and Nicholas Woods.

To improve my writing skills, I've participated in instructive programs at The Writer's Center, the Iowa Summer Writing Festival, The Second City, and Zigbone Writers Retreat. Julia Scheeres is an excellent Developmental Editor; I didn't follow all of her stellar advice, so any glaring gaffes are on me. Special thanks, or eskerrik asko, to Diana Friedman and Francisco Javier Martinez at KindWrite

Studio. Mayur Chauhan provided a touch of humor. The Shut Up & Write community in Sterling, Virginia were cheerleaders through the last mile.

Finally, I am so thankful for my amazing, supportive friends and family, who must have quietly wondered if I was ever going to finish this book. I am grateful for the many times that you asked me how the book was progressing, patiently listened as I described my latest work (or lack thereof, as was often the case), read and edited drafts, and encouraged and uplifted my spirit. Since I took so long to complete this book, if I've missed anyone, please let me know. Thank you to Avrille Blaize, Christy Dennis, David Bredbenner, Diane McAndrews, Jim Foster, Judy Foster, Linda Huffaker, Marg Watt, Marilyn Hanson, Riani Townshend, Rina Makdoom, Roanne Pitluk, Russ and Cindy Mitchell, Sahirah Caby, Sara Mastro, Susan, Matt and Grace Broyles, Varun Nikore, and Ximena Mujica. Melissa and Paul Duncan kindly accompanied me to museums and sites in Grasse, France when I'm sure they'd rather have spent time in the cafes in Cannes. Monica Elrod generously joined me for the Iowa Summer Writers Festival.

A special remembrance and thank you to the late Michael J. McAndrews, the Merry Warrior, who patiently volunteered as editor through pages and pages of drafts. Mike, I finally finished the book.

Bibliography

Abbey, Kathryn. "Efforts of Spain to Maintain Source of Information in the British Colonies before 1779." *The Mississippi Valley History Review* 15, no. 1 (June 1928).

Abbey, Kathryn Trimmer. "Spanish Projects for the Reoccupation of the Floridas during the American Revolution." *The Hispanic American Historical Review* 9, no. 3 (August 1929): 265–285.

Acosta, Jose Manuel Guerrero, ed. "Diego Maria de Gardoqui, Present at the Swearing-In of the First President of the United States." In *Recovered Memories: Spain, New Orleans and the Support for the American Revolution*. Iberdola-arte .es, pp. 274–277.

Acosta, José Manuel Guerrero, the Queen Sofia Spanish Institute, Gilder Lehrman Institute of American History. "Notes on Spain's Multicultural Militias." https://www.gilderlehrman.org/spanish-influence-american-history/ame rican-revolution/spains-multicultural-militias.

Adler, Mortimer Jerome and Wayne Moquin, eds. *The Revolutionary Years: Britannica's Book of the American Revolution*. Chicago: Encyclopedia Britannica, Inc., 1976.

Alden, John R. *A History of the American Revolution*. New York: Alfred A. Knopf, 1969.

Alexander, Leslie. "Black Americans and the American Revolution." The Great Courses Plus. Accessed April 25, 2025. https://www.thegreatcoursesplu s.com/plus-pilots-black-americans-and-the-revolutionary-war.

Alexander, Leslie and Michelle Alexander. "Fear." In Hannah-Jones, Nikole, ed. *The 1619 Project, A New Origin Story*, 97–122. New York: One World, 2021.

Allison, David K. and Larry Ferreiro, eds. *The American Revolution: A World War*. Washington, DC: Smithsonian Books, 2018.

Allison, Robert J. "The American Revolution and the Fate of the World with Richard Bell." Revolution 250 Podcast, November 11, 2025. https://www.you tube.com/watch?v=iOZyQM254-0.

Allitt, Patrick N. "The American Identity." Chantilly, VA: The Teaching Company, 2005.

Allitt, Patrick N. "American Religious History Course Guidebook." Chantilly, VA: The Teaching Company, 2001.

Amores, Juan B. *Cuba en la época de Ezpeleta (1785–1790)*. Pamplona: Ediciones Universidad de Navarra, S.A., 2000.

Anderson, Carol. "Self-Defense." In Hannah-Jones, Nikole, ed. *The 1619 Project, A New Origin Story*, 248–266. New York: One World, 2021.

Andrew, A. Piatt. "The End of the Mexican Dollar." *The Quarterly Journal of Economics* 18, no. 3 (1904): 321–356. https://doi.org/10.2307/1884074.

Andrews, John (attributed) *A History of the War With America, France, Spain, and Holland Begun in . . . 1775, and Ended in 1783*. 1787.

Antier, Jean-Jacques. *L'Admiral de Grasse*. Paris: Plon, 1965.

Augur, Helen. *The Secret War for Independence*. New York: Duell, Sloan and Pearce, 1955.

Axelrod, Alan. *The Real History of the American Revolution: A New Look at the Past*. New York: Sterling Publishing Co., Inc., 2007.

Barbier, Jacques A. and Allan J. Kuethe, eds. *The North American Role in the Spanish Imperial Economy, 1760–1819*. Manchester: Manchester University Press, 1984.

Barney, Mary. *A Biographical Memoir of the Late Commodore Joshua Barney From Autobiographical Notes and Journals in Possession of His Family, and Other Authentic Sources*. 1832. https://www.google.com/books/edition/A_Biographi cal_Memoir_of_the_Late_Commod/y2sDAAAAYAAJ?hl=en.

Basker, James G., ed. *Black Writers of the Founding Era*. New York: The Library of America, 2023.

Bate, Richard Alexander. *The Romance of George Rogers Clark and Therese de Leyba*. Louisville: The Standard Printing Co., 1929.

Baumgarten, Linda. *Eighteenth-Century Clothing at Williamsburg*. Williamsburg: The Colonial Williamsburg Foundation, 1986.

Bearss, Ed. "Last Campaign and the Battle of Yorktown." Study Tour, The Smithsonian Associates Program, Yorktown, Virginia, November 26, 2005.

Bearss, Ed. "The Philadelphia Campaign and Valley Forge." Study Tour, The Smithsonian Associates Program, Valley Forge, Pennsylvania, January 29, 2005.

Beerman, Eric. *España y la Independencia de Estados Unidos*. Málaga, Spain: Editorial Arguval, 1992.

Beerman, Eric. "Governor Bernardo de Gálvez's New Orleans Belle: Felicitas de Saint Maxent." *Universidad de Alcalá de Henares. Servicio de Publicaciones*, 1994.

Beerman, Eric. "The Last Battle of the American Revolution: Yorktown. No, the Bahamas! (The Spanish-American Expedition to Nassau in 1782)." *The Americas* 45, no. 1 (1988): 79–95. https://doi.org/10.2307/1007328.

Beerman, Eric. "'Yo Solo' Not 'Solo': Juan Antonio de Riaño." *The Florida Historical Quarterly* 58, no. 2 (1979): 174–184. http://www.jstor.org/stable/30149358.

Bell, Richard C. *The American Revolution and the Battle for India: A Forgotten Connection*. Webinar presentation, The Smithsonian Associates Program, Washington, DC, March 28, 2024.

Bell, Richard C. *The American Revolution and the Fate of the World*. New York: Riverhead Books, 2025.

Bell, Richard C. *The Battle for America: The French and Indian War*. Webinar presentation, The Smithsonian Associates Program, Washington, DC, October 17, 2023.

Bell, Richard C. *Benedict Arnold: Betrayal and Loyalty in the American Revolution*. Webinar presentation, The Smithsonian Associates Program, Washington, DC, February 6, 2025.

Bell, Richard C. *Guns, Ships, & Cows, The Spanish in the American Revolution*. Webinar presentation, The Smithsonian Associates Program, Washington, DC, April 24, 2023.

Bell, Richard C. *The Irish and the American Revolution*. Webinar presentation, The Smithsonian Associates Program, Washington, DC, December 2, 2024.

Bell, Richard C. *Privateers, Prisoners, and Britain's Black Holes: POWs in the American Revolution*. Webinar presentation, The Smithsonian Associates Program, Washington, DC, December 4, 2023.

Bell, Richard C. *The Pursuit of Happiness: The African American Diaspora in the Revolutionary War*. Webinar presentation, The Smithsonian Associates Program, Washington, DC, September 14, 2023.

Bell, Richard C. *The Real Revolution, America 1775–1783*. Webinar presentation, The Smithsonian Associates Program, Washington, DC, March 29, 2025.

Bell, Richard C. *Slavery and the American Revolution*. Webinar presentation, The Smithsonian Associates Program, Washington, DC, February 20, 2021.

Bemis, Samuel Flagg. *The Diplomacy of the American Revolution*. Bloomington: Indiana University Press, 1957. https://archive.org/details/dli.ernet.214430.

Bethell, Leslie, ed. *The Cambridge History of Latin America, Volume 1*. Cambridge: Cambridge University Press, 1984.

Bezanson, Anne, Blanche Daley, Marjorie C. Dennison, and Miriam Hussey. *Prices and Inflation During the American Revolution, Pennsylvania, 1770–1790*. Philadelphia: University of Pennsylvania Press, 1951.

Birmingham, Stephen. *The Grandees: America's Sephardic Elite*. New York: Harper & Row, 1971.

Blanchard, Claude. *The Journal of Claude Blanchard, Commissary of the French Auxiliary Army sent to the United States during the American Revolution*. Translated by William Duane and edited by Thomas Balch. New York: Arno Press, Inc., 1969.

Bodley, Temple. *George Rogers Clark: His Life and Public Services*. Boston: Houghton Mifflin Company, 1926.

Boeta, José Rudolfo. *Bernardo de* Gálvez. Madrid: Publicaciones Españolas, 1977.

Bolton, Charles K. *The Private Soldier Under Washington*. Gaansevoort, New York: Corner House Historical Publications, 1997.

Bonsal, Philip W. Private Letter to Stephen Bonsal, December 29, 1946. Unpublished manuscript. *The Papers of Stephen Bonsal*, Manuscript Division, Library of Congress, Washington, DC.

Bonsal, Stephen. *When the French Were Here*. Garden City, New York: Doubleday, Doran and Company, Inc., 1945.

Borrell, Pedro J. *Historia y Rescate del Galeon Nuestra Senora de la Concepcion*. Santo Domingo, República Dominicana: Impresion Amigo del Hogar, 1983.

Bowen, Clarence Winthrop. *History of the Centennial Celebration of the Inauguration of George Washington as First President of the United States*. New York: D. Appleton, 1892. Internet Archive. https://archive.org/details/historyofcentenn00bowe.

Brittlebank, Kate. *Tiger: The Life of Tipu Sultan*. New Delhi: Juggernaut Books, 2016.

Bryant, G.J. "British Logistics and the Conduct of the Carnatic Wars (1746–1783)." *War in History* 11, no. 3 (2004): 278–306. http://www.jstor.org/stable/26061925.

Buel, Richard, Jr. *In Irons: Britain's Naval Supremacy and the American Revolutionary Economy*. New Haven: Yale University Press, 1991.

Burns, Ken and Geoffrey C. Ward. "Book Breaks with Ken Burns and Geoffrey C. Ward on *The American Revolution: An Intimate History*." Webinar, Gilder Lehrman Institute of American History, November 9, 2025.

Burns, Ken, dir. *The American Revolution*. Walpole, NH: Florentine Films / PBS, 2025.

Calderón Cuadrado, Reyes. *Empresarios españoles en el proceso de independencia norteamericana: La casa Gardoqui e hijos de Bilbao*. Madrid: Union Editorial, S.A., 2004.

Calderón, Reyes. "Spanish Financial Aid for the Process of Independence of the United States of America: Facts and Figures." In *Legacy: Spain and the United States in the Age of Independence, 1763–1848*. Washington, DC: Smithsonian Institution, 2007.

Caron, Canon Max. *Admiral De Grasse: One of the Great Forgotten Men*. Translated by Dr. Mathilde Masse. Boston: The Four Seas Publishing Company, 1924.

Carstens, Nancy S. and Kenneth Carstens, eds. *The Life of George Rogers Clark, 1752–1818: Triumphs and Tragedies*. Westport, CT: Praeger, 2004.

Castillero Calvo, Alfredo. "La Globalización que fue." *Panorama de las Américas*, July 2009, 117–128.

Castillero Calvo, Alfredo. *Las Rutas de la Plata: La Primera Globalización*. Madrid: Ediciones San Marcos, 2004.

Caughey, John Walton. *Bernardo de Gálvez in Louisiana 1776–1783*. Berkeley: University of California Press, 1934.

Caughey, John Walton. *Bernardo de Gálvez in Louisiana 1776–1783*. Gretna: Pelican Publishing Company, 1998.

Cava Mesa, María Jesús and Begona Cava. *Diego María de Gardoqui: Un Bilbaino en La Diplomacia del Siglo XVIII*. Bilbao: Gestingraf, 1992.

Cazorla Grandos, Frank J., Rosa María García Baena, and José David Polo Rubio. *El gobernadora Luis de Unzaga (1717–1793) Precursor en el Nacimiento de los EE.UU. y en el liberalismo*. Málaga: Fundación Málaga, 2019.

Chapparo Sainz, Álvaro. "Educación y reproducción social de las élites habaneras (1776–1804)." *Revista Complutense de Historia de América* 36 (2010): 185–207.

Chávez, Thomas E. "Benjamin Franklin, Francisco Saavedra de Sangronis and Spain's Grand Strategy in the American Revolutionary War." Conference presentation, The American Revolutionary War in the West: History Conference II, September 27–29, 2024.

Chávez, Thomas E. *Revolutionary Diplomacy, Spanish Connections and the Birth of the United States*. Charlottesville: University of Virginia Press, 2025.

Chávez, Thomas E. *Spain and the Independence of the United States: An Intrinsic Gift*. Albuquerque: University of New Mexico Press, 2002.

Chernow, Ron. *Alexander Hamilton*. New York: Penguin Press, 2004.

Christelow, Allan. "Economic Background of the Anglo-Spanish War of 1762." *The Journal of Modern History* 18, no. 1 (March 1946): 22–36.

Christelow, Allan. "French Interest in the Spanish Empire during the Ministry of the Duc de Choiseul, 1759–1771." *The Hispanic American Historical Review* 21, no. 4 (November 1941): 515–537.

Clark, George P. "The Role of the Haitian Volunteers at Savannah in 1779: An Attempt at an Objective View." *Phylon* 41, no. 4 (1980): 356–366. https://doi.org/10.2307/274860.

Coakley, Robert W. and Stetson Conn. *The War of the American Revolution*. Center for Military History, United States Army. Washington, DC: US Government Printing Office, 1975.

Cobb, Daniel M. "Native Peoples of North America Course Guidebook." Chantilly, VA: The Great Courses.

Coe, Alexis. *You Never Forget Your First: A Biography of George Washington*. New York: Viking, 2020.

Coe, Samuel Gwynn. "The Mission of William Carmichael to Spain." PhD diss., Johns Hopkins University, 1926.

Commager, Henry Steele and Richard B. Morris, eds. *The Spirit of Seventy-Six: The Story of the American Revolution as Told by Participants*. New York: Da Capo Press, 1995.

Conrotte, Manuel. *La intervención de España en la independencia de los Estados Unidos de la América del Norte*. Madrid: V. Suárez, 1920.

Cooperman, Andrew. "Cahokia and the Trans-Appalachian West in the American Revolution." *The Confluence*, Spring/Summer 2015.

Couturier, Edith Boorstein. *The Silver King: The Remarkable Life of the Count of Regla in Colonial Mexico*. Albuquerque: The University of New Mexico Press, 2003.

Cribb, Joe, Barrie Cook, and Ian Carradice. *Coin Atlas: The World of Coinage from Its Origins to the Present Day*. New York: MacDonald & Co., 1990.

Cummins, Light Townsend. *Spanish Observers and the American Revolution, 1775–1783*. Baton Rouge: Louisiana State University Press, 1991.

Cuvillier, Louis A. *Admiral Francis Joseph Paul de Grasse: Hero of Yorktown*. 1931.

Dalrymple, William. *The Anarchy: The East India Company, Corporate Violence, and the Pillage of an Empire*. New York: Bloomsbury Publishing, 2019.

Davis, Burke. *The Campaign that Won America: The Story of Yorktown*. Eastern Acorn Press, 1970.

De Grasse, Compte. Letter to Marquis de Lafayette, October 26, 1781. National Archives: m247, R171, i152, v.10, p. 327.

De Grasse, Francois Joseph Paul. Letter to Rochambeau, August 30, 1781, aboard the *Ville de Paris*. Beinecke Rare Book and Manuscript Library, Yale University Library, New Haven, CT.

Delbanco, Andrew. *The War before the War: Fugitive Slaves and the Struggle for America's Soul from the Revolution to the Civil War*. New York: Penguin Press, 2018.

de Raparaz, Carmen. *Yo Solo: Bernard de* Gálvez *y la toma de Panzacola en 1781*. Barcelona: Ediciones de Serbal S.A., 1986.

Dobado, Rafael and Gustavo A. Marrero. "The Role of the Spanish Imperial State in the Mining-Led Growth of Bourbon Mexico's Economy." *The Economic History Review* 64, no. 3 (2011): 855–884. http://www.jstor.org/stable/41262480.

Dolin, Eric Jay. *Fur, Fortune, and Empire: The Epic History of the Fur Trade in America*. New York: W.W. Norton & Company, 2010.

Domingo Del Monte Collection of Spanish Colonial History. Unpublished manuscript. Manuscript Division, Library of Congress, Washington, DC, 1997.

Doniol, Henry. *La Participation De La France a l'Establissement des Etats-Unis d'Amerique*. Paris: Libraire de archive Nationales et de la Societe de L'Ecoles des chartes, 1890.

Dull, Jonathan R. *A Diplomatic History of the American Revolution*. New Haven: Yale University Press, 1985.

Dull, Jonathan R. *The French Navy and American Independence: A Study of Arms and Diplomacy, 1774–1787*. Princeton: Princeton University Press, 1975.

Dupuy, Richard Ernest, Gay M. Hammerman, and Grace P. Hayes, eds. *The American Revolution, a Global War*. New York: D. McKay Company, 1977.

DuVal, Kathleen. "The Education of Fernando de Leyba: Quapaws and Spaniards on the Border of Empires." *The Arkansas Historical Quarterly* 60, no. 1 (2001): 1–29. https://doi.org/10.2307/40028007.

DuVal, Kathleen. *Independence Lost: Lives on the Edge of the American Revolution*. New York: Random House, 2015.

Eakin, Marshall C. "The Americas in the Revolutionary Era Lecture Transcript and Course Guidebook." Chantilly, Virginia: The Teaching Company, 2004.

East, Robert A. *Business Enterprise in the American Revolutionary Era*. Gloucester: Peter Smith, 1964.

Eduardo, Miguel Antonio. "Diary of Miguel Antonio Eduardo." In *Naval Documents of the American Revolution (NDAR): American Theater: May 9, 1776–July 31, 1776, Volume 5, Appendix B*. https://www.history.navy.mil/content/dam/nhhc/research/publications/naval-documents-of-the-american-revolution/NDARVolume5.pdf, pp. 1339–1351.

Ellet, Elizabeth, ed. *Women of the American Revolution, Volumes I and II*. New York: Baker and Scribner, 1848.

Ellet, Elizabeth F. *The Women of the American Revolution, Volumes I, II, III*. Williamstown: Corner House of Publishers, 1980.

Ellis, Joseph J. *Founding Brothers: The Revolutionary Generation*. New York: Alfred A. Knopf, 2000.

Ellis, Joseph J. *His Excellency, George Washington*. New York: Alfred A. Knopf, 2004.

Emery, Noemie. *Alexander Hamilton: An Intimate Portrait*. New York: G.P. Putnam's Sons, 1982.

Enrique Hurtado de Mendoza Collection, Digital Library of the Caribbean. Cardenas Family, Marques de Cardenas de Monte Hermoso. https://dloc.com /FIHU000952/00001/pdf. Accessed July 9, 2025.

Fast, Howard. *The Crossing*. New York: Pocket Books, 1971.

Fenn, Elizabeth A. *Pox Americana: The Great Smallpox Epidemic of 1775–1782*. New York: Hill and Wang, 2001.

Ferguson, E. James, ed. *The Papers of Robert Morris, 1781–1784, Volume 1*. Pittsburgh: University of Pittsburgh Press, 1973.

Fernández y Fernández, Enrique. *Spain's Contribution to the Independence of the United States*. Embassy of Spain: United States of America, 1885.

Ferreiro, Larrie D. *Brothers at Arms: American Independence and the Men of France and Spain who Saved It*. New York: Albert Knopf, 2016.

Ferreiro, Larrie D. "The Franco-Spanish Combined Royal Navies against the British Royal Navy." Presentation, Daughters of the American Revolution and Queen Sofia Spanish Institute Symposium, Washington, DC, September 20–21, 2025.

Ferreiro, Larrie D. "The Spanish-French Bourbon Armada." In Paquette, Gabriel and Gonzalo M. Quintero Saravia, eds. *Spain and the American Revolution: New Approaches and Perspectives*. Charlottesville: University of Virginia Press, 2022.

Ferrer, Ada. *Cuba: An American History*. New York: Scribner, 2021.

Fischer, David H. *Paul Revere's Ride*. New York: Oxford University Press, 1994.

Fischer, David H. *Washington's Crossing*. New York: Oxford University Press, 2004.

Fisher, Redwood. "Revolutionary Reminiscences Connected with the Life of Robert Morris, Esq." *Graham's Magazine* 44 (January 1854).

Fox, Ebenezer. *The Adventures of Ebenezer Fox in the Revolutionary War*. Boston: Charles Fox, 1838.

Freeman, H. Ronald. *Savannah Under Siege*. Savannah, Georgia: Freeport Publishing, 2002.

Gaitán, Antonio Ignacio Laserna. *El Fondo Saavedra*. Granada: Universidad de Granada, 1995.

Galloway, Joseph. *A Letter to the People of America Lately Printed at New York; Now Re-Published by an American. With a Postscript, by the Editor, Addressed to*

*Sir W***** H****. London: T. Becket, 1778. https://jstor.org/stable/comm unity.34338609.

Gálvez, Bernardo de. "Diario de las operaciones de la expedicion contra la Plaza de Panzacola concluida por las Armas de S. M. Católica, baxo las órdenes del mariscal de campo D. Bernardo de Gálvez." Mexico, 1781.

Gálvez, José. Unpublished manuscript, Havana Cuba, February 16, 1782. Manuscript Division, Library of Congress, Washington, DC. Domingo del Monte Collection, Cuba, 182–186, B11–45, Box 4, fol. 2.

García Baena, Rosa María and Frank J. Cazorla Grandos. "La Cosmopolita Isabel Saint Maxent de Unzaga, Filántropa y Mecenas de la Educación Ilustrada." *Transatlantic Studies Network*, no. 11 (2021): 174–186. https://transatlanticstudiesnetwork.uma.es/wpcontent/uploads /2022/03/tsn_11_especial_3_compressed.pdf.

García Melero, Luis Ángel. *La Independencia de los Estados Unidos de Norteamérica a Través de la Prensa Española*. Madrid: Ministerio de Asuntos Exteriores, 1977.

Gardoqui, Diego de. "Regulación of Diego de Gardoqui." 1793. Archival manuscript material, Library of Congress Collection.

Gardoqui García, José Luis Diego Cano. "Diego de Gardoqui in Spain and America." In Acosta, Jose Manuel Guerrero, ed. *Recovered Memories: Spain, New Orleans and the Support for the American Revolution*. Iberdola-arte.es.

Gibson, Carrie. *El Norte: The Epic and Forgotten Story of Hispanic North America*. New York: Atlantic Monthly Press, 2019.

Gilbert, Arthur N. "Recruitment and Reform in the East India Company Army, 1760–1800." *Journal of British Studies* 15, no. 1 (1975): 89–111. http://www.jstor.org/stable/175240.

Goldstein, Erik. "'To Arms!' Weapons of the American Revolutionary War." Conference presentation, The American Revolutionary War in the West: History Conference II, September 27–29, 2024.

Golway, Terry. *Washington's General: Nathanael Greene and the Triumph of the American Revolution*. New York: Henry Holt and Company, 2005.

Grasse, Francois Joseph Paul. Letter to Rochambeau at Chesapeake, August 30, 1781. Unpublished manuscript. Beinecke Rare Book and Manuscript Library, Yale University Library, New Haven.

Griffin, Martin I. J. "Requiem for Don Juan Miralles." *American Catholic Historical Researches* 6 (1889).

Guelzo, Allen C. "The American Revolution Lecture Transcript and Course Guidebook." Chantilly, VA: The Teaching Company, 2008.

Hackett, David. "George Washington's Crossing of the Delaware: A Pivotal Moment in American History." Lecture, the Smithsonian Associates Program, Washington, DC, April 2004.

Halstead, Murat. *The Story of Cuba: Her Struggles for Liberty . . . The Cause, Crisis and Destiny of the Pearl of the Antilles*. Akron: The Werner Company, 1897.

Hannah-Jones, Nikole, ed. *The 1619 Project, A New Origin Story*. New York: One World, 2021.

Haring, C. H. *The Spanish Empire in America*. New York: Harcourt Brace Jovanovich, Publishers, 1947.

Hibbert, Christopher. *Redcoats and Rebels: The American Revolution through British Eyes*. New York: Avon Books, 1990.

Hiden, Philip Wallace. "The Money of Colonial Virginia." *The Virginia Magazine of History and Biography* 51, no. 1 (1943): 36–54. http://www.jstor.org/stable/4245216.

Hilton, Sylvia L. "Spain and North America, 1763–1821." In *Legacy: Spain and the United States in the Age of Independence, 1763–1848*. Washington, DC: Smithsonian Institution, 2007.

Hoffman, Phillip W. *Simon Gurty Turncoat Hero, The Most Hated Man on the Early American Frontier*. Franklin, Tennessee: American History Imprints, 2009.

Hough, Granville W. and Nancy C. Hough. *Spain's California Patriots in Its 1779–1783 War with England During the American Revolution, Part 2*. Midway City, CA: Society of Hispanic Historical and Ancestral Research, 1999.

Howarth, David and Stephen Howarth. *Lord Nelson, The Immortal Memory*. New York: Viking Penguin, 1999.

Irigoin, Alejandra and Bridget Millmore. "Piece of Eight." In *New World Objects of Knowledge: A Cabinet of Curiosities*, edited by Mark Thurner and Juan Pimentel, 41–46. London: University of London Press, 2021. http://www.jstor.org/stable/j.ctv1vbd275.8.

James, James Alton. *The Life of George Rogers Clark*. New York: AMS Press, 1970.

James, James Alton. "Oliver Pollock, Financier of the Revolution in the West." *Mississippi Valley Historical Review* 16 (1929).

James, James Alton. *Oliver Pollock: The Life and Times of an Unknown Patriot*. Freeport, New York: Books for Libraries Press, 1937.

James, James Alton. "Spanish Influence in the West During the American Revolution." *The Mississippi Valley Historical Review* 4, no. 2 (September 1917): 193–208.

Johnson, Raymond. "Stewart-deJaham Genealogy Pages." RaymondJohnson.net. https://www.raymondjohnson.net/genealogy/familychart.php?familyID=F651&tree=stewart. Retrieved August 21, 2025.

Johnson, Sherry. *The Social Transformation of Eighteenth-Century Cuba*. Gainesville: University of Florida Press, 2001.

Kaliamurthy, G. *Second Anglo-Mysore War (1780–1784)*. Delhi: Mittal Publications, 1987.

Kalman, Bobby. *18th Century Clothing*. New York, Ontario, Oxford: Crabtree, 1993.

Kamen, Henry. *Empire: How Spain Became a World Power: 1492–1763*. New York: HarperCollins Publishers, 2003.

Kantak, M.R. *The First Anglo-Maratha War 1774–1783: A Military Study of Major Battles*. Bombay: Popular Prakashan Private Ltd., 1993.

Kaplan, Roger. "The Hidden War: British Intelligence Operations during the American Revolution." *William and Mary Quarterly*, 3rd ser., 47, no. 1 (January 1990): 115–138.

Ketchum, Richard M. *Victory at Yorktown: The Campaign that Won the Revolution*. New York: Henry Holt and Company, 2004.

Kling, Stephen L., Jr., ed. *The American Revolutionary War in the West*. St. Louis: THGC Publishing, 2020.

Kling, Stephen L., Jr., Kristine Sjostrom, and Marysia Lopez. *The Battle of St. Louis, the Attack on Cahokia, and the American Revolution in the West*. St. Louis: THGC Publishing, 2017.

Knight, Vick, Jr. *"Send for Haym Salomon!"*. Alhambra, California: Borden Publishing Company, 1970.

Kuethe, Allan J. *Cuba, 1753–1815: Crown, Military, and Society*. Knoxville: The University of Tennessee Press, 1986.

Kuethe, Allan J. "The Development of the Cuban Military as a Sociopolitical Elite, 1763–83." *The Hispanic American Historical Review* 61, no. 4 (1981): 695–704. https://doi.org/10.2307/2514610.

Kuethe, Allan J. "Guns, Subsidies, and Commercial Privilege: Some Historical Factors in the Emergence of the Cuban National Character, 1763–1815." *Cuban Studies* 16 (1986): 123–138. http://www.jstor.org/stable/24485979.

Kuethe, Allan J. and G. Douglas Inglis. "Absolutism and Enlightened Reform: Charles III, the Establishment of the Alcabala, and Commercial Reorganization in Cuba." *Past and Present*, no. 109 (November 1985).

Kurlansky, Mark. *The Basque History of the World*. New York: Walker & Company, 1999.

Lacour-Gayet, Georges. *La Marine Militaire de La France sous Le Regne de Louis XVI*. Paris: Librarie speciale pour L'Histoire de la France et de ses Anciennes Provinces, 1905.

Lancaster, Bruce. *The American Revolution*. New York: American Heritage Press, 1985.

Landers, H.L. "The Virginia Campaign and the Blockade and Siege of Yorktown 1781." Senate Document 273, 71st Congress, 3rd Session. Washington: US Government Printing Office, 1931.

Langguth, A.J. *Patriots: The Men Who Started the American Revolution*. New York: Simon and Schuster, 1988.

Langley, Lester D. *The Americas in the Age of Revolution, 1750–1850*. New Haven: Yale University Press, 1998.

Larrabee, Harold A. *Decision at the Chesapeake*. New York: Bramhall House, 1964.

Larson, Edward J. "Book Breaks with Edward J. Larson on 'Declaring Independence: Why 1776 Matters.'" Webinar presentation, The Gilder Lehrman Book Breaks, December 21, 2025.

Lawler, Andrew. *A Perfect Frenzy: A Royal Governor, His Black Allies, and the Crisis That Spurred the American Revolution*. New York: Atlantic Monthly Press, 2025.

Leal, Guillermo Calleja. "Spain Financially Sustained the Continental Congress and its Army During the American Revolutionary War." In Acosta, Jose

Manuel Guerrero, ed. *Recovered Memories: Spain, New Orleans and the Support for the American Revolution*. Iberdola-arte.es.

Lee, Richard Henry. *Life of Arthur Lee, LL.D.* Boston: Wells and Lilly, 1829.

Leguizamo, John (Creator) and Ben DeJesus (Director). "Voces American Historia: The Untold History of Latinos." Documentary film. Public Broadcasting Service (PBS), 2024.

Lengel, Edward G. *General George Washington, A Military Life*. New York: Random House, 2005.

Levenson, Jay. *Encompassing the Globe: Portugal and the World in the 16th and 17th Centuries*. Washington, DC: Smithsonian Institution, 2007.

Levy, B.H. *Mordecai Sheftall: Jewish Revolutionary Patriot*. Savannah: Georgia Historical Society, 1999.

Lewis, Charles Lee. *Admiral de Grasse and American Independence*. Annapolis: U.S. Naval Institute, 1973.

Lewis, James A. "Las Damas de La Havana, El Precursor, and Francisco de Saavedra: A Note on Spanish Participation in the Battle of Yorktown." *The Americas: A Quarterly Review of Inter-American Cultural History* 37, no. 1 (July 1980).

Lewis, James A. *Neptune's Militia: The Frigate South Carolina during the American Revolution*. Kent, Ohio: The Kent State University Press, 1999.

Lipscomb, Terry W. *Battles, Skirmishes, and Actions of the American Revolution in South Carolina*. Columbia: South Carolina Department of Archives and History, 1991.

Lockhart, Paul. "Steuben Comes to America." *The Quarterly Journal of Military History* 22, no. 2 (Winter 2010).

Loliannette, Emmanuelli. "Spanish Diplomatic Policy and Contribution to the Independence 1775–1783." University of Massachusetts, 1990. Ann Arbor, Michigan: UMI.

López Cantos, Angel. *Don Francisco de Saavedra, segundo intendente de Caracas*. Sevilla: Consejo Superior de Investigaciones Científicas. Escuela de Estudios Hispano-Americanos, 1973.

Lucena-Giraldo, Manuel. "Foreseeing What Great Occasions Might Come: American Independence and Spanish Naval Reforms." In Paquette, Gabriel and Gonzalo M. Quintero Saravia, eds. *Spain and the American Revolution: New*

Approaches and Perspectives, 91–99. Charlottesville: University of Virginia Press, 2022.

Magro, Ángel Bahamonde and José Gregorio Cayuela Fernández. "La Creación de Nobleza En Cuba Durante El Siglo XIX." *Historia Social*, no. 11 (1991): 56–82. http://www.jstor.org/stable/40340288.

Mahajan, V.D. *Modern Indian History From 1707 to the Present Day*. 17th ed. New Delhi: S. Chand & Company Pvt. Ltd., 2014.

Mahan, Alfred Thayer. *The Major Operations of the Navies in the War of American Independence*. New York: Greenwood Press Publishers, 2005.

Maldonado, Cecilia. *America & Spain250 – Discovering Spain's Role in the American Revolution*. Webinar presentation, The Queen Sofia Spanish Institute, New York, New York, July 31, 2025.

Mancall, Peter C. "Origins and Ideologies of the American Revolution Lecture Transcript and Course Guidebook." Chantilly, VA: The Teaching Company, 2006.

Mann, Barbara Alice. *George Washington's War on Native America*. Lincoln: University of Nebraska Press, 2005.

Marlantes, Karl. *Matterhorn: A Novel of the Vietnam War*. New York: Atlantic Monthly Press, 2010.

Marshall, P.J. *The Making and Unmaking of Empires: Britain, India, and America c.1750–1783*. Oxford: Oxford University Press, 2007.

Martin, Joseph Plumb. *Private Yankee Doodle: Being a Narrative of Some of the Adventures, Dangers and Sufferings of a Revolutionary Soldier*. Edited by George F. Scheer. Canada: Little, Brown & Company, Inc., 1962.

Martín-Merás, Luisa. "The Capture of Pensacola through Maps, 1781." In *Legacy: Spain and the United States in the Age of Independence, 1763–1848*. Washington, DC: Smithsonian Institution, 2007.

McCadden, Helen Matzke. "Juan de Miralles and the American Revolution." *The Americas* 29, no. 3 (January 1973).

McCullough, David. *1776*. New York: Simon and Schuster, 2005.

McCullough, David. *John Adams*. New York: Simon and Schuster, 2001.

McDermott, John Francis, ed. *The Spanish in the Mississippi Valley 1762–1804*. Urbana, IL: University of Illinois Press, 1974.

McLoughlin, William G. *Rhode Island: A Bicentennial History*. New York: W.W. Norton & Company, Inc., 1978.

McNeil, Keith and Rusty McNeil. *Colonial & Revolution Songs with Historical Narration*. Riverside, CA: McNeil Music, Inc.

Mendez, Manuel Cruz. *Santo Domingo a fines del Siglo 18: Documentos y Comentarios y Glosas*. Santo Domingo, República Dominicana: Universidad Autónoma de Santo Domingo, 1999.

Mesa, Begona Cava. "Enlightenment Figure, Trader and Diplomat, The Historical Contribution of Diego de Gardoqui to the Independence of the United States." In Acosta, Jose Manuel Guerrero, ed. *Recovered Memories: Spain, New Orleans and the Support for the American Revolution*. Iberdola-arte.es.

Miles, Alfred Hart. *The Yorktown Campaign and Admiral Count de Grasse*. Washington, DC: U.S. Navy, 1931.

Miles, Tiya. "Dispossession." In Hannah-Jones, Nikole, ed. *The 1619 Project, A New Origin Story*, 135–155. New York: One World, 2021.

Millar, John F. *American Ships of the Colonial & Revolutionary Periods*. New York: W.W. Norton & Company, Inc., 1978.

Miranda, Francisco de. *Colombia 1781–1783*. Caracas: Ediciones de la Presidencia de la República, 1979.

Miranda, Francisco de. *The New Democracy in America: Travels of Francisco de Miranda in the United States, 1783–84*. Translated by Judson P. Wood, edited by John S. Ezell. Norman, Oklahoma: University of Oklahoma Press, 1963.

Mollo, John and Malcolm McGregor. *Uniforms of the American Revolution in Color*. New York: Macmillan Publishing Company, 1975.

Montemayor, Ernest A., ed. *Yo Solo*. New Orleans: Polyanthos, Inc., 1978.

Moreno, Roberto. "Regimen de trabajo en la mineria del siglo XVIII." In *El Trabajo y Los Trabajadores En La Historia De México: Ponencias y Comentarios Presentados En La V Reunión De Historiadores Mexicanos y Norteamericanos, Pátzcuaro, 12 al 15 de Octubre de 1977*, 242–267. Mexico: El Colegio de México.

Morison, Samuel Eliot. *John Paul Jones: A Sailor's Biography*. Annapolis, Maryland: Bluejacket Books, 1999.

Morris, Richard B. *John Jay: The Making of a Revolutionary, Unpublished Papers 1745–1780*. New York: Harper & Row, 1975.

Nagy, John A. *Rebellion in the Ranks: Mutinies of the American Revolution*. Yardley: Westholme Publishing, LLC, 2008.

Nash, Gary B. *The Unknown American Revolution*. New York: Viking, 2006.

Neeser, Robert Wilden, ed. *Letters and Papers Relating to the Cruises of Gustavus Conyngham: A Captain of the Continental Navy 1777–1779*. Port Washington: Kennikat Press, 1970.

Neimeyer, Charles Patrick. *America Goes to War: A Social History of the Continental Army*. New York: New York University Press, 1996.

Nelson, Craig. *Thomas Paine: Enlightenment, Revolution, and the Birth of Modern Nations*. New York: Viking, 2006.

Nemours, Alfred. "Haiti Et La Guerre to L'indépendance Américaine." Port-au-Prince: Haiti, H. Deschamps, 1952.

Nucete-Sardi, Jose. *Aventura y Tragedia de Don Francisco de Miranda*. Caracas: Departamento De Publicaciones, 1964.

Oberholtzer, Ellis P. *Robert Morris: Patriot and Financier*. New York: The MacMillan Company, 1903.

Okoye, F. Nwabueze. "Chattel Slavery as the Nightmare of the American Revolutionaries." *The William and Mary Quarterly* 37, no. 1 (1980): 4–28. https://doi.org/10.2307/1920967.

Olwell, Robert A. "'Domestick Enemies': Slavery and Political Independence in South Carolina, May 1775–March 1776." *The Journal of Southern History* 55, no. 1 (1989): 21–48. https://doi.org/10.2307/2209718.

Opatrny, Josef. *Historical Pre-Conditions of the Origin of the Cuban Nation*. Lewiston: The Edwin Mellen Press, 1993.

O'Donnell, Patrick K. *The Indispensables: The Diverse Soldier-Mariners Who Shaped the Country, Formed the Navy, and Rowed Washington Across the Delaware*. New York: The Atlantic Monthly Press, 2022.

O'Shaughnessy, Andrew Jackson. *The Men Who Lost America: British Leadership, the American Revolution, and the Fate of the Empire*. New Haven: Yale University Press, 2014.

Padrón, Francisco Morales. "Mexico y La Independencia de Hispanoamerica en 1781 segun un comisionado region: Francisco de Saavedra." In *Homenaje a Ciriaco Perez-Bustamente*, 335–358. Vol. 1969.

Padrón, Francisco Morales. *Spanish Help in American Independence*. Madrid: Publicaciones Españolas, 1952.

Padrón, Francisco Morales, ed. *Journal of Don Francisco Saavedra de Sangronis, 1780–1783*. Gainesville: University of Florida Press.

Padrón, Francisco Morales, ed. *Los Decenios (Autobiografía de una Sevillano de la Ilustracion): Francisco de Saavedra*. Sevilla: Servicio de Publicaciones Excmo. Ayuntamiento de Sevilla, 1995.

Paine, Thomas. "The American Crisis." A series of 16 pamphlets published between 1776 and 1783.

Pangle, Thomas L. "The Great Debate: Advocates and Opponents of the American Constitution Lecture Transcript and Course Guidebook." Chantilly, VA: The Teaching Company, 2007.

Paquette, Gabriel and Gonzalo M. Quintero Saravia, eds. *Spain and the American Revolution: New Approaches and Perspectives*. Charlottesville: University of Virginia Press, 2022.

Parcero Torre, Celia María. *La Pérdida de la Habana y Las reformas Borbónicas en Cuba*. Spain: Junta de Castilla y León Consejería y Cultura.

Patton, Robert H. *Patriot Pirates: The Privateer War for Freedom and Fortune in the American Revolution*. New York: Pantheon Books, 2008.

Paulo Pavia, Francisco de. "Descripcion del apresamiento del gran convey ingles en 1780 por la escuadra combinada de España y Francia al mando del general don Luis de Cordoba." *La revista militar: periódico de arte, ciencia y literatura militar* 8 (Madrid, 1851): 153–162.

Perez-Alonzo, Manuel Ign. *War Mission in the Caribbean: The Diary of Don Francisco de Salvadora (1780–1783)*. Washington, DC: Graduate School of Georgetown University, 1955.

Pérez Cabrera, Dr. José Manuel. *Miranda en Cuba (1780–1783)*. La Habana: La Academia de La Historia de Habana, 1950.

Peters, Madison C. *Haym Salomon, The Financier of the American Revolution: An Unwritten Chapter in American History*. New York: Trow Press, 1911.

Petrie, Sir Charles. *King Charles III of Spain: An Enlightened Despot*. New York: The John Day Company, 1971.

Pond, Shepard. "The Spanish Dollar: The World's Most Famous Silver Coin." *Bulletin of the Business Historical Society* 15, no. 1 (1941): 12–16. https://doi.org/10.2307/3111072.

Portell-Vila, Herminio. *Los Otros Extranjeros en la Revolución Norteamericana*. Miami, Florida: Ediciones Universal, 1978.

Quarles, Benjamin. *The Negro in the American Revolution*. New York: W.W. Norton & Company, 1961.

Racine, Karen. *Francisco de Miranda: A Transatlantic Life in the Age of Revolution*. Wilmington: Scholarly Resources, Inc., 2003.

Randall, William Sterne and Nancy Nahra. *Forgotten Americans: 15 Footnote Figures Who Changed American History*. New York: Barnes & Noble, 1998.

Raphael, Ray. *A People's History of the American Revolution: How Common People Shaped the Fight for Independence*. New York: Perennial, 2002.

Ratcliffe, Sam D. "'Escenas de Martirio': Notes on 'The Destruction of Mission San Sabá.'" *The Southwestern Historical Quarterly* 94, no. 4 (1991): 507–534. http://www.jstor.org/stable/30238793.

Rauch, Steven J. "Southern (Dis)Comfort: British Phase IV Operations in South Carolina and Georgia, May–September 1780." *Army History*, no. 71 (2009): 34–50. http://www.jstor.org/stable/26296758.

Reed, William, ed. *Reprint of the Original Letters from Washington to Joseph Reed, during The American Revolution*. Philadelphia: A. Hart, Late Carey, Hart, 1852.

Reparaz, Carmen De. *Yo Solo: Bernardo de Gálvez y la toma de Panzacola en 1781*. Barcelona: Ediciones del Serval S.A., 1986.

Reynolds, Donald E. "Ammunition Supply in Revolutionary Virginia." *Virginia Magazine of History and Biography* 73, no. 1 (1965).

Ribera, Nicholas Joseph de. *Descripción de la Isla de Cuba y algunas consideraciones sobre su poblacion y comercios*. 1767. Reprint ed. Havana: Ministerio del Cultura de Cuba, 1975.

Ribes, Vicent. "Nuevos Datos Biográficos sobre Juan de Miralles." *Revista de Historia Moderna*, no. 16 (1997): 363–374.

Robertson, William Spence. *The Life of Miranda*. Chapel Hill: The University of North Carolina Press, 1929.

Robertson, William Spence. "Miranda's Testamentary Dispositions." *The Hispanic American Historical Review* 7, no. 3 (August 1927): 279–298.

Rodrigues de Alonso, Josefina. *Francisco de Miranda: Colombia Primer Seccion Miranda Subdito Español 1781–1783, Tomo II.*

Rodriguez, Amalia, ed. *Cinco diarios del sitio de la habana: toma de la habana por los ingleses en 1762*. Havana: Biblioteca Nacional de José Martí, Departamento de Coleccion Cubana, 1963. https://search.catalog.loc.gov /instances/14b54fd1-17c9-535f-b879-17acc00623a3.

Rodriguez, Laura. "The Spanish Riots of 1766." *Past and Present*, no. 59 (May 1973): 117–146.

Rodrique, Cristina de Santiago. "Women in the 18th Century: Reality Versus Theoretical Dogma in the Age of Change." In Acosta, Jose Manuel Guerrero, ed. *Recovered Memories: Spain, New Orleans and the Support for the American Revolution*. Iberdola-arte.es.

Rosenfeld, Richard N. *American Aurora*. New York: St. Martin's Griffin, 1997.

Ross, Dave. "How the East India Company Became the World's Most Powerful Monopoly." https://www.history.com/articles/east-india-company-england -trade.

Rueda, Natividad. *La compañia comercial "Gardoqui e Hijos 1760–1800": sus relaciones políticas y económicas con Norteamérica (1770–1780)*. San Sebastián: Eusko Jaurlaritzaren Argitalpen Zerbitzu Nagusia, 1992.

Rush, N. Orwin. *The Battle of Pensacola: Spain's Final Triumph Over Great Britain in the Gulf of Mexico*. Tallahassee: Florida State University, 1966.

Sagredo Santos, Antonio. "Imágenes de La Revolución Americana y de la época Formativa de los Estados Unidos En la Historiografía Española." *Orbis Incognitivs: Avisos y Legajos del Nuevo Mundo. XII Congreso International de la AEA*, 301–308.

Sagredo Santos, Antonio. "Personal Connections between Spaniards and Americans in the Revolutionary Era: Pioneers in Spanish-American Diplomacy." In *Legacy: Spain and the United States in the Age of Independence, 1763–1848*. Washington, DC: Smithsonian Institution, 2007.

Salay, David L. "The Production of Gunpowder in Pennsylvania during the American Revolution." *The Pennsylvania Magazine of History and Biography* 99, no. 4 (October 1975).

Salvucci, Linda K. "Merchants and Diplomats: Philadelphia's Early Trade with Cuba." *Pennsylvania Legacies* 3, no. 2 (2003): 6–10. http://www.jstor.org/stab le/27764891.

Santiago, Pedro J. *Estudiamos Sobre Comercio Maritimo, Naufragios y Rescates Submarinos en La República Dominicana*. Santo Domingo, República Domini-cana: Comision de Rescate Arqueologico Submarino, 1990.

Saravia, Gonzalo M. Quintero. *Bernardo de Gálvez: Spanish Hero of the Amer-ican Revolution*. Chapel Hill: The University of North Carolina Press, 2018.

Saravia, Gonzalo M. Quintero. "Felicitas and Bernardo: The Power Couple of Spanish Louisiana." Webinar presentation, Historic New Orleans Collection, New Orleans, LA, January 19, 2023.

Saravia, Gonzalo M. Quintero. "Felicitas St. Maxent, Wife of Bernardo de Gálvez: From French New Orleans Belle to Exiled Spanish Dowager Countess." The Gilder Lehrman Institute. https://www.gilderlehrman.org/history-resources/essays/felicitas-st-maxent-wife-bernardo-de-galvez-french-new-orleans-belle.

Schama, Simon. *Rough Crossings: Britain, The Slaves and the American Revolution*. New York: Harper Collins Publishers, 2006.

Schiff, Stacy. *A Great Improvisation: Franklin, France, and the Birth of America*. New York: Henry Holt and Company, LLC, 2005.

Schneider, Elena A. *The Occupation of Havana: War, Trade, and Slavery in the Atlantic World*. Williamsburg, VA: The Omohundro Institute of Early American History and Culture, 2018.

Schurz, William Lytle. "The Spanish Lake." *The Hispanic American Historical Review* 5, no. 2 (1922): 181–194. https://doi.org/10.2307/2506024.

Selesky, Harold E. *A Demographic Survey of the Continental Army that Wintered at Valley Forge 1777–1778*. New Haven, Connecticut, 1987.

Selvon, Sydney. *A Comprehensive History of Mauritius*. Mauritius: Mauritius Printing Specialists, 2001.

Sen, Dr. Sailendra Nath. *Anglo-Maratha Relations During the Administration of Warren Hastings 1772–1785*. Bombay: Popular Prakashan Pvt Ltd, 1961.

Shea, J.G. *The Operations of the French Fleet Under the Count De Grasse in 1781–1782*. New York: Da Capo Press, 1971.

Sjostrom, Kristine L. *Fernando de Leyba (1734–1780): A Life of Service and Sacrifice in Spanish Louisiana*. 2022.

Sjostrom, Kristine L. "Leyba & Clark: Spanish American Collaboration in the Illinois Country during the American Revolutionary War." Conference presentation, The American Revolutionary War in the West: History Conference II, September 27–29, 2024.

Sparks, Jared, ed. *The Diplomatic Correspondence of the American Revolution, Volumes 1–12*. Boston: Nathan Hale and Gray & Bowen, 1829.

Stahr, Walter. *John Jay: Founding Father*. New York: Continuum International Publishing Group, 2005.

Stephenson, Orlando W. "The Supply of Gunpowder in 1776." *The American Historical Review* 30, no. 2 (January 1925).

Stephenson, R. Scott. *Clash of Empires: The British, French & Indian War 1754–1763*. Pittsburgh: Senator John Heinz Pittsburgh Regional History Center, 2005.

Stern, Mark A. *David Franks, Colonial Merchant*. University Park: Pennsylvania State University Press, 2010. https://archive.org/details/davidfran kscolon0000ster/page/128/mode/2up?q=Mischianza+.

Steward, Theophilus G. "How the Black St. Domingo Legion Saved the Patriot Army in the Siege of Savannah, 1779." *The American Negro Academy. Occasional Papers*, no. 5 (1899). https://www.gutenberg.org/ebooks/31256.

Sumner, W.G. "The Spanish Dollar and the Colonial Shilling." *The American Historical Review* 3, no. 4 (1898): 607–619. https://doi.org/10.2307/ 1834139.

Sumner, William Graham. *Robert Morris: The Financier and Finances of the American Revolution, Volumes I and II*. New York: Dodd, Mead and Company, 1891. Reprinted in 2000 by Beard Books.

Taylor, Alan. *The Internal Enemy: Slavery and War in Virginia, 1772–1832*. New York: W.W. Norton & Company, 2013.

Taylor, Dale. *The Writer's Guide to Everyday Life in Colonial America: From 1607 to 1783*. Cincinnati, Ohio: Writer's Digest Books, 1997.

Tejera, Eduardo J. *The Cuban Contribution to the American Independence.* Miami: Ediciones Universal, 1972.

Tejera, Eduardo J. *La Ayuda de España y Cuba a la Independencia Norteamericana, Una Historia Olvidada*. The Little French eBooks, 2016.

Thomas, Hugh. *Cuba or The Pursuit of Freedom*. New York: Da Capo Press, 1971.

Thomson, Buchanan Parker. *Spain: Forgotten Ally of the American Revolution*. North Quincy: Christopher Publishing House, 1976.

Thonhoff, Robert H. *The Texas Connection with the American Revolution*. Austin, TX: Eakin Press, 1981.

Topping, Aileen Moore. "Alexander Gillon in Havana, 'This Very Friendly Port.'" *South Carolina Historical Magazine* 83, no. 1 (January 1982). http s://www.jstor.org/stable/27567722.

Topping, Aileen Moore. "Mission of Francisco Rendón." Unpublished manuscript. Aileen Moore Topping Collection Concerning a Spanish Diplomatic Mission to the United States. Library of Congress Manuscript Collection, 1995.

Topping, Aileen Moore. "Mission of Juan de Miralles." Unpublished manuscript. Aileen Moore Topping Collection Concerning a Spanish Diplomatic Mission to the United States. Library of Congress Manuscript Collection, 1995.

Tornquist, Karl Gustaf. *The Naval Campaigns of Count de Grasse during the American Revolution 1781–1783*. Philadelphia: Swedish Colonial Society, 1942.

Trollope, Anthony. *The West Indies and the Spanish Main*. New York: Carroll & Graf Publishers, Inc., 1999.

Tuchman, Barbara W. *The First Salute: A View of the American Revolution*. New York: Ballantine Books, 1988.

U.S. Congress. Senate. Committee on Revolutionary Claims. *Report on the Memorial of H. M. Salomon, for Indemnification for Advances of Money, Made by His Father during the Revolutionary War*. Report 353. 35th Congress, 2nd Session. Washington, DC: US Senate, 1859.

U.S. Congress. Senate. Committee on Revolutionary Claims. *Report Relative to Advances of Money to the United States during the Revolutionary War*. Report 178. 69th Congress, 2nd Session. Washington, DC: US Senate, 1925.

Van Lohuizen, Jan. "War with the British, 1781–1783." In *The Dutch East India Company and Mysore 1762–1790*, 115–134. Brill, 1961. http://www.js tor.org/stable/10.1163/j.ctvbqs37w.9.

Van Wyck Mason, F. *Eagle in the Sky*. Philadelphia: J.B. Lippincott Company, 1948.

Wagner, Frederick. *Robert Morris: Audacious Patriot*. New York: Dodd, Mead & Company, 1976.

Waller, George M. *The American Revolution in the West*. Chicago: Nelson-Hall, Inc. Publishers, 1976.

Warren, Mercy Otis. *History of the Rise, Progress and Termination of the American Revolution Interspersed with Biographical, Political, and Moral Observations*. Indianapolis: Liberty Fund, 1989.

Watson, Thomas D. "Strivings for Sovereignty: Alexander McGillivray, Creek Warfare, and Diplomacy, 1783–1790." *The Florida Historical Quarterly* 58, no. 4 (1980): 400–414. http://www.jstor.org/stable/30140492.

Weber, David J. *The Spanish Frontier in North America*. New Haven: Yale University Press, 1992.

Weddle, Kevin J. "The Saratoga Campaign: 'The Compleat Victory.'" Webinar presentation, The Smithsonian Associates Program, Washington, DC, March 5, 2024.

Wharton, Francis. *The Revolutionary Diplomatic Correspondence of the United States*. Washington: Government Printing Office, 1889.

Wheeler, Richard. *Voices of 1776: The Story of the American Revolution in the Words of Those Who Were There*. New York: Penguin Books, 1972.

Whitaker, Arthur P. "The Pseudo-Aranda Memoir of 1783." *The Hispanic American Historical Review* 17, no. 3 (August 1937): 287–313.

Wilbur, C. Keith, MD. *Revolutionary Medicine 1700–1800*. Philadelphia: Chelsea House Publishers, 1980.

Willcox, William, ed., *The American Rebellion. Sir Henry Clinton's Narrative of his Campaigns, 1775–1782, with an Appendix of Original Documents*. Binghamton, New York: Yale University Press, 1954.

Williams, Eric. *From Columbus to Castro: The History of the Caribbean 1492–1969*. London: André Deutsch Limited, 1970.

Williams, Stephen. *Cuba: The Land, The History, The People, The Culture*. Philadelphia: Running Press, 1994.

Wood, Gordon S. *The American Revolution: A History*. New York: Modern Library Chronicles, 2002.

Wood, Gordon S. *The Radicalism of the American Revolution*. New York: Vintage, 1991.

Worcester, Donald E. "Miranda's Diary of the Siege of Pensacola, 1781." *The Florida Historical Quarterly* 29, no. 3 (January 1951): 163–196.

Yagi, George, Jr. "Junípero Serra — Meet the Spanish Missionary Who Rallied California to Support the American Revolution." MilitaryHistoryNow.com, July 2, 2023. https://militaryhistorynow.com/2023/07/02/junipero-serra-meet-the-spanish-missionary-who-rallied-california-to-support-the-american-revolution/.

Yela-Utrilla, Dr. Juan F. *España ante La Independencia de los Estados Unidos, Volumes 1 and 2*. Lerida, España: Graficos Academia Mariana, 1925.

Zepeda Cortés, María Bárbara. "Jose's Secrets: Minister Gálvez's Master Plan for Spain's Participation in the American Revolution." In Paquette, Gabriel and

Gonzalo M. Quintero Saravia, eds. *Spain and the American Revolution: New Approaches and Perspectives*, 77–90. Charlottesville: University of Virginia Press, 2022.

Endnotes

Prequel to the American Revolution

1. Schneider, Elena A., *The Occupation of Havana: War, Trade, and Slavery in the Atlantic World*. Williamsburg, VA: The Omohundro Institute of Early American History and Culture, 2018, p. 63

2. Kamen, Henry, *Empire: How Spain became a World Power: 1492-1763*. New York: Harper Collins Publishers, 2003, p. 181

3. Schneider, op. cit., p. 17

4. Rodriguez, Amalia, ed., *Cinco diarios del sitio de la* La Habana. Toma de La Habana por los ingleses en 1762. Biblioteca Nacional de José Martí, Departamento de Coleccion Cubana, La Habana, 1963, p. 106

5. Kuethe, Allan J. "Guns, Subsidies, and Commercial Privilege: Some Historical Factors in the Emergence of the Cuban National Character, 1763–1815." *Cuban Studies* 16 (1986): 123–38. http://www.jstor.org/stable/24485979.

6. Halstead, Murat, *The Story of Cuba Her Struggles for Liberty... The Cause, Crisis and Destiny of the Pearl of the Antilles*. Akron: The Werner Company, 1897, p. 220

7. Schneider, op. cit., pp. 114-119

8. Johnson, Sherry, *The Social Transformation of Eighteenth-Century Cuba*. Gainesville: University of Florida Press, 2001, p. 41

9. Schneider, op. cit., p. 131

10. Parcero Torre, Celia María, *La Pérdida de la Habana y Las reformas Borbónicos*. Spain: Junta de Castilla y Léon Consejería y Cultura, p. 152

11. Parcero Torre, Celia María, *La Pérdida de la Habana y Las reformas Borbónicos en Cuba*. Spain: Junta de Castilla y Léon Consejería y Cultura, p. 128-133

12. Schneider, op. cit., p. 137

13. Parcero Torre, *La Pérdida de la Habana*, op. cit., p. 132

208

14. Parcero Torre, *La Pérdida de la Habana*, op. cit., p. 15

15. Ferrer, Ada, *Cuba: An American History*. New York: Scribner 2021, p. 49

16. Halstead, op. cit., p. 233

17. Parcero Torre, *La Pérdida de la Habana*, op. cit., p. 152

18. Halstead, op. cit., pp. 234-235

19. Schneider, op. cit., p. 202

20. Halstead, op. cit., pp. 234-235

21. Parcero Torre, *La Pérdida de la Habana*, op. cit., p. 158

22. Schneider, op. cit., pp. 202-207

23. Parcero Torre, *La Pérdida de la Habana*, op. cit., p. 162

24. Thomas, Hugh, *Cuba or The Pursuit of Freedom*. New York: Da Capo Press, 1971, p. 61

25. Foard, Douglas W., Ph. D., *"The Imperious Laird": John Campbell Fourth Earl of Loudoun*. Sterling, VA: Better Impressions, 2007, p. 29

26. Stephenson, R. Scott, *Clash of Empires: The British, French & Indian War 1754-1763*. Pittsburgh: Senator John Heinz Pittsburgh Regional History Center, 2005, p. 20

27. Foard, op. cit., p. 66

28. Kamen, op. cit., p. 209

29. Dalrymple, William, *The Anarchy: The East India Company, Corporate Violence, and the Pillage of an Empire*. New York: Bloomsbury Publishing, 2019

30. Kamen, op. cit., p. 483

31. Castillero Calvo, Alfredo, *Las Rutas de la Plata: La Primera Globalización*. Madrid: Ediciones San Marcos, 2004

32. Castillero Calvo, Alfredo, "La Globalización que fue" in *Panorama de las Américas*, July 2009, p. 123

33. Kamen, op. cit., p. 481

34. Ferrer, op. cit., p. 54

35. Schneider, op. cit., p. 8

36. Williams, Stephen, *Cuba: The Land, The History, The People, The Culture*. Philadelphia: Running Press, 1994, p. 23

37. Schneider, op. cit., p. 220

38. Ferrer, op. cit., p. 54

39. Williams, op. cit., p. 23

40. Kuethe, Allan J., *Cuba, 1753-1815: Crown, Military, and Society*. Knoxville: The University of Tennessee Press, 1986, pp. 28-30

41. Ibid., pp. 41-42

42. Ferrer, op. cit., pp. 54-55

43. Ibid., pp. 54-55

44. Weber, David J., *The Spanish Frontier in North America*. New Haven: Yale University Press, 1992, p. 6

45. Petrie, Sir Charles, *King Charles III of Spain: An Enlightened Despot*. New York: The John Day Company, 1971, p. 228

46. Ibid., p. 118

47. Ferreiro, Larrie D., *Brothers at Arms: American Independence and the Men of France and Spain who Saved It*. New York: Albert Knopf, 2016, pp. 339-340. This calculation uses the Economy Cost Comparator based on the national gross domestic product (GDP) calculator.

48. Nash, Gary B., *The Unknown American Revolution*. New York: Viking, 2006, p. 45

49. Garcia Melero, Luis Angel, *La Independencia de los Estados Unidos de Norteamérica a Traves de la Prensa Española*. Madrid: Ministerio de Asuntos Exteriores, 1977, p. 10

50. Fernández y Fernández, Enrique, *Spain's Contribution to the independence of the United States*. Embassy of Spain: United States of America, 1885, p. 4

Days and Days without a "Mexican"

1. Reed, William, ed., Reprint of the original letters from Washington to Joseph Reed, during The American Revolution. Philadelphia: A. Hart, Late Carey, Hart, 1852, pp. 44-45

2. Chávez, Thomas E., *Spain and the Independence of the United States: An Intrinsic Gift*. Albuquerque: University of New Mexico Press, 2002

3. Taylor, Dale, *The Writer's Guide to Everyday Life in Colonial America: From 1607 to 1783*. Cincinnati, Ohio: Writer's Digest Books, 1997, pp 182-183

4. Wood, Gordon S., *The American Revolution: A History*. New York: Modern Library Chronicles, 2002, p. 14

5. Wood, Gordon S., *The Radicalism of the American Revolution*. New York: Vintage 1991, pp. 137-138

6. Bolton, Charles K., *The Private Soldier Under Washington*. Gaansevoort, New York: Corner House Historical Publications, 1997

7. Stephenson, Orlando W., "The Supply of Gunpowder in 1776", *The American Historical Review*, Vol. 30, No. 2 (January 1925), pp. 271-277

8. Fox, Ebenezer, *The Adventures of Ebenezer Fox in the Revolutionary War*. Boston: Charles Fox, 1838

9. David H. Fischer, *Paul Revere's Ride*. New York: Oxford University Press, 1994, p. 34

10. Bell, Richard C., *The American Revolution and the Fate of the World with Richard Bell*. New York: Riverhead Books, 2025, p. 251

11. Mancall, Peter C., "Origins and Ideologies of the American Revolution Lecture Transcript and Course Guidebook", Chantilly, VA: The Teaching Company: 2006, p. 28

12. Fischer, op. cit., pp. 95-96

13. Stephenson, op. cit., pp. 272-276

14. Salay, David L., "The Production of gunpowder in Pennsylvania during the American Revolution", *The Pennsylvania Magazine of History and Biography*, October 1975, Volume XCIX Number 4, p. 423

15. Ibid., pp. 437-438

16. Augur, Helen, *The Secret War for Independence*. New York: Duell, Sloan and Pearce, 1955, pp. 84-86

17. Jared Sparks, ed., *The Diplomatic Correspondence of the American Revolution*. Boston: Nathan Hale and Gray & Bowen, 1829-1830, Volume 1, p. 201

18. Wilbur, C. Keith, MD, *Revolutionary Medicine 1700 – 1800*. Philadelphia: Chelsea House Publishers, 1980, pp. 29-30

19. Goldstein, Erik, (2024, September 27-29) *"To Arms!" Weapons of the American Revolutionary War* [Conference Presentation]. The American Revolutionary War in the West: History Conference II

20. Chernow, Ron, *Alexander Hamilton*. New York: Penguin Press, 2004, p. 103

21. Axelrod, Alan, *The Real History of the American Revolution: A New Look at the Past*. New York: Sterling Publishing Co., Inc., 2007, p. 137

22. Mollo, John, *Uniforms of the American Revolution in color*. New York: Macmillan Publishing Company, Inc., 1975

23. Allison, David K. and Ferreiro, Larry, eds., *The American Revolution A World War*. Washington, DC: Smithsonian Books, 2018, p. 88

24. Taylor, op. cit., p. 107

25. Baumgarten, Linda, *Eighteenth-Century Clothing at Williamsburg*. Williamsburg: The Colonial Williamsburg Foundation, 1986, p. 10

26. Taylor, op. cit., p. 108

27. Ibid., p. 113

28. Stephenson, op. cit., p. 281

29. Berkin, Carol, *Revolutionary Mothers: Women in the Struggle for America's Independence*. New York: Alfred A. Knopf 2005, p. 42

GoFundUs a Revolution

1. Eakin, Marshall C., "The Americas in the Revolutionary Era Lecture Transcript and Course Guidebook" Chantilly, Virginia: The Teaching Company, 2004

2. Ibid., 119-120

3. Cribb, Joe, Barrie Cook, Ian Carradice, *Coin Atlas: The World of Coinage from Its Origins to the Present Day*. New York: MacDonald & Co., 1990, p. 16

4. Bethell, Leslie, Ed., *The Cambridge History of Latin America, Volume 1*. Cambridge: Cambridge University Press, 1984, p. 321

5. Irigoin, Alejandra, and Bridget Millmore. "PIECE OF EIGHT." In *New World Objects of Knowledge: A Cabinet of Curiosities*, edited by Mark Thurner and Juan Pimentel, 41–46. University of London Press, 2021. http://www.jstor.org/stable/j .ctv1vbd275.8.

6. Castillero Calvo, op. cit., p. 78

7. Leguizamo, John (Creator), DeJesus, Ben (Director). (2024) "Voces American Historia: The Untold History of Latinos" [Documentary Film]. Public Broadcasting Service (PBS)

8. Coe, Michael D. and Koontz, Rex, *Mexico: from the Olmecs to the Aztecs*. London: Thames & Hudson, 2002, p. 153

9. Cobb, Daniel M., "Native Peoples of North America Course Guidebook." Chantilly, VA: The Great Courses, p. 16

10. Irigoin, op. cit., pp. 41-46

11. Cribb, op. cit., p. 291

12. Dobado, Rafael, and Gustavo A. Marrero. "The Role of the Spanish Imperial State in the Mining-Led Growth of Bourbon Mexico's Economy." *The Economic History Review* 64, no. 3, p. 860 (2011): 855–84. http://www.jstor.org/stable/41262480.

13. Moreno, Roberto, "Regimen de trabajo en la mineria del siglo XVIII", *El Trabajo y Los Trabajadores En La Historia De México: Ponencias y Comentarios Presentados En La V Reunión De Historiadores Mexicanos y Norteamericanos, Pátzcuaro, 12 Al 15 De Octubre De 1977*. Mexico: El Colegio de México; pp. 242 - 267

14. Bethell, op. cit., pp. 420-422

15. Ratcliffe, Sam D. "'Escenas de Martirio': Notes on 'The Destruction of Mission San Sabá.'" *The Southwestern Historical Quarterly* 94, no. 4 (1991): 507–34. http://www.jstor.org/stable/30238793 ., p. 509

16. Couturier, Edith Boorstein, *The Silver King: The Remarkable Life of the Count of Regla in Colonial Mexico*. Albuquerque: The University of New Mexico Press, 2003, pp. 7-8

17. Ratcliffe, op. cit., p. 512

18. Couturier, op. cit., p. 49

19. Ibid., pp. 26-27

20. Irigoin, op. cit., pp. 41-46

21. Bell, Richard C., (2023, April 24) *Guns, Ships, & Cows, The Spanish in the American Revolution*. [Webinar presentation] The Smithsonian Associates Program, Washington, DC

22. Royal Bank of Scotland Archives Records of John and Henry Drummond, as Contractors to the Treasury as Paymaster to His Majesty's Forces in North America, 1767-83, Reference code: GB 1502 DR/464/

23. Rodrique, Cristina de Santiago, "Women in the 18th Century: Reality Versus Theoretical Dogma in the Age of Change" in *Recovered Memories: Spain, New Orleans and the Support for the American Revolution*. Iberdola-arte.es https://www.iberdrola-arte.es/FicherosIberdrola/Publicaciones/8/48add1ac-6593-46d2-9e98-0ee6a201b527.pdf , p. 89

24. Kurlansky, Mark, *The Basque History of the World*. New York: Walker & Company, 1999, p. 57

25. Rueda, Natividad, *La compania comercial "Gardoqui e Hijos 1760 – 1800" sus relaciones políticas y económicas con Norteamérica (1770-1780)*. San Sebastián: Vitoria-Gasteiz: Eusko Jaurlaritzaren Argitalpen Zerbitzu Nagusia, 1992, pp. 43- 48

26. Calderón, Reyes, "Spanish Financial Aid for the Process of Independence of the United States of America: Facts and Figures" in *Legacy: Spain and the United States in the Age of Independence, 1763-1848*. Washington, DC: Smithsonian Institution, 2007, p. 66

27. "Benjamin Franklin to Jonathan Williams, Sr., 13 January 1772," *Founders Online,* National Archives, https://founders.archives.gov/documents/Franklin/01-19-02-0015. [Original source: *The Papers of Benjamin Franklin,* vol. 19, *January 1 through December 31, 1772,* ed. William B. Willcox. New Haven and London: Yale University Press, New Haven and London, 1975, pp. 32–34.]

28. Rueda, op. cit., p. 206

29. Calderón Cuadrado, Reyes, *Empresarios españoles en el proceso de independencia norteamericana: La casa Gardoqui e hijos de Bilbao*. Madrid: Union Editorial, S. A. 2004, pp. 206-208

30. Rueda, op. cit., p. 51

31. Calderón, op. cit., p. 69

32. Cava y Begona Cava, María Jesús, Diego María de Gardoqui: Un Bilbaino en La Diplomacia del Siglo XVIII. Bilbao: Gestingraf, 1992, p. 26

33. Chávez, *Spain and the Independence of the United States*, op. cit., p. 224

34. Thompson, Buchanan Parker, *Spain: forgotten ally of the American Revolution.* North Quincy: Christopher Publishing House, 1976, p. 56

35. Yela, Dr. Juan F. Utrilla, *España ante La Independencia de los Estados Unidos Volumes 1 and 2.* Lerida, España: Graficos Academia Mariana, 1925, Volume II, p. 16

36. Ibid., Volume I, p. 22

37. Ibid., Volume I, pp. 44-45

38. Thompson, op. cit., pp. 24-25

39. Coakley, Robert W. and Stetson Conn, *The War of the American Revolution. Center for Military History, United States Army.* Washington, D. C.: US Government Printing Office, 1975, p. 32

40. Ibid., p. 132

41. Cazorla Grandos, Frank J., Rosa María García Baena, José David Polo Rubio, *El gobernador Luis de Unzaga (1717-1793) Precursor en el Nacimiento de los EE.UU. y en el liberalism*. Málaga: Fundación Málaga, 2019, p. 86

42. Ibid., p. 77

43. "From George Washington to Colonel Joseph Reed, 30 November 1776," *Founders Online,* National Archives, https://founders.archives.gov/documents/Washington /03-07-02-0171. [Original source: *The Papers of George Washington*, Revolutionary War Series, vol. 7, *21 October 1776–5 January 1777*, ed. Philander D. Chase. Charlottesville: University Press of Virginia, 1997, pp. 237–239.]

44. Cazorla Grandos, op. cit., p. 77

45. Yela, op. cit., Volume I, p. 103

46. Saint-Domingue is modern-day Haiti on the western portion of the island formerly known as Hispaniola. Santo Domingo was the Spanish colonial city of Hispaniola, now the Republic of Santo Domingo. Agreed, it's confusing, Domingo was a very popular saint.

47. Cazorla Grandos, op. cit., p. 86

48. Chávez, Thomas E., *Revolutionary Diplomacy, Spanish Connections and the Birth of the United States*. Charlottesville: University of Virginia Press 2025, p. 36

49. Dull, Jonathan R., *A Diplomatic History of the American Revolution*. New Haven: Yale University Press, 1985, pp. 61-62

50. Augur, op. cit., p. 125

51. Chávez, *Revolutionary Diplomacy*, op. cit., p. 112

52. Thompson, op. cit., p. 67

The Spies Who Loved Us

1. Cummins, Light Townsend, *Spanish Observers and the American Revolution, 1775-1783*. Baton Rouge: Louisiana State University Press, 1991, p. 40

2. Ibid., pp. 39-40

3. Buel, Richard, Jr., *In Irons: Britain's Naval Supremacy and the American Revolutionary Economy*. New Haven: Yale University Press, 1991 pp. 31-33

4. Eduardo, Miguel Antonio, N*aval Documents of the American Revolution* (*NDAR*) *American Theater: May 9, 1776–July 31, 1776, Volume 5 Appendix B*, "Diary of Miguel Antonio Eduardo",]https://www.history.navy.mil/content/dam/nhhc/research/publications/naval-documents-of-the-american-revolution/NDARVolume5.pdf , p. 1339

5. Eduardo, Miguel Antonio, N*aval Documents of the American Revolution* (*NDAR*) *American Theater: May 9, 1776–July 31, 1776, Volume 5 Appendix B*, "Diary of Miguel Antonio Eduardo", p. 1341

6. Eduardo, Miguel Antonio, N*aval Documents of the American Revolution* (*NDAR*) *American Theater: May 9, 1776–July 31, 1776, Volume 5 Appendix B*, "Diary of Miguel Antonio Eduardo", p. 1343

7. Abbey, Kathryn, "Efforts of Spain to Maintain Source of Information in the British Colonies before 1779", *The Mississippi Valley History Review*, Vol. XV, No. 1, June 1928, p. 60

8. Saravia, Gonzalo M. Quintero, *Bernardo de Gálvez: Spanish Hero of the American Revolution*. The University of North Carolina Press, 2018, p. 5

9. Ibid., pp. 9-10

10. Lewis, James A., *Neptune's Militia: the Frigate South Carolina during the American Revolution*. Kent, Ohio: The Kent State University Press, 1999, p. 54

11. Topping, Aileen Moore, "Mission of Juan de Miralles", unpublished manuscript, Library of Congress Manuscript Collection, Cuba AGI 1290, San Ildefenso, August 26, 1777, José de Gálvez to Diego José Navarro

12. Topping, Aileen Moore, "Mission of Juan de Miralles", unpublished manuscript, Library of Congress Manuscript Collection, AGI 1227, Havana, December 11, 1777, Diego José Navarro to José de Gálvez

13. Ribes, Vicent, "Nuevas Datos Biográficos sobre Juan de Miralles", *Revista de Historia Moderna No. 16* (1997), p. 371

14. Ibid., pp. 364-366

15. Schneider, op. cit., p. 162

16. Abbey, op. cit., p. 63

17. Cummins, op. cit., pp. 101-102

18. Abbey, op. cit., pp. 67-68

19. Cummins, op. cit., pp. 104-106

20. Topping, Aileen Moore, "Mission of Juan de Miralles", unpublished manuscript, Library of Congress Manuscript Collection. AGI: Cuba 1227 Havana 17 December 1777, Diego José Navarro to José de Gálvez

21. Topping, Aileen Moore, "Mission of Juan de Miralles", unpublished manuscript, Library of Congress Manuscript Collection, AGI Cuba 1290, Navarro to Gálvez, 3 January

22. Yela, op. cit., Volume 1, p. 386

23. Topping, Aileen Moore, "Mission of Juan de Miralles", unpublished manuscript, Library of Congress Manuscript Collection, AGI: Cuba 1281, Juan de Miralles to José de Gálvez, Box 1, Folder 1

24. Ribes, op. cit., p. 374

25. Sumner, William Graham, *Robert Morris: The Financier and Finances of the American Revolution: Volumes I and II*. New York: Dodd, Mead and Company, 1891. Reprinted in 2000 by Beard Books. 2:126

26. Topping, Aileen Moore, "Mission of Juan de Miralles", unpublished manuscript, Library of Congress Manuscript Collection, AGI: Cuba 1281, Juan de Miralles to Diego José Navarro.

27. Sagredo Santos, Antonio, "Personal Connections between Spaniards and Americans in the Revolutionary Era: Pioneers in Spanish-American Diplomacy", in *Legacy: Spain and the United States in the Age of Independence, 1763-1848*. Washington, DC: Smithsonian Institution, 2007, p. 54

28. Topping, Aileen Moore, "Mission of Juan de Miralles", unpublished manuscript, Library of Congress Manuscript Collection, AGI Cuba 1281, Philadelphia, July 22, 1779, Juan de Miralles to Diego José Navarro.

29. Griffin, Martin I. J., "Requiem for Don Juan Miralles", American Catholic Historical Researches, II, (April 1889), p. 62

30. Ribes, op. cit., pp. 371-372

31. Topping, Aileen Moore, "Mission of Juan de Miralles", unpublished manuscript, Library of Congress Manuscript Collection, AGI: Cuba 1281, Juan de Miralles to Diego José Navarro, Philadelphia, February 15, 1779.

32. Topping, Aileen Moore, "Mission of Juan de Miralles", unpublished manuscript, Library of Congress Manuscript Collection, AGI 1606, Philadelphia, October 20, 1778, Juan de Miralles to José de Gálvez

33. Ribes, op. cit., p. 368

34. Topping, Aileen Moore, "Mission of Juan de Miralles", unpublished manuscript, Library of Congress Manuscript Collection, AGI: Cuba 1290, Havana, August 11, 1779, Diego José Navarro to Juan de Miralles

35. Topping, Aileen Moore, "Mission of Juan de Miralles", [Unpublished Manuscript, 1995] Library of Congress Manuscript Collection, AGI Cuba 1281, Philadelphia, May 4, 1779, Juan de Miralles to Diego José de Navarro.

36. Topping, Aileen Moore, "Mission of Juan de Miralles", unpublished manuscript, Library of Congress Manuscript Collection, AGI 1606, Philadelphia, May 10, 1779, Juan de Miralles to José de Gálvez.

37. Sagredo Santos, op. cit., p. 54

38. Cummins, op. cit., p. 164

39. Griffin, op. cit., pp. 64-66

40. Topping, Aileen Moore, "Mission of Francisco Rendón", Library of Congress Manuscript Collection, AGI Cuba 1319, Philadelphia, April 20, 1782, Francisco Rendón to José de Gálvez, Box 2, Folder 1

41. Cummins, op. cit., p. 181

42. Ibid., pp. 184-186

43. Topping, Aileen Moore, "Mission of Francisco Rendón", Library of Congress Manuscript Collection, AGI Cuba 1319, Philadelphia, October 7, 1781, Francisco Rendón to Bernardo de Gálvez, Box 2, Folder 1

44. Topping, Aileen Moore, "Mission of Francisco Rendón", Library of Congress Manuscript Collection, AGI Cuba 1319, Philadelphia, October 12, 1781, George Washington to Francisco Rendón, Box 2, Folder 1

45. Cummins, op. cit., p. 187

46. Topping, Aileen Moore, "Mission of Francisco Rendón", Library of Congress Manuscript Collection, AGI Cuba 1319, Philadelphia, July 30, 1782, Francisco Rendón to José de Gálvez, Box 2, Folder 2

47. Cummins, op. cit., pp. 187-188

48. Topping, Aileen Moore, "Mission of Francisco Rendón", unpublished manuscript, Library of Congress Manuscript Collection, AGI Cuba 1319, Philadelphia, July 30, 1782, Francisco Rendón to José de Gálvez, 1782-105.

49. Topping, Aileen Moore, "Mission of Francisco Rendón", unpublished manuscript, Library of Congress Manuscript Collection, "AGI SD 2597, Philadelphia, August 31, 1783, Francisco Rendón "Memorial on the Commerce of the United States", 1783-119 to 1783-120

50. Topping, Aileen Moore, "Mission of Francisco Rendón", unpublished manuscript, Library of Congress Manuscript Collection, "AGI SD 2597, Philadelphia, August 31, 1783, Francisco Rendón "Memorial on the Commerce of the United States", 1783-87 to 1783-134

The American Crisis

1. Ellet, Elizabeth, ed., *Women of the American Revolution, Volumes I and II*. New York: Baker and Scribner, New York, 1848, Volume 1, pp. 114-115

2. Ellet, Elizabeth F., *The Women of the American Revolution*. Williamstown: Corner House of Publishers, 1980, Volume I, pp. 337-340

3. Morison, Samuel Eliot, *John Paul Jones: A Sailor's Biography*. Annapolis, Maryland: Bluejacket Books, 1999, pp 94-95

4. Ellet, The Women of the American Revolution [1980 ed.], op. cit., Volume I, p. 343

220

5. Bezanson, Anne, Blanche Daley, Marjorie C. Dennison, and Miriam Hussey. *Prices and Inflation During the American Revolution, Pennsylvania, 1770-1790*. University of Pennsylvania Press, 1951. http://www.jstor.org/stable/j.ctv4v3334 ., p. 91

6. Topping, Aileen Moore, "Mission of Juan de Miralles", unpublished manuscript, Library of Congress Manuscript Collection, AGI:SE 2598, Philadelphia, August 17, 1779, Juan de Miralles to José de Gálvez

7. Quarles, Benjamin, *The Negro in the American Revolution*. New York: W. W. Norton & Company, 1961. p. xi

8. Ellet, The Women of the American Revolution [1980 ed.], op. cit., Volume I, pp. 306

9. Ibid., Volume III, p. 195

10. Coe, Alexis, *You Never Forget Your First: A Biography of George Washington*. Viking, 2020, pp. 71-72

11. Ellet, The Women of the American Revolution [1980 ed.], op. cit., Volume II, p. 293

12. Ibid., Volume I, p. 227

13. Ibid., Volume I, p. 296

14. Fischer, David H., *Washington's Crossing*. New York: Oxford University Press, 2004, p. 101

15. Coakley and Conn, op. cit., pp. 98-100

16. Lengel, Edward G., *General George Washington, A Military Life*. New York: Random House, 2005, p. 196

17. Larson, Edward J., (December 21, 2025), Book Breaks with Edward J. Larson on "Declaring Independence: Why 1776 Matters". [Webinar presentation] The Gilder Lehrman Book Breaks

18. Paine, Thomas, "The American Crisis", a series of 16 pamphlets published between 1776 and 1783

19. Fischer, op. cit., pp. 140-141

20. Fast, Howard, *The Crossing*. New York: Pocket Books, 1971, p. 136

21. Kaplan, Roger, "The Hidden War: British Intelligence Operations during the American Revolution." *William and Mary Quarterly*, Third Series, Volume 47, Issue 1 (January 1990), p. 115

22. Fast, op. cit., p. 178

23. O'Donnell, Patrick K., *The Indispensables: The Diverse Soldier-Mariners Who Shaped the Country, Formed the Navy, and Rowed Washington Across the Delaware.* New York: The Atlantic Monthly Press, 2022

24. Martin, Joseph Plumb, *Private Yankee Doodle: Being a Narrative of Some of the Adventure, Dangers and Sufferings of a Revolutionary Soldier.* Copyright by George F. Sheer, Editor. Canada: Little, Brown & Company, Inc., 1962, p. 69

25. Kaplan, op. cit., p. 116

26. Willcox, William B., ed., *The American Rebellion. Sir Henry Clinton's Narrative of his Campaigns, 1775-1782, with an Appendix of Original Documents.* Binghamton, New York: Yale University Press, 1954. pp. xiii – xvii

27. Bell, Richard C., (March 29, 2025) *The Real Revolution, America 1775–1783* [Webinar presentation] The Smithsonian Associates Program, Washington, DC

28. Axelrod, op. cit., p. 245

29. Martin, op. cit., p. 96

30. Fischer, op. cit.

31. Golway, Terry, *Washington's General: Nathanael Greene and the Triumph of the American Revolution.* New York: Henry Holt and Company, 2005, p. 159

32. Ellis, Joseph J., *His Excellency, George Washington.* New York: Alfred A. Knopf, 2004, pp. 80-81

33. Selesky, Harold E., "A Demographic Survey of the Continental Army that Wintered at Valley Forge 1777-1778". New Haven, Connecticut: 1987, pp. 26-32

34. Burns, Ken, dir., *The American Revolution.* Walpole, New Hampshire, 2025, Episode 5, 12:40.

35. Selesky, op. cit., p. 30

36. Kaplan, op. cit., p. 115

37. Kaliamurthy, G., *Second Anglo-Mysore War (1780-1784)*. Mittal Publications: Delhi, 1987, p. 5

38. Lockhart, Paul, "Steuben Comes to America", *The Quarterly Journal of Military History*, Winter 2010, Volume 22, Number 2, p. 30

39. Ibid., pp. 28-29

40. Burns, The American Revolution [2025 film], op. cit., Episode 5, 24:50

41. Coakley and Conn, op. cit., p. 63

Two Tales of Two Cities

1. Chávez, *Spain and the Independence of the United States*, op. cit., p. 52

2. Lee, Richard Henry, *Life of Arthur Lee, LL.D.* Boston: Wells and Lilly, 1829, p. 53

3. Bemis, Samuel Flagg, *The Diplomacy of the American Revolution*. Bloomington: Midland Books, 1957 by Indiana University Press, p. 59

4. Sparks, op. cit., 1:408

5. Francis Wharton, ed., *The Revolutionary Diplomatic Correspondence of the United States* Washington: Government Printing Office, 1889, 2:279–280.

6. Lee, op. cit., p. 278

7. Dull, op. cit., p. 63

8. Warren, Mercy Otis, *History of the Rise, Progress and Termination of the American Revolution interspersed with Biographical, Political, and Moral Observations*. Indianapolis: Liberty Fund, 1989, p. 289

9. Dull, op. cit., p. 64

10. Chávez, *Revolutionary Diplomacy*, op. cit., p. 61

11. Warren, op. cit., p. 292

12. Patton, Robert H., *Patriot Pirates : The Privateer War for Freedom and Fortune in the American Revolution*. New York : Pantheon Books, 2008, p. 226

13. Morris, Richard B., *John Jay: The Making of a Revolutionary, Unpublished Papers 1745-1780*. New York: Harper & Row, 1975, p. 705

14. Ibid., p. 697

15. Stahr, Walter, *John Jay: Founding Father*. Continuum International Publishing Group, 2005, pp. 129-133

16. Sparks, op. cit., Volume 8, p. 11

17. Ibid., Volume 8, p. 85

18. Ibid., Volume 8, p. 49

19. Ibid., Volume 2, pp. 344-345

20. Ibid., Volume 8, p. 104

21. Ibid., Volume 8, p. 104

22. Patton, op. cit., p. 155

23. Chávez, *Revolutionary Diplomacy*, op. cit., p. 128

24. Sparks, op. cit., Volume 9, p. 191

25. Ibid., Volume 9, p. 192

26. Ibid., Volume 4, p. 346

27. Ibid., Volume 4, p. 347

28. Ibid., Volume 4, p. 408

29. Ibid., Volume 4, p. 349

30. Rueda, op. cit., pp. 51-52

31. Sparks, op. cit., Volume 4

Pirates of the Caribbean, Atlantic and Pacific

1. McCadden, Helen Matzke, "Juan de Miralles and the American Revolution", *The Americas*, Volume XXIX, Number 3, January 1973

224

2. Chávez, *Revolutionary Diplomacy*, op. cit., p. 97

3. Dupuy, Richard Ernest; Hammerman, Gay M; Hayes, Grace P., eds. *The American Revolution, a Global War.* D. McKay Company, 1977, pp. 286-287

4. US Naval History and Heritage Command, "Vessels of the Continental Navy" https://www.history.navy.mil/research/library/online-reading-room/title-list-alphabetically/v/vessels-of-the-continental-navy.html

5. Buel, op. cit., p. 94

6. Beerman, Eric. "The Last Battle of the American Revolution: Yorktown. No, the Bahamas!. The Spanish-American Expedition to Nassau in 1782." *The Americas* 45, no. 1, 1988, p 84. https://doi.org/10.2307/1007328.

7. John Adams to John Jay, Paris Hotel de Valois, February 22, 1780. https://founders.archives.gov/documents/Adams/06-08-02-0226

8. Selvon, Sydney, *A Comprehensive History of Mauritius.* Mauritius: Mauritius Printing Specialists, 2001, p. 149

9. Patton, op. cit., p. xvi

10. "George Washington to John Hancock, 4 December 1775," Founders Online, National Archives, https://founders.archives.gov/documents/Washington/03-02-02-0437.

11. Yela, op. cit., Volume 2, p. 260

12. Sparks, op. cit., Volume 8, p. 38

13. Ibid., Volume 7, p. 216

14. Patton, op. cit., pp. 56-57

15. US Naval History and Heritage Command, "John Paul Jones the Pirate", Glasgow:Printed for the Booksellers. [circa 1820] https://www.history.navy.mil/content/history/nhhc/research/library/online-reading-room/title-list-alphabetically/h/history-of-paul-jones-the-pirate.html

16. Morison, op. cit., pp. 174-175

17. Ibid., p. 94

18. Dupuy, op. cit., p. 221

19. Benjamin Franklin to John Paul Jones, Paris Jany 16th [–18]. 1778. https://found ers.archives.gov/documents/Franklin/01-25-02-0381

20. Neeser, Robert Wilden, ed., *Letters and Papers Relating to the Cruises of Gustavus Conyngham A Captain of the Continental Navy 1777-1779*. Port Washington: Kennikat Press, 1970, pp. 100-104

21. Ibid., p. 115

22. Patton, op. cit., pp. 177-179

23. Lewis, Neptune's Militia, op. cit., p. 14

24. Yela, op. cit., Volume 1, p. 378

25. Topping, Aileen Moore, "Alexander Gillon in Havana, 'This Very Friendly Port,'" in *South Carolina Historical Magazine* Volume 83 Number 1 January 1982, p. 39 https://www.jstor.org/stable/27567722

26. Ibid., p. 40

27. Lewis, Neptune's Militia, op. cit., pp. 53-54

28. Ibid., p. 1

29. Ibid., p. 5

30. Ibid., p. 23

31. Ibid., p. 36

32. Ibid., pp. 43-45

33. Ibid., p. 126

34. Fox, op. cit., p. 45

35. Ibid., p. 56

36. Ibid., pp. 95-104

37. Ibid., p. 223

38. "George Washington to Henry Laurens," 11 November 1778, Founders Online, National Archives, https://founders.archives.gov/documents/Washington/03-18 -02-0103.

39. Ferreiro, Larrie D., "The Franco-Spanish combined Royal Navies against the British Royal Navy." Presentation, Daughters of the American Revolution and Queen Sofia Spanish Institute, Symposium, Washington, DC, September 20-21, 2025

40. Ibid.

Friendship, Love and War on the Western Front

1. Chávez, *Spain and the Independence of the United States*, op. cit., p. 31

2. Tejera, Eduardo J., *La Ayuda de España y Cuba a la Independencia Norteamericana, Una Historia Olvidada*. The Little French eBooks, 2016, p. 188

3. James, James Alton, *Oliver Pollock: The Life and Times of an Unknown Patriot*. Freeport, New York: Books for Libraries Press, 1937, p. 4

4. Caughey, John Walton, *Bernardo de Gálvez in Louisiana 1776-1783*. Gretna: Pelican Publishing Company, 1998, p. 87

5. García Baena, Rosa María; Cazorla Grandos, Frank J. (2021). "La Cosmopolita Isabel Saint Maxent de Unzaga, Filántropa y Mecenas de la Educación Ilustrada" *TSN* No. 11. p. 178

6. Beerman, Eric. "'Yo Solo' Not 'Solo': Juan Antonio de Riaño." The Florida Historical Quarterly 58, no. 2 (1979): 174–84. http://www.jstor.org/stable/30149358.

7. García Baena, op. cit., pp. 174-186

8. Johnson, Raymond, "Stewart- deJaham Geneaology Pages", RaymondJohnson .net. https://www.raymondjohnson.net/genealogy/familychart.php?familyID=F6 51&tree=stewart Retrieved on August 21, 2025

9. Boeta, José Rudolfo, *Bernardo de Gálvez*. Madrid: Publicaciones Españolas, 1977

10. Saravia, Gonzalo M. Quintero, (January 19, 2023) *Felicitas and Bernardo: The Power Couple of Spanish Louisiana*. [Webinar presentation] Historic Nueva Orleans Collection, Nueva Orleans, LA

11. Saravia, Gonzalo M. Quintero, *Felicitas St. Maxent, Wife of Bernardo de Gálvez: From French Nueva Orleans Belle to Exiled Spanish Dowager Countess.* The Gilder Lehrman Institute. https://www.gilderlehrman.org/history-resources/essays/felicitas-st-maxent-wife-bernardo-de-galvez-french-new-orleans-belle

12. Caughey, John W., *Bernardo de Gálvez in Louisiana 1776-1783.* Berkley, California: University of California Press, 1934, pp. 89-90

13. Thompson, op. cit., p. 152

14. Caughey, *Bernardo de Gálvez in Louisiana 1776–1783* [1934], op. cit., p. 90

15. Ibid., pp. 90-93

16. Dupuy, op. cit., p. 136

17. James, Oliver Pollock, op. cit., pp. 120-124

18. Dolin, Eric Jay, *Fur, Fortune, and Empire, The Epic History of the Fur Trade in America.* New York: W.W. Norton & Company 2010, pp. 120-121

19. Kling, Stephen L., Jr., Sjostrom, Kristine, Lopez, Marysia, *The Battle of St. Louis, the Attack on Cahokia, and the American Revolution in the West.* St. Louis: THGC Publishing, 2017, pp. 125-133

20. Sjostrom, Kristine L., *Fernando de LEYBA (1734-1780): A Life of Service and Sacrifice in Spanish Louisiana.* 2022, p. 127

21. Kling, Stephen L., Jr., ed., *The American Revolutionary War in the West.* St. Louis: THGC Publishing, 2020 pp. 67-68

22. Caughey, *Bernardo de Gálvez in Louisiana 1776–1783* [1934], op. cit., pp. 98-99

23. Sjostrom, Kristine L., (2024, September 27-29) *"Leyba & Clark: Spanish American Collaboration in the Illinois Country during the American Revolutionary War"* [Conference Presentation]. The American Revolutionary War in the West: History Conference II

24. Kling, *The Battle of St. Louis*, op. cit., p. 133

25. Sjostrom, *Fernando de Leyba*, op. cit., p. 170

26. James, James Alton, *The Life of George Rogers Clark*. New York: AMS Press, 1970, pp. 123-124

27. Sjostrom, *Fernando de Leyba*, op. cit., pp. 164-170

28. Ibid., p. 139

29. Ibid., pp. 171-172

30. Carstens, Nancy S. and Carstens, Kenneth, eds., *The Life of George Rogers Clark, 1752-1818: Triumphs and Tragedies*. Praeger: 2004, p. 64

31. Bate, Richard Alexander, *The Romance of George Rogers Clark and Therese de Leyba*. *Louisville: The Standard Printing Co.*, 1929

32. Kling, *The Battle of St. Louis*, op. cit., p. 75

33. Ibid., pp. 85-87

34. Ibid., p. 102

35. Ibid., p. 93

36. Ibid., p. 87

The Civil War and the Desperate Pursuit of Happiness

1. Quarles, op. cit., p. x

2. Marshall, P.J., *The Making and Unmaking of Empires: Britain, India, and America c.1750-1783*. Oxford: Oxford University Press, 2007, p. 25

3. Lawler, Andrew. *A Perfect Frenzy: A Royal Governor, His Black Allies, and the Crisis That Spurred the American Revolution*. New York: Atlantic Monthly Press, 2025. p. 9

4. Ibid., p. 93

5. Alexandria Black History Museum, Alexandria, VA. Wall plaque, *British officer with General Braddock in Alexandria, VA, April 1755*

6. Burns, Ken, Ward, Geoffrey C., *"Book Breaks with Ken Burns and Geoffrey C. Ward on The American Revolution: An Intimate History."* Webinar, Gilder Lehrman Institute of American History, November 9, 2025.

7. Allison and Ferreiro, op. cit., p. 220

8. The Gilder Lehrman Institute of American History, Lord Dunmore's Proclamation, 1775https://www.gilderlehrman.org/history-resources/spotlight-primary-source/lord-dunmores-proclamation-1775

9. Lawler, op. cit., p. 93

10. Taylor, Alan, *The Internal Enemy: Slavery and War in Virginia, 1772-1832*. New York: W.W. Norton & Company, 2013, p. 25

11. Bell, The Real Revolution [webinar], op. cit.

12. DuVal, Kathleen, *Independence Lost: Lives on the Edge of the American Revolution*. New York: Random House, 2015, p. 57

13. Lawler, op. cit., pp. 234-235

14. Ibid., pp. 242-250

15. Ibid., p. 300

16. George Washington, "From George Washington to Richard Henry Lee," December 26, 1775, *Founders Online*, National Archives https://founders.archives.gov/documents/Washington/03-02-02-0568

17. Lawler, op. cit., p. 127

18. Ibid., p. 373

19. Ibid., p. 386

20. Quarles, op. cit., p. 112

21. Schama, Simon, *Rough Crossings: Britain, The Slaves and the American Revolution*. New York: Harper Collins Publishers, 2006, pp. 105-106

22. National Museum of African American History and Culture, *Double Victory: The African American Military Experience*. Smithsonian Institution: Washington, DC. April 2025

23. Neimeyer, Charles Patrick, *America Goes to War: A Social History of the Continental Army. New York: New York University Press, 1996, p. 77*

230

24. Lawler, op. cit., p. 340

25. Schama, op. cit., pp. 100-108

26. Ibid., pp. 112-113

27. Alexander, Leslie, "Black Americans and the American Revolution". The Great Courses Plus. Accessed April 25, 2025 https://www.thegreatcoursesplus.com/plus -pilots-black-americans-and-the-revolutionary-war

28. Basker, James G., editor, Black Writers of the Founding Era. New York: The Library of America, 2023, p. xlvii

29. Schama, op. cit., pp. 115-116

30. Alexander, op. cit.

31. Taylor, op. cit., pp. 22-23

32. Basker, op. cit., p. 484

33. Taylor, op. cit., p. 27

34. Ibid., p. 27

35. Basker, op. cit., pp. 80-81

36. Ibid., p. 367

37. Ibid., p. 134

38. Ibid., pp. 36-37

39. Ibid., p. 103

40. George Washington to Phillis Wheatley, 28 February 1776," *Founders Online,* National Archives, https://founders.archives.gov/documents/Washington/03-03-02 -0281.

41. Freeman, H. Ronald, *Savannah Under Siege.* Savannah, Georgia: Freeport Publishing, 2002, pp. 4-5

42. The George Washington Presidential Library at Mount Vernon https://www.mountvernon.org/library/digitalhistory/digital-encyclopedia/article/first-continental-congress#

43. Quarles, op. cit., p. 113

44. Freeman, op. cit., pp. 5-6

45. Schama, op. cit., p. 93

46. Coakley and Conn, op. cit., p. 115

47. Schama, op. cit., p. 93

48. Coakley and Conn, op. cit., pp. 115-116

49. Schama, op. cit., p. 101

50. Ibid., p. 102

51. Ferreiro, *Brothers at Arms*, op. cit., pp. 200-201

52. Quarles, op. cit., p. 82

53. Steward, Theophilus G., "How the Black St. Domingo Legion Saved the Patriot Army in the Siege of Savannah, 1779", The American Negro Academy. Occasional Papers No. 5, 1899, p. 7 https://www.gutenberg.org/ebooks/31256

54. Freeman, op. cit., p. 132

55. Nemours, Alfred, "Haiti Et La Guerre to L'indépendance Américaine". Port-au-Prince: Haiti, H. Deschamps, 1952.

56. Freeman, op. cit., p. 135

57. Coakley and Conn, op. cit., p. 119

58. Ferreiro, *Brothers at Arms*, op. cit., pp. 212-214

59. Schama, op. cit., p. 104

60. Ibid., pp. 106-107

61. Ibid., p. 99

62. Coakley and Conn, op. cit., p. 123

63. Ferreiro, *Brothers at Arms*, op. cit., p. 218

Spain and Latin America on the Southern Front

1. Tejera, op. cit., pp. 232-233

2. Caughey, *Bernardo de Gálvez in Louisiana* [1998], op. cit., p. 149

3. Ferreiro, *Brothers at Arms*, op. cit., p. 115

4. Tejera, op. cit., p. 7

5. Bell, Guns, Ships, & Cows [webinar], op. cit.

6. Caughey, *Bernardo de Gálvez in Louisiana 1776–1783* [1998], op. cit., p. 153

7. Thonhoff, Robert H., *The Texas Connection with the American Revolution*. Austin, TX: Eakin Press, 1981, p. 10

8. Ibid., p. 46

9. Saravia, Bernardo de Gálvez, op. cit., p. 60

10. Beerman, Eric, *España y la Independencia de Estados Unidos*. Málaga, Spain: Editorial Arguval, 1992, p. 49

11. James, Oliver Pollock, op. cit., p. 195

12. DuVal, op. cit., pp. 150-151

13. James, Oliver Pollock, op. cit., pp. 197-198

14. Caughey, *Bernardo de Gálvez in Louisiana 1776–1783* [1998], op. cit., p. 171

15. Boeta, op. cit., pp. 92-93

16. Topping, Aileen Moore, "Mission of Juan de Miralles", unpublished manuscript, Library of Congress Manuscript Collection, Container 1, Folder 4, pp. 487-501

17. Coakley and Conn, op. cit., pp. 123-125

18. Kuethe, op. cit., p. 104

19. Caughey, *Bernardo de Gálvez in Louisiana 1776–1783* [1998], op. cit., pp. 175-177

20. Saravia, Bernardo de Gálvez, op. cit., p. 235

21. Caughey, *Bernardo de Gálvez in Louisiana 1776–1783* [1998], op. cit., pp. 177-178

22. DuVal, op. cit., p. 176

23. Caughey, *Bernardo de Gálvez in Louisiana 1776–1783* [1998], op. cit., p. 190

24. Ibid., p. 192

25. Kuethe, op. cit., pp. 106-107

26. Lucena-Giraldo, Manuel, "Foreseeing what great occasions might come, American independence and Spanish Naval Reforms", Paquette, Gabriel and Quintero Saravia, Gonzalo M. (editors), *Spain and the American Revolution New Approaches and Perspectives*. Charlottesville: University of Virginia Press, 2022, pp. 91-99

27. Saravia, Bernardo de Gálvez, op. cit., p. 201

28. Chávez, *Spain and the Independence of the United States*, op. cit., pp. 188-191

29. Martín-Merás, Luisa, "The Capture of Pensacola through Maps, 1781" in *Legacy: Spain and the United States in the Age of Independence*, 1763-1848. Washington, DC: Smithsonian Institution, 2007, p. 81

30. Rush, N. Orwin, *The Battle of Pensacola: Spain's Final Triumph Over Great Britain in the Gulf of Mexico*. Tallahassee: Florida State University, 1966, p. 51

31. Beerman, "Yo Solo" Not "Solo," op. cit., pp. 174-84

32. Rush, op. cit., p. 57

33. Taylor, op. cit., pp. 170-171

34. Ferreiro, *Brothers at Arms*, op. cit., p. 268

35. Worcester, Donald E., "Miranda's Diary of the Siege of Pensacola", 1781, *The Florida Historical Quarterly*, Vol. 29, No. 3 (January 1951), pp. 180-182

36. Martín-Merás, op. cit., p. 82

37. Worcester, op. cit., p. 171

38. Montemayor, Ernest A., ed., *Yo Solo*. Nueva Orleans: Polyanthos, Inc., 1978, p. 22

39. Martín-Merás, op. cit., p. 84

40. Maldonado, Cecilia (July 31, 2025) *America & Spain250 – Discovering Spain's Role in the American Revolution,* [Webinar presentation] The Queen Sofia Spanish Institute, New York, New York

41. Ferreiro, *Brothers at Arms,* op. cit., p. 253

42. Allison and Ferreiro, op. cit., p. 190

43. Worcester, op. cit., p. 176

44. Ibid., pp. 191-192

45. Dupuy, op. cit., p. 153

46. Ferreiro, *Brothers at Arms,* op. cit., p. 14

47. Chávez, *Spain and the Independence of the United States,* op. cit., pp. 151-152

48. Yela, op. cit., Volume 1, p. 219

49. Tejera, op. cit., p. 232

50. Ibid., pp. 247-248

51. Acosta, José Manuel Guerrero, the Queen Sofia Spanish Institute, Gilderman Lehrman Institute of American History, "Notes on Spain's Multicultural Militias", https://www.gilderlehrman.org/spanish-influence-american-history/american-revolution/spains-multicultural-militias

52. Chávez, Thomas E., (2024, September 27-29) *"Benjamin Franklin, Francisco Saavedra de Sangronis and Spain's Grand Strategy in the American Revolutionary War"* [Conference Presentation]. The American Revolutionary War in the West: History Conference II

53. Marlantes, Karl, *Matterhorn: A Novel of the Vietnam War*. New York: Atlantic Monthly Press, 2010. Please note that Barbara repurposed this work for the 18th century Central American war.

54. Howarth, David and Howarth, Stephen, *Lord Nelson, The Immortal Memory*. New York: Viking Penguin, 1999, p. 35

55. Bell, Guns, Ships, & Cows [webinar], op. cit.

56. Ferreiro, *Brothers at Arms*, op. cit., p. 256

"Now or never"

1. National Archives, Founders Online, From George Washington to John Laurens, 9 April 1781. https://founders.archives.gov/documents/Washington/99-01-02-05 346

2. Elizabeth A. Fenn, *Pox Americana: The Great Smallpox Epidemic of 1775-1782*. (New York: Hill and Wang, 2001)

3. Sparks, op. cit., Volume 9, pp. 68-69

4. Coakley and Conn, op. cit., p. 72

5. Sumner, op. cit., Volume 2, p. 134

6. Willcox, op. cit., p. 305

7. George Washington's Mount Vernon, "Washington's Winters". https://www.mountvernon.org/george-washington/so-hard-a-winter

8. Coakley and Conn, op. cit., p. 125

9. Ferreiro, *Brothers at Arms*, op. cit., p. 212

10. Martin, op. cit., pp. 144-145

11. Ibid., p. 158

12. Nagy, John A., *Rebellion in the Ranks: Mutinies of the American Revolution*. Yardley: Westholme Publishing, LLC, 2008, p. xix

13. Coakley and Conn, op. cit., p. 121

14. Nagy, op. cit., pp. 77-80

15. Ibid., pp. 176-185

16. Sumner, op. cit., Volume I, pp. 3-4

17. Oberholtzer, Ellis P., *Robert Morris: Patriot and Financier*. New York: The MacMillan Company, 1903, p. 18

18. Chernow, op. cit., p. 155

19. Ferguson, E. James, Ed., *The Papers of Robert Morris, 1781 –1784*. Pittsburgh: University of Pittsburgh Press, 1973, p. xviii

20. Birmingham, Stephen, *The Grandees: America's Sephardic Elite*. New York: Harper & Row, 1971, pp. 52-55

21. Peters, Madison C., *Haym Salomon, The Financier of the American Revolution An Unwritten Chapter in American History*. New York: Trow Press: 1911, p. 14

22. U.S. Congress. Senate. The Committee on Revolutionary Claims. The Committee on Revolutionary Claims, Relative to Advances of Money to the United States during the Revolutionary War. Report 178. 69th Congress, 2nd Session, Washington, DC: US Senate, 1925. P. 5

23. Birmingham, op. cit., p. 153

24. Peters, op. cit., p. 20

25. Ferguson, op. cit., pp. 311-314

26. Sumner, op. cit., Volume 1, p. 34

27. Ibid., Volume 1, pp. 302-303

28. Ibid., Volume 1, p. 308

29. Ibid., Volume 2, p. 95

30. Warren, op. cit., Volume 2, p. 417

31. Ferreiro, *Brothers at Arms*, op. cit., pp. 192-193

32. Chávez, *Spain and the Independence of the United States*, op. cit., p. 214

33. Long de Fernández de Mesa, Mary Ann (Molly) and Long Startz, Mary Anthony, UnveilingMemories.com https://www.unveilingmemories.com/events/the-donativos-finding-the-silver-that-dropped-through-the-floor/

34. Ibid.

35. Chávez, *Spain and the Independence of the United States*, op. cit., p. 143

36. Ferreiro, *Brothers at Arms*, op. cit., pp. 196-197

37. Paulo Pavia, Francisco de, "Descripcion del apresamiento del gran convey ingles en 1780 por la escuadera combinada de Expana y Francia al mando del general don Luis de Cordoba", *La revista militar: periódico de arte, ciencia y literatura militar*, Volumen 8, Madrid, 1851, pp. 153-162

38. Ferreiro, *Brothers at Arms*, op. cit., pp. 196-197

39. Stern, Mark A., *David Franks, Colonial Merchant*. University Park: Pennsylvania State University Press, 2010, p. 128

40. Kaplan, op. cit., p. 124

41. The US National Security Agency Kids Reference, "What is a Cipher?" at https://www.nsa.gov/kids/ciphers.swf , retrieved on 10-April-2016

42. Bell, *The American Revolution and the Fate of the World*, op. cit., p. 321

43. Chernow, op. cit., p. 141

44. Kaplan, op. cit., p. 130

45. Willcox, op. cit., pp. 305-306

La Habana, The Key to the New World

1. Johnson, op. cit., p. 42

2. Kuethe, op. cit., p. 125

3. Johnson, op. cit., p. 42

4. Kuethe, op. cit., p. 125

5. Johnson, op. cit., p. 25

6. Ibid., pp. 9-13

7. Ibid., p. 44

8. Ibid., p. 9

9. Lewis, Charles Lee, *Admiral de Grasse and American Independence*. Annapolis: U.S. Naval Institute, 1973, p. 138

10. Yela, op. cit., Volume 1, p. 455

11. Padrón, Francisco Morales, ed., Aileen Moore Topping, translator, *Journal of Don Francisco Saavedra de Sangronis, 1780-1783*. Gainesville: University of Florida Press., 1988, p. 54

12. Saravia, Bernardo de Gálvez, op. cit., p. 68

13. Ibid., p. 1

14. Ibid., p. 192

15. Rochambeau to Louis Philippe, Marquis et Comte de Ségur, Philadelphia, September 4, 1781. unpublished manuscript, The Library of Congress Manuscript Division. Translated by John F. Gough, New Jersey, December 9, 1930.

16. Bonsal, op. cit., p. 118

17. Padrón, *Journal of Don Francisco Saavedra de Sangronis*, op. cit., pp. 207-208

18. Bonsal, Philip W., 1946 Private Letter to Stephen Bonsal, December 29, 1946, unpublished manuscript, *The Papers of Stephen Bonsal* in The Collections of the Manuscript Division, Library of Congress, Washington, DC. p. 8

19. Bonsal, Philip W., 1946 Private Letter to Stephen Bonsal, December 29, 1946, unpublished manuscript, *The Papers of Stephen Bonsal* in The Collections of the Manuscript Division, Library of Congress, Washington, DC. p. 5

20. Cagigal, Juan Manual de, Letter to Josef de Gálvez, June 22, 1781, AGI Santo Domingo 1232, unpublished manuscript Archivo General de Indias, Sevilla, Spain

21. Cagigal, Juan Manual de, Letter to Francisco Aimar de Monteil, El Cavallero [Knight] de Monteil, June 15, 1781, AGI Santo Domingo 1232, unpublished manuscript, Archivo General de Indias, Sevilla, Spain

22. Padrón, *Journal of Don Francisco Saavedra de Sangronis*, op. cit., pp. 204-205

23. Shea, J.G., *The Operations of the French Fleet Under the Count De Grasse in 1781-1782*. New York: Da Capo Press, 1971 p. 151

24. Padrón, *Journal of Don Francisco Saavedra de Sangronis*, op. cit., pp. 209-210

25. Lewis, James A., "Las Damas de La Havana, El Precursor, and Francisco de Saavedra: A Note on Spanish Participation in the Battle of Yorktown. *The Americas. A Quarterly Review of Inter-American Cultural History*, Academy of American Franciscan History. July 1980, Volume XXXVII, Number 1, p. 95

26. Padrón, Francisco Morales, ed., *Los Decenios (Autobiografia de una Sevillano de la Ilustracion) Francisco de Saavedra*. Sevilla: Servicio de Publicaciones Excmo. Ayutamiento de Sevilla, 1995, p.163

27. Padrón, *Journal of Don Francisco Saavedra de Sangronis*, op. cit., p. 211

28. Ferreiro, *Brothers at Arms*, op. cit., p. 259

29. Chapparo Sainz, Álvaro, "Educación y reproducción social de las élites habaneras (1776-1804)", Revista Complutense de Historia de América, 2010, vol. 36, p. 187

30. Johnson, op. cit., p. 35

31. Bonsal, Philip W., 1946 Private Letter to Stephen Bonsal, December 29, 1946, [Unpublished Manuscript 1946], *The Papers of Stephen Bonsal* in The Collections of the Manuscript Division, Library of Congress, Washington, DC. p. 14

32. Cagigal, Juan Manual de, Letter to Josef de Gálvez, February 16, 1782, Santo Domingo 1234, unpublished manuscript, Archivo General de Indias, Sevilla, Spain.

33. Cagigal, Juan Manual de, Letter to Josef de Gálvez, February 16, 1782, Santo Domingo 1234, unpublished manuscript, Archivo General de Indias, Sevilla, Spain.

34. Kuethe, op. cit., pp. 183-187

35. Ibid., p. 59

36. Lewis, "Las Damas de La Havana," op. cit., p. 96

37. Kuethe, op. cit., p. 188

240

38. Enrique Hurtado de Mendoza Collection, Digital Library of the Caribbean. Cardenas Family, Marques de Cardenas de Monte Hermoso, https://dloc.com/FIHU 000952/00001/pdf . Accessed July 9, 2025

39. Bonsal, Philip W., 1946 Private Letter to Stephen Bonsal, December 29, 1946, unpublished manuscript, *The Papers of Stephen Bonsal* in The Collections of the Manuscript Division, Library of Congress, Washington, DC

40. Magro, Ángel Bahamonde, and José Gregorio Cayuela Fernández. "La Creación de Nobleza En Cuba Durante El Siglo XIX." *Historia Social*, no. 11 (1991): 56–82. http://www.jstor.org/stable/40340288 . p. 4

41. Kuethe, op. cit., p. 119

42. Bonsal, Philip W., 1946 Private Letter to Stephen Bonsal, December 29, 1946, unpublished manuscript, *The Papers of Stephen Bonsal* in The Collections of the Manuscript Division, Library of Congress, Washington, DC

43. Lewis, "Las Damas de La Havana," op. cit., p. 88

44. Miranda, Francisco de (Translated by Judson P. Wood, Edited by John S. Ezell), *The New Democracy in America: Travels of Francisco de Miranda in the United States, 1783-84.* Norman, Oklahoma: University of Oklahoma Press, Publishing Division, 1963, p. xvi

45. Racine, Karen, *Francisco de Miranda: A Transatlantic Life in the Age of Revolution.* Wilmington: Scholarly Resources, Inc. 2003, pp. 90-96

46. Miranda, op. cit.

47. Padrón, *Journal of Don Francisco Saavedra de Sangronis*, op. cit., pp. 200-211

48. Padrón, *Los Decenios*, op. cit., p. 159

49. Dull, op. cit., pp. 243-244

50. Ibid., pp. 242-243

51. Shea, op. cit., p. 152

52. Davis, Burke, *The Campaign that won America: The Story of Yorktown.* Eastern Acorn Press, 1970. p. 166

53. Ketchum, Richard M., *Victory at Yorktown: The Campaign that won the Revolution*. New York: Henry Holt and Company, 2004, p. 168

54. Grasse, Francois Joseph Paul, August 30, 1781 to Rochambeau at Chesapeake, Maryland. unpublished manuscript, New Haven: Yale University Library, Beinecke Rare Book and Manuscript Library.

55. "John Laurens to John Adams, 28 April 1781," *Founders Online,* National Archives, https://founders.archives.gov/documents/Adams/06-11-02-0212.

56. Rochambeau to Aranda, October 24, 1784, Camp in York. unpublished manuscript, Library of Congress Manuscript Division.

57. Ferreiro, *Brothers at Arms*, op. cit., p. 266

58. Blanchard, Claude, *The Journal of Claude Blanchard, Commissary of the French Auxiliary Army sent to the United States during the American Revolution*. Translated by William Duane and edited by Thomas Balch. New York: Arno Press, Inc., 1969, p. 143

59. Willcox, op. cit., pp. 306-307

60. Topping, Aileen Moore, "Mission of Francisco de Rendón", [Unpublished Manuscript, 1995] Library of Congress Manuscript Collection unpublished manuscript, AGI: Cuba 1319, Philadelphia, September 15, 1781, Francisco Rendón to Juan Manual de Cagigal.

61. Topping, Aileen Moore, "Mission of Francisco de Rendón", [Unpublished Manuscript, 1995] Library of Congress Manuscript Collection, AGI: Cuba 1319, Philadelphia, September 21, 1781, Francisco Rendón to Juan Manual de Cagigal.

62. Topping, Aileen Moore, "Mission of Francisco de Rendón", [Unpublished Manuscript, 1995] Library of Congress Manuscript Collection, AGI: Cuba 1319, Philadelphia, July 30, 1782, Francisco Rendón to Bernardo de Gálvez, pp. 900-901

63. Topping, Aileen Moore, "Mission of Francisco de Rendón", [Unpublished Manuscript, 1995] Library of Congress Manuscript Collection, AGI: Cuba 1319, Philadelphia, July 30, 1782, Francisco Rendón to Bernardo de Gálvez, pp. 897-906

64. Topping, Aileen Moore, "Mission of Francisco de Rendón", [Unpublished Manuscript, 1995] Library of Congress Manuscript Collection, AGI: Cuba 1319, Philadelphia, October 22, 1781, Francisco Rendón to Juan Manual de Cagigal

65. Topping, Aileen Moore, "Mission of Francisco de Rendón", [Unpublished Manuscript, 1995] Library of Congress Manuscript Collection, AGI:SD 2598, No. 44, Philadelphia, December 10, 1781, Francisco Rendón to Jose de Gálvez. 942-943

66. Topping, Aileen Moore, "Mission of Francisco de Rendón", [Unpublished Manuscript, 1995] Library of Congress Manuscript Collection, AGI: Cuba 1319, Philadelphia, July 30, 1782, Francisco Rendón to José de Gálvez. 1782-105

67. Topping, Aileen Moore, "Mission of Francisco de Rendón", [Unpublished Manuscript, 1995] Library of Congress Manuscript Collection, AGI:SD 2598, No. 44, Philadelphia, December 10, 1781, Francisco Rendón to Jose de Gálvez. 943-944

The Rocky Road to Peace

1. O'Shaughnessy, Andrew Jackson, *The Men Who Lost America: British Leadership, the American Revolution, and the Fate of the Empire (The Lewis Walpole Series in Eighteenth-Century Culture and History)*. New Haven: Yale University Press, 2014, p. 46

2. Ferreiro, *Brothers at Arms*, op. cit., p. 292

3. Allison, Robert J., "The American Revolution and the Fate of the World with Richard Bell", Revolution 250 Podcast, Nov. 11, 2025, https://www.youtube.com/watch?v=iOZyQM254-0

4. Chávez, *Spain and the Independence of the United States*, op. cit., p. 165

5. Topping, Aileen Moore, "Mission of Francisco Rendón", Library of Congress Manuscript Collection, Box 2, Folder 2, p. 1782-71

6. Topping, Aileen Moore, "Mission of Francisco Rendón", unpublished manuscript, Library of Congress Manuscript Collection, Box 2, Folder 2, pp.1782-72 – 1782-73

7. Buel, op. cit., p. 220

8. Ibid., p. 220

9. Topping, Aileen Moore, "Mission of Francisco Rendón", unpublished manuscript, Library of Congress Manuscript Collection, Box 2, Folder 2, p.1782-73

10. Topping, Aileen Moore, "Mission of Francisco Rendón", unpublished manuscript, Library of Congress Manuscript Collection, AGI Cuba 1354, Philadelphia, February 28, 1783, Francisco Rendón to Jose de Gálvez, Box 2, Folder 3

11. Topping, Aileen Moore, "Mission of Francisco Rendón", unpublished manuscript, Library of Congress Manuscript Collection, Box 2, Folder 3, p. 1783-14-15

12. Cummins, op. cit., p. 174

13. Buel, op. cit., p. 190

14. Ellis, op. cit., pp. 139-144

15. Chernow, op. cit., pp. 180-184

16. Basker, op. cit., p. 253

17. Schama, op. cit., p. 128

18. Ibid., pp. 147-150

19. Basker, op. cit., p. 253

20. Schama, op. cit., p. 153

21. Cummins, op. cit., p. 191

22. Ferreiro, *Brothers at Arms*, op. cit., p. 287

23. Beerman, España y la Independencia de Estados Unidos, op. cit., pp. 251-257

24. Ferreiro, *Brothers at Arms*, op. cit., p. 73

25. Dupuy, op. cit.

26. Dull, op. cit., p. 111

27. Beerman, "The Last Battle of the American Revolution," op. cit., pp. 79-95

28. Ibid., p. 85

29. Ibid., pp. 87-88

30. Lewis, Neptune's Militia, op. cit., pp. 107-108

31. Saravia, Felicitas and Bernardo [webinar], op. cit., pp. 252-253

32. Topping, Aileen Moore, "Mission of Francisco Rendón", unpublished manuscript, Library of Congress Manuscript Collection, AGI Cuba 1319, Philadelphia, June 25, 1782, Francisco Rendón to Juan Manuel de Cagigal, p. 1782-98

33. Kaliamurthy, G. *Second Anglo-Mysore War (1780–1784)*. Delhi: Mittal Publications, 1987, p. 22

34. Ibid., p. 13

35. Dupuy, op. cit., p. 240

36. Kaliamurthy, op. cit., pp. 67-68

37. Dalrymple, op. cit., p. 251

38. Bell, Richard C., (March 28, 2024) *The American Revolution and the Battle for India: A Forgotten Connection* [Webinar presentation] The Smithsonian Associates Program, Washington, DC

39. Dalrymple, op. cit., pp. 250-255

40. Allison and Ferreiro, op. cit., p. 102

41. Gilbert, Arthur N. "Recruitment and Reform in the East India Company Army, 1760-1800." *Journal of British Studies* 15, no. 1 (1975): 89–111. http://www.jstor.org/stable/175240. P. 99

42. Benjamin Rush to Horatio Gates, 5 September 1781, The University of Virginia press https://rotunda.upress.virginia.edu/founders/default.xqy?keys=RUSH-info-log-in

43. Bonsal, Stephen, *When the French Were Here*. Garden City, New York: Doubleday, Doran and Company, Inc., 1945, pp. 172-173

44. Barney, Mary, *A Biographical Memoir of the Late Commodore Joshua Barney From Autographical Notes and Journals in Possession of His Family, and Other Authentic Sources.* 1832, p. 120.

45. Dupuy, op. cit., pp. 245-246

46. "Thomas Jefferson to André Limozin, 18 June 1788," Founders Online, National Archives, https://founders.archives.gov/documents/Jefferson/01-13-02-0164

47. Allison and Ferreiro, op. cit., pp. 102-103

48. Dull, op. cit., pp. 140-141

49. Ibid., pp. 148-149

50. "John Jay's Diary of the Peacemaking, 12–29 October 1782," *Founders Online*, National Archives, https://founders.archives.gov/documents/Jay/01-03-02-0062.

51. Dull, op. cit., pp. 149-150

52. Ibid., pp. 149-150

53. Sparks, op. cit., Volume 10, p. 26

54. Dull, op. cit., p. 147

55. Topping, Aileen Moore, "Mission of Francisco Rendón", Library of Congress Manuscript Collection, Box 2, Folder 3, p. 1783-33 to 1783-34

56. Coe, Samuel Gwynn, "The Mission of William Carmichael to Spain" (PhD Diss., Johns Hopkins University, 1926), p. 50

57. Ibid., pp. 51-52

58. Ferreiro, *Brothers at Arms*, op. cit., p. 300

59. Gardoqui García, José Luis Diego Cano, "Diego de Gardoqui in Spain and America", in Acosta, Jose Manuel Guerrero, ed., *Recovered Memories: Spain, New Orleans and the Support for the American Revolution*. Iberdola-arte.es https://www.iberdrola-arte.es/FicherosIberdrola/Publicaciones/8/48add1ac-6593-46d2-9e98-0ee6a201b527.pdf, p. 115

60. Mesa, Begona Cava, "Enlightenment Figure, Trader and Diplomat, The Historical Contribution of Diego de Gardoqui to the Independence of the United States", in Acosta, Jose Manuel Guerrero, ed., *Recovered Memories: Spain, New Orleans and the Support for the American Revolution*. Iberdola-arte.es https://www.iberdrola-arte.es/FicherosIberdrola/Publicaciones/8/48add1ac-6593-46d2-9e98-0ee6a201b527.pdf, p. 130

61. Bowen, Clarence Winthrop, *History of the Centennial celebration of the Inauguration of George Washington as first President of the United States*. New York: D. Appleton, 1892, p. 32

62. Ibid., p. 47

63. Mount Vernon, Washington Library Center for Digital History, "President Washington's Inauguration", https://www.mountvernon.org/george-washington/the-first-president/inauguration/timeline

64. Mount Vernon, Washington Library Center for Digital History, "Diego María de Gardoqui y Arriquíbar", https://www.mountvernon.org/library/digitalhistory/digital-encyclopedia/article/diego-maria-de-gardoqui-y-arriquibar-1735-1789

65. Ferreiro, *Brothers at Arms*, op. cit., pp. 309-310

66. Bowen, op. cit., p. 46

Index

www.ingramcontent.com/pod-product-compliance
Lightning Source LLC
Chambersburg PA
CBHW030431160726
47991CB00005B/1680